From Snake Pits to Cash Cows

To Vicki

With regards

Pat C...

From Snake Pits
to Cash Cows

Politics and Public Institutions in New York

Paul J. Castellani

State University of New York Press

Published by
State University of New York Press, Albany

For information, address State University of New York Press,
90 State Street, Suite 700, Albany, NY 12207

Production by Judith Block
Marketing by Fran Keneston

Library of Congress Cataloging-in-Publication Data

Castellani, Paul J., 1942–
   From snake pits to cash cows : politics and public institutions in New York /
Paul J. Castellani.
       p. cm.
   Includes bibliographical references and index.
   ISBN 0-7914-6439-3 (hardcover : alk. paper) — ISBN 0-7914-6440-7 (pbk. :
alk. paper)
   1. People with mental disabilities—Institutional care—New York (State)—
History. 2. Developmentally disabled—Institutional care—New York
(State)—History. 3. State Hospitals—New York (State)—History. I. Title.

HV3006.N69C37 2005
362.2'1'09747—dc22   2004014225

10 9 8 7 6 5 4 3 2 1

To Donna

Contents

Part 4   Closing and Not Closing Institutions

Tables

Acknowledgments

Hundreds of people in public and private organizations around the country, especially in the New York State Office of Mental Retardation and Developmental Disabilities, described, explained, and gave me unexpected insights on the features of policy and practice covered in this book. I risk leaving out thanks to many if I try to list them all.

Several individuals provided support at crucial times in the project. David Braddock, Director of the Coleman Institute for Cognitive Disabilities at the University of Colorado; Valerie Bradley, President of the Human Services Research Institute; and Colleen Wieck, Executive Director of the Minnesota Governor's Council on Developmental Disabilities, gave me opportunities to develop early versions of parts of this book. At a later stage, Jim Mansell of the Tizard Centre at the University of Kent and Kent Ericsson at the University of Uppsala hosted forums that allowed me to rethink earlier assumptions and get different perspectives on my research. Frank Thompson, Dean of the Nelson A. Rockefeller College of Public Affairs, University at Albany, State University of New York, supplied the encouragement and resources to finish the project. Librarians Alan Carter and Paul Hillengas located archives and documents and recommended source materials I hadn't considered. Nan Carroll, Dawn Guinan, and Clare Yates at the Center for Legislative Development provided a congenial atmosphere in which to work as well as a great deal of assistance.

Donna Castellani made an enormous contribution in editing the final draft as well as getting me through the many hard parts in this project.

Introduction

The Perseverance and Vitality of Public Institutions

Images of the future are usually caricatures of the present. They inflate some recognizable features of contemporary life to extravagant proportions, and out of fear or hope respond to every vagary of historical experience, as if it were a sign of destiny.

— Paul Starr, Medicine and the Waning of
Professional Sovereignty, *Daedalus*

Prologue

September 17, 1987 was a clear, crisp day on Staten Island in New York City. Several hundred people milled about waiting for speeches by ex-Governor Hugh Carey, talk-show host Geraldo Rivera, and former resident Bernard Carabello that were to mark the formal closing of Willowbrook. There was the atmosphere of a college reunion. Attorneys for plaintiffs and respondents, parents, and various public officials greeted old friends and adversaries in the crowd, gossiped, took care of a little business, and reminisced about colleagues who had retired, died, or moved on in the twenty-two years since Senator Robert F. Kennedy charged that Willowbrook was a "snake pit." It had been sixteen years since Geraldo Rivera's televised exposé and fifteen years since parents sued the state in federal court for relief of the appalling conditions at the institution whose name became synonymous with abuse and neglect.

When the ceremony got underway, the speakers recalled victories and setbacks in what became known as the Willowbrook Wars and declared that other public institutions like Willowbrook should be closed. Earlier that year

Governor Mario Cuomo, in his State of the State address, said that in addition to the already announced closures of Willowbrook and Westchester Developmental Centers, five more of the state's twenty public institutions would be closed by 1991.

In 1991, toward the end of the round of closures begun in 1987, Governor Cuomo, in his Message to the Legislature, declared that he was directing the Office of Mental Retardation and Developmental Disabilities to "develop a long term plan to close the remaining developmental centers." The governor's decision endorsed the conclusion of that state agency's policy paper, *A Mandate for the 1990s: Closing Developmental Centers in New York State*, reflected the positions taken by the major provider associations, advocacy groups, and public employee unions, and echoed the recommendation of the Chairman of the State Senate's Committee on Mental Hygiene "that all developmental centers in the State of New York be permanently closed by the year 2000."

Shortly after the inauguration of Governor George Pataki in January 1995, New York suspended the closure of all developmental centers pending a review of the 1991 decision. The suspension became a "case-by-case" policy as two previously announced closures were completed, another canceled, and no others were slated for the remainder of the 1990s.

In September 1998, Governor Pataki announced that the state would build its first new institution in thirty years. The governor said the Center for Intensive Treatment would protect the public by providing appropriate services in secure settings for people with mental retardation who violated the law. Those attending the ceremony in Norwich were reported to be "very pleased" at the "great news" that the facility would employ more than 200 full-time staff in addition to the more than 500 construction jobs required to build the center. The state had already added capacity to secure units at existing institutions and planned the expansion of facilities for other special populations.

In August 1998, the governor announced to "a beaming mix of state officials, voluntary providers, advocates, families, and consumers" a five-year plan to eliminate the waiting list for residential services by adding 4,900 new beds to the more than 30,000 in congregate residential settings operated by state and private agencies. Admissions to developmental centers continued, and at the end of 1999, almost two thousand individuals lived in the remaining eight public institutions, and the agency's billing to the federal government topped $2,000 per day per resident.

The Perseverance and Vitality of Public Institutions

What explains the perseverance and vitality of public institutions for people with developmental disabilities in a state in which those institutions have been condemned for the past sixty years and public policy has called for their closure for the past thirty? The closure of Willowbrook and several other developmental centers and Governor Cuomo's broadly endorsed directive to plan for the closure of all developmental centers by 2000 appeared to be the death knell for these institutions in New York. But they did not close. Their closure was suspended, reversed, and ultimately transformed into a policy to build new institutions.

Why did the public officials from both political parties, advocates, and interest group representatives who endorsed the 1991 plan to close all developmental centers not protest the suspension of closure plans in 1995? Why were the same public officials, providers, parents, consumers, and advocates who applauded the closing of institutions beaming at announcements of the building of new institutions and funding of new congregate care beds? Why does the contemporary literature on public institutions focus almost exclusively on describing and explaining their inevitable downsizing and closure?

Public institutions for people with developmental disabilities persevere and remain vital in New York because these institutions adapted to perform new roles for different kinds of people. They became functionally integrated with private and public community services. They generate federal revenues that exceed their costs to state taxpayers and underwrite a substantial proportion of the costs of private and public community services. They, along with public and private community services, are significant elements in many local economies. These various supports for the perseverance of public institutions are not coincidental but central to a long-term strategy that turned political adversaries into allies, parents into providers, and competitors into partners. That strategy, forged in the mid-1970s, emerged from forty years of conflict and failure to solve the problem of public institutions. The plan to close all public institutions was reversed when closure threatened the fiscal, operational, and political foundations of developmental services in the state.

The Problem of Public Institutions for People with Developmental Disabilities

Public institutions have been the focus and fulcrum of public policy for people with developmental disabilities (those with mental retardation, cerebral palsy, autism, epilepsy, and related neurological impairments) since the mid-nineteenth century (Ferguson 1994; Rothman 1971; Rothman 1980; Rothman and Rothman 1984; Scheerenbeger 1987; Tyor and Bell 1984). While public services for these individuals were often intermingled with those for people with mental illness in county poor houses and asylums, their distinct institutional history clearly emerges in the mid-nineteenth century when states, first Massachusetts and soon after New York, created separate custodial asylums for "mental defectives" (Ferguson 1994; Scheerenberger 1987).

Histories of public institutions differ about their roles in social control vis-à-vis more humane rationales for their existence, but they are unanimous in portraying abandonment, abuse and neglect, unsuccessful attempts at reform, and ultimately, their failure to provide humane care for their residents (Ferguson 1994; Trent 1994). Their titles convey a profound pessimism: Blatt and Kaplan's (1966) *Christmas in Purgatory*; Blatt's (1970) *Exodus from Pandemonium*; Ferguson's (1994) *Abandoned to Their Fate*; the Rothmans' (1984) *The Willowbrook Wars*; and Trent's (1994) *Inventing the Feeble Mind*.

These portrayals of the failures of public institutions are not simply modern judgments on the misguided actions in an earlier era. Post-World War II exposés of state institutions for the mentally ill (which wove in references to care for the mentally retarded), such as Deutsch's (1948) *The Shame of the States* and Ward's (1946) *The Snake Pit* were based on widely circulated articles in newspapers and such popular magazines as *Reader's Digest*. They followed investigations and reports on conditions in state institutions that found appalling abuse and neglect and were not only well-publicized but became issues in statewide political contests (Moreland 1944; Beyer 1979).

By the mid-1960s, smaller institutions and group homes in the community were seen as remedies for poor conditions. Advocates argued that services in communities were more appropriate to normal lives and were less likely to lead to abuse and neglect. They maintained that these services were superior to those in institutions, were preferred by clients and parents, and produced better outcomes (Bank-Mikkelson 1969; Gollay et al. 1978; Nirje 1969; President's Commission 1965; Wolfensberger 1972).

By the 1970s, the notion that large public institutions were inherently harmful and should be closed became a central tenet of the dominant political ideology in the developmental disabilities field and was expressed in a variety of statutes, federal court decisions, and other public policies (Castellani 1987). A number of states were sued in federal courts, and the *Wyatt v. Stickney* case in Alabama, the *Halderman v. Pennhurst* case in Pennsylvania, and the *ARC v. Rockefeller* (Willowbrook) case in New York were important catalysts for downsizing. By the 1980s, "deinstitutionalization" became the term used to describe this large-scale downsizing and creation of community alternatives.

In the 1980s, states began to close rather than reform public institutions when group homes, supports to parents caring for children at home, free and appropriate public education, and community day services became more available. Braddock and his colleagues tracked the drop in states' public institution numbers and census and suggested that interest group advocacy and civil rights suits explained much of the decline (Braddock et al. 1985). There was also an argument (which achieved axiomatic status) that community services were less expensive than institutions. In explaining what he called "the abandonment of the institution after 1970," Trent (1994) wrote, "As I argue, the federal policy of deinstitutionalization resulted from an ironic convergence of developments:

a combination of civil-libertarian and advocacy groups joined with state officials hoping to trim the ever-rising costs of state institutions" (4–5). A related claim was that the unattractiveness of large institutions lowered demand for admissions and resulted in excess capacity and higher costs to the states (Anderson et al. 1998). Advocates and analysts argued that closing public institutions was not only the "right thing to do," it was also the smart thing to do.

In 1984, New York decided to close Willowbrook, and in 1987, the state decided to close several more of its twenty developmental centers. New Hampshire and Vermont closed their single state institutions, and, in 1991, New York announced its intention to close all of its remaining public institutions by 2000. By the end of the twentieth century, the census of public institutions for people with developmental disabilities dropped to 48,496 from their peak in the late 1960s when states operated 345 institutions housing more than 150,000 individuals (Anderson et al. 1999; Lakin et al. 1999). Seven states (Arkansas, Hawaii, Maine, New Hampshire, New Mexico, Vermont, and West Virginia) had closed all their public institutions. Braddock and his colleagues chronicled these trends in several editions of *The State of the States in Developmental Disabilities* (1984–2002).

Institution closures, especially in the 1970s and early 1980s, were politically controversial and operationally challenging (Castellani 1992; Mansell and Erricsson 1996; Rothman and Rothman 1984). The Rothmans cast the conflict at Willowbrook "as between the court and a bureaucracy dominated by a civil service that may be impervious to both the legislature and the executive" (1984, 355). Other analyses described the struggle as one between advocates for people with disabilities, allied with private community agencies, and state governments, allied with public employees and a small remaining cadre of parents frightened by horror stories of life in the community (Crissey and Rosen 1986; Disability Experience 1998; Ferguson 1994). Nonetheless, every contemporary history cast public institutions as expensive and regressive relics of a bygone era contrasted with less-costly and more humane options in communities. Episodes that seemed to support keeping institutions open, such as the debate around institution vis-à-vis community mortality rates, were viewed as rear-guard actions and near-terminal spasms (Borthwick-Duffy et al. 1998; Strauss and Kastner 1996). The story of public institutions was one in which the outcome, if not the timing, had been decided.

Gaps and Anomalies in the Descriptions and Explanations about Closing Institutions

Many descriptions and analyses of the closing of public institutions miss important parts of the problem. Most importantly, explanations for their predicted extinction do not account for the reversal of public policy to close them all in New York or their perseverance in a myriad of other forms in New York and other states.

Public and Other Institutions Remain Open

Tens of thousands of individuals still live in public institutions in almost every state—decades after federal and state statutory, judicial, and administrative policy declared them to be fundamentally antithetical to the appropriate care of people with developmental disabilities and analysts maintained that they were fiscally and operationally dysfunctional (Lakin et al. 1999). New York not only failed to close all its developmental centers by 2000, but during the most severe fiscal crisis in generations, none of its remaining centers were proposed for closure. Preoccupation with the decline in the numbers of formally designated public institutions nationwide ignores the fact that tens of thousands of individuals with developmental disabilities live in other types of large public and private institutions and nursing homes. Descriptions of closure and deinstitutionalization also fail to account for large clusters of congregate "community" facilities housing scores, sometimes hundreds, of former residents on the perimeters of "closed" public institutions. In 2000, there were 47,374 individuals residing in large (more than 15 beds) public institutions, and 69,153 people with developmental disabilities living in other institutions: 34,743 in nursing homes and 34,410 in private and other large (more than 15 beds) institutions (Braddock et al. 2002).

These descriptions do not explain why some states downsized and closed public institutions while similar states kept them open (Braddock et al. 1995; Anderson et al. 1999; Lakin et al. 1999; Parish 2002). Moreover, there are large and unexplained variations among states in the number of residential beds per thousand, the amounts of day services, the amounts of ancillary support services, and spending relative to fiscal capacity (Braddock et al. 2002; Prouty and Lakin 1997). Moral and pragmatic rationales that apparently led some states to close their public institutions were not compelling in similar states.

There are large variations among states in where people with different developmental disabilities are served. People with cerebral palsy and autism are often grouped with people with physical and mental disabilities, and individuals who are involved in the criminal justice system are dealt with in separate facilities in the prison system or in separate facilities in disabilities services systems (Castellani 2000). The observation made by Krugel (1969) in the report to the President's Committee on Mental Retardation that "states differ dramatically in how many and what types of their retarded they serve" remained accurate thirty years later.

There are also wide variations among states in the history of their use of public institutions. New York, for example, built new institutions and refurbished older ones well into the era of downsizing and closure that began in the 1970s. This followed an extensive post-World War II construction program aimed at reducing overcrowding, which followed a pre-war expansion of institutional capacity. Most importantly, the era of downsizing and closure was followed by the creation of new institutions at the end of the twentieth century. A portrayal of public institutions as shadows of nineteenth and early twentieth century asylums inexorably moving toward extinction is belied by modern facilities recently built to serve "special populations."

Deinstitutionalization or Reinstitutionalization

"Deinstitutionalization" established an implicit dichotomy between public institutions and the community programs created to serve former residents. However, most community services are congregate programs that have many of the same features and problems of traditional public institutions even though they are smaller, disaggregated, and operated by private agencies. Congregate day services—sheltered workshops, clinics, and day treatment programs—also remain vibrant. Some of these smaller and dispersed public and private facilities in communities have replicated the abuse, neglect, and abandonment found in larger public institutions (CQC 1984; 1986; 1995c).

The bulk of late twentieth and early twenty-first century expansion in community developmental services continues to be in congregate settings rather than individual, self-directed supports. The overwhelming majority of individuals living in group homes lead lives largely governed by institutional norms and routines, although the distances between the residences and day programs are covered in yellow vans instead of a walk across the campus, and the rhetoric of "beds" and day "slots" has changed to "opportunities." Advocates of a "supported living" approach have described the medicalized and bureaucratized features of most community programs, although their critiques have not linked the problems to their integration with institutions (Ferguson et al. 1990; Gardner 1992; Mount 1994; O'Brien and O'Brien 1994; Taylor, Bodgon, and Racino 1991).

Finally, almost all descriptions of institutions and community services focus on specific services and program models. Virtually none consider the institutional implications of a concentration of services, even so-called individualized services, in large, private, specialized developmental services agencies that are often vertically and horizontally integrated by age and service, that hold a monopoly on the provision of services in many locales, and that serve hundreds, sometimes thousands, of individuals in their various programs.

Changing Institutions and Integration with Community Programs

Descriptions of downsizing and closure and the concomitant creation of community programs convey an image of the emptying of static, custodial public institutions and the creation and expansion of privately operated community agencies. But neither the statistical summaries nor histories describe the new roles these institutions assumed, how those new roles were played in relation to public and private community programs, and how the specialization and integration of roles among public institutions and public and private community programs were mutually reinforcing.

Before World War II, New York's institutions housed relatively less disabled and more indigent adults. After the war, large numbers of severely disabled infants and children were admitted, and new rationales were created for institutions. As the era of deinstitutionalization and closure began, New York's institutions housed a varied mix of residents similar to those living in the community (OMRDD 1978; 1980; 1984). By the 1990s, the remaining public institutions had a census split largely between infirm aged, behaviorally problematic, and forensically involved individuals (OMRDD 1995). Changes in the characteristics of the residents and the adaptation in roles institutions played needs to be part of a full description and explanation. Private agencies grew to serve individuals with different clinical needs, service histories, and personal and family characteristics in different organizational and geographic contexts. As community programs expanded to meet varying needs and circumstances, public institutions evolved, and the service functions and clientele of each were inextricably linked.

Public Institutions: Neither Adequately Described nor Explained

Public institutions persevere at the beginning of the twenty-first century, and explaining why along contrasting institution-community, public-private, and large-small axes produces contradictions and anomalies rather than a coherent description or explanation. The various advocacy, civil rights, and cost-cutting explanations for downsizing and closure fail to account for why public institutions persevere in large numbers in almost every state, vary widely among similar states, and seem revitalized in New York.

This book takes a new approach to explaining the perseverance and vitality of public institutions by examining all public institutions and other public and private institutional and community developmental services in New York from 1935 to 2000 and the early years of the twenty-first century. This approach takes social, economic, and political factors, slowly emerging over sixty-five years, into account and considers public institutions in the larger organizational context within which they are embedded. An in-depth investigation shows how technical, fiscal, and operational issues had long-term ramifications. This broad, long, and deep approach overcomes the limitations of national surveys and summaries. The experience of New York provides important lessons for dealing with institutions, policy, and practice in other states, federal-state relations, and Medicaid policy in this and related areas.

Public Institutions in New York

New York's experience has important implications and lessons for other states since virtually every significant phenomenon involving policy and practice on public institutions, developmental services, and intergovernmental finance was played out in New York on a grand scale. New York's suspension of the plan to close all its public institutions by 2000 and the construction of a new public institution was a startling reversal of what had been viewed as a virtually inevitable process of closure. The absence of serious protest over the suspension of the plan to close all institutions and the widespread support for the new institution is a significant challenge to the prevailing moral and pragmatic arguments, especially in a state where its top public officials proclaimed that closing institutions was "the right thing to do" (Webb 1988; New York State Senate 1990).

The history of public institutions for people with developmental and other mental disabilities is, to a large extent, their history in New York, going back 150 years to the 1851 creation of the second state institution in the country (Ferguson 1994; Grob 1991, 1994; Rothman 1971, 1980; Rothman and Rothman 1984). New York also had the largest number of these institutions and, at their zenith, the largest numbers of people in public institutions. At the end of 1967, there were 27,554 people in twenty state schools and "discrete mental retardation units" on the grounds of state psychiatric centers (DMH 1968). This was more than twice the number in the next largest state (California, with 12,610) and almost 15 percent of the 192,493 individuals estimated to be in the 150 public institutions at the time (Butterfield 1969).

New York's public institutions have always drawn national attention, first as models of care, but later as prime examples of abuse and neglect, as this indictment and Willowbrook became synonymous. The Willowbrook suit (*ARC v. Rockefeller*) became a vehicle for the important changes in policy and practice as new concepts of normalization and services in communities, new federal and state statutes, and new federal and state funding for community services were played out in New York to, at first, a national media audience, and, later, to virtually every expert in the field who testified in the case, served on an oversight panel, or visited the state (Castellani 1987; Rothman and Rothman 1984).

With Willowbrook and Medicaid funding as the legal and fiscal engines, New York embarked on the largest and proportionately fastest deinstitutionalization and creation of community services in the country, with the census in the state's developmental centers dropping from 20,062 to 11,162 in the ten years following the Willowbrook Consent Decree in 1975. With hundreds of group homes and day services created in new and expanded private agencies and in publicly operated community programs, New York is a prime arena for examining the various aspects of deinstitutionalization that led to closures of public institutions.

In 1984, New York decided to close Willowbrook, and in 1987, the announcement of the intention to close several of its remaining developmental centers by 1991 was the most ambitious closure policy initiative among the states where only a few were planning to close single facilities. New York's closure of several institutions and plan to close them all by 2000 is the best example of policymaking and implementation on this central issue. The reversal of that plan is another important reason for examining New York's experience.

New York's institutional experience is also embedded in a large and complex array of publicly and privately operated developmental services that provide an important context and relevance to other states. By the end of the 1990s, New York had converted the majority of its funding to the Medicaid Home and Community-Based Services waiver. With 46,209 recipients, the waiver had become the largest in the country and substantially larger than the next largest user, California, with 39,391 recipients (Lakin et al. 2001). New York also provided exceptionally high levels of services with more than 35,000 total public and private residential beds, second only to California in total residential capacity. New York is in the top quintile of residential capacity per 100,000 and fifth in dollars spent per consumer (Braddock et al. 1998; OMRDD 2000). New York established self-determination and supported living pilots that achieved about the same level of participation as in other states.

Methods and Sources

This book began as a study of the policy development and implementation of developmental center closures announced by New York in 1987. It expanded to include a study of closure of all developmental centers in New York by 2000 and closure policy and implementation in several other states. When the plan to close all developmental centers was suspended, then reversed, and later transformed into plans to build new institutions and linked with funding for more congregate residential programs in communities, the central question became explaining the perseverance and vitality of public institutions. A reconsideration of New York's closure policies and implementation and a closer examination of the experience in other states revealed the gaps and anomalies outlined previously and pointed to the necessity of broadening the perspective to encompass all public and private developmental services.

Looking back from the 1987 decision, the literature on public institutions was so focused on the abuse and neglect that it became a rationale for public policy changes in the 1970s. It appeared that advocates, social policy analysts, and historians could conceive of no outcome other than the institutions' inevitable demise. This led back to earlier research and reconsideration of the author's experience in fiscal and operational roles, especially during the Rockefeller era. Since the construction of new institutions that accelerated in the Rockefeller years was based in large part on frustration with the slow pace of construction to meet pent-up demand, this required a look back to assess the strength and depth of these forces. It became apparent that this review of the history of public institutions from the end of World War II needed to take into account the forces underway before and during the war that caused such radical changes immediately after. The starting point became 1935 when, with the closing of the last municipal hospital for people with developmental disabilities, New York's modern system of public institutions was in place.

Examining all public institutions as well as public and private developmental services from 1935 required using a wide and rich array of sources. The literature on public institutions was important: histories from colonial times, statistical analyses of institution census changes, and the many articles and chapters on deinstitutionalization and closure. Political histories of New York, biographies of governors, studies of public administration and management, and analyses of New York's economy and finances were also important in providing the political and economic context for the evolution of public institutions.

Large numbers of government documents were examined and analyzed: *Annual Reports* of the New York State Office of Mental Retardation and Developmental Disabilities and its predecessor agency, the Department of Mental Hygiene; the *Executive Budgets*, governors' budget messages; and related documents were important sources for describing the fiscal and programmatic history of institutions in the state. Scores of annual, three-year, five-year, master, comprehensive, and special plans issued by New York, the federal government, and various other agencies were also important sources. Other government documents went deeper into particular features of institutions: fiscal and program audits, reviews by oversight bodies, reports of legislative committees, consultant reports, and the reports of special investigations by various governmental commissions. Still deeper in this vein were letters, memoranda, fiscal and program analyses, handbooks, guidelines, and rate-setting manuals. A large number of documents from private agencies were also used: annual reports, legislative proposals, and fiscal analyses.

Hundreds of interviews were conducted on policy making and implementation in New York and other states: public officials, chief executives and senior staff of federal, state, and local government agencies, legislators, directors of private agencies, administrative staff in central and field offices, direct care staff, clinicians, union representatives, parents, advocates, and consumers. Individuals who played significant roles in the executive offices of Governors Nelson Rockefeller, Hugh Carey, Mario Cuomo, and George Pataki were also interviewed on the politics and policies affecting institutions and developmental services.

Thirty-five years of public service in New York made participant observation a very important source for this book. Working in the Office of State Comptroller and subsequently in the budget office of the Department of Mental Hygiene in the mid- to late 1960s when many new institutions were being built and bonded and Medicaid funding was being increasingly tapped provided important insights into the fiscal foundations of institutions. Thirty-five years as a fiscal analyst, researcher, and administrator meant participating in innumerable meetings related to the central issues of this book. Formal and informal inter and intra-departmental committees, inter-agency task forces, budget reviews, legislative hearings, conferences, and constituency group presentations were important sources of information about decisions, strategies, assessments, and expectations on policy and practice related to public institutions as well as discussion, debate, review, and coordination of decisions made in other meetings. These included the peculiar bureaucratic phenomena called "pre-meetings" and what Bruce Vladeck called "walking around and talking to people"—other sources, but more importantly, guides for interpreting and cross-referencing reorganizations, reassignments, and other soft signs in large organizations that added texture and provided important reality checks.

Plan of the Book

The history of public institutions in New York from 1935 to 2000 does not follow regular patterns of social, economic, political, and operational causes and effects. Slowly emerging changes in social attitudes and decades-long deterioration in local economies formed the ground against which the figures of shorter-term political battles, fiscal crises, and opportunistic policy decisions stood out. Long-simmering problems erupted into brief and intense periods of change. Dramatic events such as those at Willowbrook often obscured less visible but equally significant developments such as the Medicaid Plan of Compliance. What appeared to be decisions of strategic consequence became, over time, relatively minor adjustments in the status quo. Virtually invisible and purportedly technical changes in fiscal mechanisms had profound and long-lasting implications for public institutions and other developmental services. Public institutions and other developmental services went through distinct phases when certain factors moved to the fore and particular events and decisions had critical importance. These overlap and are not rigid, but they help focus on those periods in the evolution of public institutions when unanticipated turns were made toward unexpected outcomes.

Part 1: Drift and Conflict

Part 1 of the book examines the forty years between 1935 and 1965 during which the state failed to resolve either the radical shift in institutionalization of profoundly disabled infants or demands for community services for less-disabled individuals. It describes how prewar and wartime fault lines in organization, staffing, and clientele widened as the state's decision to admit infants without increasing capacity led to overcrowding, increasingly abysmal conditions, and growing waiting lists. Part 1 describes the conflict between the state and emerging parent organizations over the state's failure to fund the community services its rhetoric promoted. It shows how multiple, overlapping, and inconsistent state and federal plans fueled tensions between the state and constituency groups rather than establishing guidelines for the future. This part of the book explains how the state's attempt to address chronic and severe fiscal crises through moral obligation bonding, public authorities, and reliance on Medicaid financing led to political confrontations that collapsed the old order but also laid the fiscal and organizational foundations for the future of public institutions and community services.

Part 2: Sweeping Away the Old Order

Part 2 of the book examines the crucial period from 1965 to 1972 during which important components in the foundation of services for people with developmental disabilities were replaced. It explains how a new political ideology about people with disabilities, a new source of funding in Medicaid, a new role for federal courts in policymaking, and the presidential ambitions of Nelson Rockefeller and Robert Kennedy meshed with long-simmering cleavages and swept away the old order. This part of the book explains how New York took advantage of the many unanticipated features of Medicaid and the ICF/MR program to refinance its public institutions.

Part 3: The Big Bang

Part 3 of the book covers a short and intense period, beginning in 1975, in which a new universe of developmental services was created. It describes the Willowbrook Consent Decree and the ICF Plan of Compliance and shows how they worked in tandem to set a new direction for developmental services in New York by requiring rapid deinstitutionalization and the use of existing and new community organizations to provide services. It describes the new and aggressive approaches to financing community services and explains how they had strategic consequences for the fiscal and operational integration of public and private institution and community services. Part 3 also examines the factors driving New York's deinstitutionalization and explains why New York's rapid and large-scale deinstitutionalization, using the Medicaid-funded ICF/MR program and Medicaid-funded day programs, replicated institutional formats in communities. This part of the book explains how resolving the political controversies surrounding the opening of new institutions and special facilities resulted in historic agreements with state employee unions, advocates, and parent organizations that shaped the foundations of the organization of services in the state for the remainder of the century. It also describes how the state began using surpluses from Medicaid maximization of institutional costs to make developmental centers "cash cows" critical to financing private as well as public community services.

Part 4: Closing and Not Closing Institutions

Part 4 of the book examines the period between 1984 and 1995 when New York decided to close Willowbrook and several other developmental centers, planned the closing of all developmental centers, suspended that plan, and eventually decided to keep some developmental centers open while it built new ones. This part describes the factors leading to these decisions and explains why closure was intended to solve the fiscal imbalances that resulted from the institution-financed system as well as maintaining the political, economic, and operational balance of developmental services in the state.

Part 4 describes the success of the 1987 closure policy, the positive outcomes of implementation, and the crafting of a policy to close all institutions. It examines the state's deepening fiscal deficits and the problems emerging in closure. It describes how rifts in the consensus around closing all institutions were growing at the same time the governor was directing that a plan be developed to close all institutions by 2000. It explains how public institutions were transformed into specialized facilities for a frail elderly, behaviorally problematic, and criminally involved clientele with no constituency demanding closure. This part of the book explains why institutionalization of these "special populations" was a guarantee for stable and higher paying jobs for public employees and a source of greatly increased Medicaid reimbursement. This part of the book explains how this revenue exceeded the costs of the entire state operation of developmental services and reduced the proportion of the overall costs paid by New York's public and private agencies to a fraction of what it had been thirty years earlier. Part 4 of the book explains why political leaders from both parties, public employees, major advocacy organizations, and the private provider industry were "the dogs that didn't bark" when it appeared that closing all institutions threatened to undermine central fiscal and economic foundations on which the organization of services rested. It explains why, at the end of the century, rather than closing all institutions, the claim that "institutions as we knew them had closed" was being made, congregate care programs in the community were being expanded, and new institutions were being built.

The Conclusion reviews the key factors and events in the history of public institutions and developmental services in New York from 1935 to 2000. It explains why the perseverance and vitality of public institutions at the end of the century emerged from the collapse of the old system around Willowbrook and the opportunities of a new system that emerged from Medicaid. It explains why, instead of the death knell of institutions that most foretold, the elements of a strategy were put into place that ultimately led to the perseverance of public institutions.

The Conclusion of the book explains why New York's experience with public and private, large and small institutions shows that the seemingly intractable problems in Medicaid financing of health and human services for people with disabilities were not all outcomes of anomalies or unintended consequences. It explains why people with developmental disabilities went from being fiscal burdens to sources of revenue for public and private agencies, why public institutions became vibrant and resilient components in the organization of developmental services, and why public institutions became cash cows.

Part I

Drift and Conflict

Chapter 1

Fault Lines: 1935 to 1945

Features of the building program [include] additional facilities for 'problem' children; and special buildings at the state schools for mentally defective infants and children.

The latter provisions represent a radical departure in the state's policy which heretofore left to families, or to county and municipal authorities, the responsibility for institutional care of defective children under the age of five. Only the most urgent and distressing cases can be occasionally accommodated now, but eventually, when the projected new facilities are constructed, the state will be able to care for mental defectives of all ages.

—Department of Mental Hygiene, *Annual Report* 1946

The New York State Department of Mental Hygiene's announcement that it would admit a limited number of infants under the age of five and "care for mental defectives of all ages" was called a "radical departure." It was a decision that shaped the nature of institutions and all services for people with developmental disabilities for more than a half-century. It would begin an era when chronic overcrowding would reach catastrophic levels, and ranks of cribs holding severely and profoundly retarded infants would replace the squeezed cots of comparatively able adults. Although the farms and workshops of rural institutions remained for many years, infant infirmaries would define this era, and "snake pits" would endure for decades as the label for institutions for people with mental disabilities.

Commissioner Frederick MacCurdy called the admission of infants a new direction when he announced the policy in 1945, but it was an acceleration of practices and an accommodation to pressures that had been building for ten years. It was only one of several important movements taking place in the state's institutional system. Institutions were admitting younger, more severely disabled children while the eight-hour day and World War II drained staff from those facilities. As more infants filled the wards, the state closed colonies and other extramural programs and concentrated care in the institutions proper. Fewer "higher grade" residents were "paroled" and were pressed into service as institution laborers. The cumulative impact of these events exacerbated scandalous conditions and led to a special investigation into mismanagement that became entwined in state and presidential politics.

Changes in the organization of the state's institutions, the characteristics of their residents, the services and staffing, and the ways they were financed and administered were tectonic plates moving in different directions. The pressures along these fault lines produced a series of large tremors in the mid-1940s that presaged the cataclysmic ruptures that occurred in the 1970s around the San Andreas Fault in the state's institution system—Willowbrook. Many of the explanations for what happened at Willowbrook and other public institutions, how and why services for people with disabilities were reorganized and refinanced, and why institutions persevered begin with understanding the shape and direction of pressures that built for decades.

State Institution System: 1935 to 1945

Dynamic, complex, and diverse are not terms usually associated with "state institutions for mental defectives and epileptics" in the midst of the Depression. Nonetheless, New York State's facilities for people with developmental disabilities in 1935 were much different than the isolated, stagnant institutions filled with one-way admissions that provoked post-war reformers. In 1935, there were six "state institutions for mental defectives and epileptics" administered by the New York State Department of Mental Hygiene: five state schools (Letchworth Village, Newark, Rome, Syracuse, and Wassaic), and Craig Colony, an institution for the care of epileptics, which was incorporated into the state school system in 1958. The pre-war institutions had distinct identities that grew out of their unique historical roots, original missions, and even the personalities of their superintendents.

Established in 1851 as the New York Asylum for Idiots, Syracuse State School was the oldest institution in the state for the care of mental defectives and the second oldest in the country after the first state school Massachusetts created in 1848. The New York State Custodial Asylum at Newark was established in 1878 as an experimental program for "custodial care and sequestration of idiotic and feeble minded girls and women, for their protection and the protection of the State from hereditary increase of that class of dependents on public charity" (Lerner 1972, 75). In 1893, the state legislature recreated the Oneida County poorhouse as the Oneida State Custodial Asylum (later renamed the Rome State Custodial Asylum) for "unteachable mental defectives" and "low-grade and delinquent cases" (Ferguson 1994; Lerner 1972).

Craig Colony began its existence in 1896 as the first and ultimately only state institution specifically devoted to the care of persons with epilepsy. In addition to providing a site for the scientific study and treatment of epilepsy, the care at Craig involved small groups of individuals living in cottages scattered throughout the 2,000 acre property in New York's Finger Lakes region at Sonyea, which local lore attributed to "State of New York Epilepsy Asylum" despite clear Native American roots for the name. Letchworth Village State School, in Rockland County, employed Frederick Law Olmstead in the design of the grounds, and opened in 1911 as "The Eastern New York Custodial Asylum." It was expected to be a model school for the feeble-minded emphasizing vocational training, although Trent (1994) points out that shelling peas for the dining rooms and mopping the floors of the wards were part of the training. Wassaic State School opened in 1930 to relieve the overcrowding in the existing state schools, especially for individuals from New York City where there was no state school.

Characteristics of the Residents of State Institutions

Higher-grade educables, women of childbearing age, low-grade delinquents, and unteachable mental defectives are terms so inimical to contemporary usage that they can deflect attention away from the complex reality behind them. Behind these archaic labels, the *Annual Reports* of the Department of Mental Hygiene describe a resident population that, in 1935, was much different than the one that characterized these institutions after World War II that would require a radical change in admissions policy. Although the differences among the six institutions had important implications for later changes in policy and practice, the 16,318 individuals "on the books" at the end of the 1934–1935 fiscal year, were generally older, comparatively less disabled, and poorer than the typical residents of the post-war era (DMH 1935, 297).

The annual statistical summaries for average age at admission, death, and length of stay at death show that a large percentage of residents died within a year of admission: 53.9 percent of those who died in 1935 had been in the institution less than two years (DMH 1936). However, those who survived the first year after admission lived relatively long lives. In the mid-1930s, the state schools housed a significant proportion of "higher grade mental defectives." In 1935, 52.1 percent of first admissions were classified as "morons" [higher grade], while only 11.5 percent were classified as "idiots" [lower grade], and 30.7 percent classified as imbeciles (DMH 1935).

In 1935, New York's Mental Hygiene Law stipulated that the institutions of the Department of Mental Hygiene were to be maintained "for the care and treatment of poor and indigent persons." The Commissioner could, however, "permit persons who are neither poor nor indigent to be received and maintained in an institution conditioned upon prompt and regular payment for their care and treatment" (Mental Hygiene Law Sec. 24-a). The reports on the economic status of first admissions confirm that state schools were largely places for the poor. Of the 1,789 first admissions in 1935, 65.3 percent were classified as "dependent," 30.7 percent as "marginal," and only 2.7 percent as "comfortable." There were only 326 paying patients in the state schools (DMH 1935).

The Organization of Care: Institutional and Extramural Programs

A picture of large, overcrowded, isolated warehouses dominates the history of large institutions in New York and other states. However, one of the most striking features of the state's institutional system before World War II was the large numbers of individuals who lived outside the institutions proper. Of the 16,318 individuals "on the books" at the state schools in 1935, only 12,797 were in the institutions: 1,716 were "on parole," and 1,805 lived in colonies (DMH 1936).

The colony system was not developed by Dr. Charles Bernstein (Superintendent of Rome State School for forty years), but he and Rome became identified with this important form of extra-institutional care (Ferguson 1994; Trent 1994). Bernstein established a series of self-sustaining colonies off the campus at specific work sites. The first colonies were farms. Later there were industrial colonies in local mills, colonies for women working as domestics in private homes, and a reforestation colony of young men planting trees in the Adirondacks for the state. In the 1920s, Bernstein set up junior colonies for young children and summer vacation colonies. In the midst of the Depression more pressure was placed on the state for admissions, and colonies increasingly became places to house more capable and docile inmates apart from the increasingly disabled and "delinquent" individuals who were filling the infirmaries and locked wards of the institutions. At their peak in 1940, Rome operated sixty colonies across the state.

Colonies were not the only form of extra-institutional care. In 1935, the state formally established Family Care, which began informally in 1931 when residents of Newark State School were boarded with local families (DMH 1936). The experiment proved successful, and legislation provided, "There be allocated from the money appropriated for maintenance and operation of any institution in the Department of Mental Hygiene a sum not to exceed twenty thousand dollars for the purpose of establishing a community care for legally admitted patients and inmates at rates not exceeding four dollars per week"

(Chapter 27, Laws 1935). By the end of the 1936 fiscal year, there were 137 individuals in Family Care from the state schools.

Parole was the term used for individuals who had been admitted to an institution but were conditionally released to the care of their families. It was not until 1945 that this term was changed to "convalescent care." Throughout the 1930s, approximately ten percent of individuals "on the books" were on parole (DMH 1936, 1940).

Admissions, Discharges, Deaths, and Overcrowding

There was a great deal of movement in and out of the institutions during the 1930s. In 1935 there were 1,789 first admissions, 158 readmissions, 823 transfers-in, 812 transfers-out, 831 discharges, and 215 deaths. A substantial amount of the movement was related to the opening of Wassaic State School and the transfer of residents from the New York City Children's Hospital on Randall's Island.

Overcrowding became the central focus of policy on institutions from World War II to the era of deinstitutionalization in the 1980s. In 1935, 12,376 individuals resided in the five state schools (1,157 over their rated capacity of 9,414—a 12.3 percent over capacity rate). The burden of overcrowding was not equally distributed among the institutions. Syracuse was five residents under capacity, and Letchworth, Newark, and Rome were 23.3, 18.4, and 20.9 percent over capacity. The newly opened Wassaic State School was at capacity (DMH, 1935).

Services Outside the State Department of Mental Hygiene

In addition to the state schools and Craig Colony, there were state institutions for defective delinquents, private schools, and the New York City municipal hospital on Randall's Island.

Randall's Island, New York City

In 1870, New York City created the New York City Children's Hospital on Randall's Island to provide temporary care for mentally defective and epileptic children from New York City. However, the lack of accommodations in state institutions made those stays permanent for most children. The opening of Wassaic State School and increased accommodations in other state institutions allowed the transfer of the patients to state schools. The population of the Children's Hospital declined rapidly, and its closing marked the end of formal public care in municipal hospitals.

Institutions for Defective Delinquents

In 1923, New York established the State Institution for Defective Delinquents in Naponoch, New York, which was operated by the Department of Corrections and inspected by the Department of Mental Hygiene. This institution was intended to provide academic and industrial training as well as positive habit training and discipline for the 400 juvenile mentally retarded offenders it was designed to serve. It was, nonetheless, a prison, which allowed the other state schools to get rid of, or avoid admitting, troublesome and dangerous residents (Scheerenberger 1983). While parole was possible for those who demonstrated an ability to adjust to society, it was largely at the discretion of the superintendent, and most defective delinquents were held indefinitely. The state later established an Institution for Female Defective Delinquents at Albion. By 1935, the census was 1,006 at Naponoch and 217 at Albion (DMH 1935, 18).

Public Schools, Day Services, and Private Institutions

Following the creation of the first special class in a public school in Providence, Rhode Island in 1896, other American cities began establishing classes for children with mental retardation. New York City established its first class in 1902 (Lerner 1972). In 1917, state law mandated special classes for "educable" children, but the classes fell far short of the letter and spirit of the law (Lerner 1972). In the 1920s, there were less than a third of the number of classes required, and additions were impeded by a lack of teachers and reluctance of school districts to create and operate these classes. Enrollment in these classes was virtually flat during the 1930s. Most special classes were in New York City, which also had a handful of classes for visually and hearing impaired children with mental retardation, but these classes were not widely available in the city or anywhere else in the state (Scheerenberger 1983). Few special classes were available outside the large city districts, and they were virtually absent in rural areas. Moreover, those not "educable" were routinely excluded from public schools, and children deemed "trainable" might get some assistance such as home training manuals from social welfare agencies or child guidance clinics. At the end of the 1935 fiscal year, there were 362 individuals in eleven private licensed institutions for mental defectives (DMH 1935, 18).

Expansion of Services and Emerging Problems: 1935 to 1941

The movement of residents from the New York City Children's Hospital on Randall's Island completed the transfer of responsibility for public housing of "mental defectives" to the state. The now-unified state system was remarkably diverse with a variety of services outside the institutions proper, with approximately one-quarter of those "on the books" living in colonies, in family care, or on parole. The individuals in the care of the state were typically high functioning (in comparison to the populations in later years), poor adults who engaged in one of the "manual arts" that were the primary activities of the institutions. The conditions were not Arcadian, but the prewar organization of services belied the notion that institutions were always isolated warehouses filling with one-way admissions.

Expansion of Existing State Schools

The Great Depression and the 1930s have become synonymous with notions of uniform deprivation. World War II and the years just before Pearl Harbor are often portrayed as a period during which the American economy pulled out of the Depression and a boom began that would last for decades. In many ways, for people with developmental disabilities in New York, the conditions were reversed. During the Depression, New York took advantage of the federal Works Projects Administration to substantially increase its institutional capacity. Wassaic State School opened in 1930 and was rapidly filled with transfers from Randall's Island. New and remodeled buildings at Letchworth Village State School added 660 beds to its capacity in 1936, and the completion of new buildings at Rome State School enlarged the capacity of that institution by 552 beds (DMH 1936).

Between 1935 and 1940, the number of individuals on the books of the state schools increased by over 25 percent, from 13,839 to 17,498, and the institutional census jumped from 12,797 to 15,952 (DMH 1935, 1940). However, every expansion in capacity resulted in increased overcrowding (from 12.3 to 17.0 over capacity between 1935 and 1940). This perverse phenomenon would plague the state for decades.

A New State School at Willowbrook

Willowbrook, the institution whose name became synonymous with overcrowding, abuse and neglect, was designed to be a major solution to these problems. In its *Annual Report* for 1939, the Department of Mental Hygiene announced plans for a new state school.

"To meet the need for additional accommodations for mental defectives from New York City, the Legislature of 1938 appropriated $5,100,000 for the acquisition of a site for a new state school and for the commencement of construction work thereon. Accordingly, the Department of Mental Hygiene purchased in December, 1938 a tract of 375 acres at Willowbrook on Staten Island for a site for the new institution. The new school will probably be opened in 1941 and may ultimately provide treatment for as many as 5,000 patients." (DMH 1939, 62)

Reduction in Expenditures

Following the formal introduction of Family Care in 1935 with 45 individuals reported in this new service, the numbers increased exponentially: 135 in 1936, 203 in 1937, to 316 in 1938 (DMH 1937,1939). However, the program proved to be highly sensitive to the amount the state paid for the board of patients. The *Annual Report* for 1940 reported a drop from 315 to 279 people in the program, and attributed the drop to "an unfortunate reduction in the appropriation for food from which money was drawn to pay the board of patients" (DMH 1940, 72).

The legislature did increase the appropriation for food in 1941, but the state institutions suffered from overall declines in expenditures. The number of the individuals "on the books" increased from 16,318 in 1935 (with 12,797 in the institutions proper) to 20,487 (with 15,592 in the institutions) in 1940, but expenditures for Maintenance and Operations of the facilities remained almost flat: $2,249,177 in 1935 and $2,259,160 in 1940 (DMH 1936, 1941). Admissions continued to outpace increases in capacity, and by 1940 over-crowding jumped to 17.0 percent over capacity from 12.3 percent in 1935 (DMH 1936, 1941).

The Eight-Hour Day

In his *Executive Budget* for 1936–1937, Governor Lehman proposed an eight-hour day and acknowledged its impact on staffing in the state institutions.

> "It is unfortunate that many ward attendants, guards, nurses and other institutional employees immediately engaged in nursing and custodial care of inmates, patients, and other wards of the state have been required to work twelve hours daily".... "The eight-hour day will ultimately require the employment of as many as five thousand additional men and women at an annual cost of possibly five million dollars (x–xi)."

While the eight-hour day became law, there were no large increases in the numbers of employees in the institutions. In fact, after the large increases in total numbers of employees in the institutions from 2,458 in 1935 to 3,243 in 1937, the numbers remained essentially flat (3,349 in 1938, 3,318 in 1939, 3,428 in 1940, and 3,297 in 1941) before the drastic drops experienced during the war (DMH 1936–1942). The *Executive Budgets* in the late 1930s and early 1940s included routine requests for overtime pay for the same number of employees working the same "unfortunate" hours. Moreover, according to Trent, Bernstein at Rome State School "complained that he did not have sufficient attendants for the three shifts and turned to the 'higher grade morons' as a source of institution labor" (1994, 220).

The use of residents as institution laborers was also exacerbated by the increasing difficulties in discharging residents, placing them in colonies, or putting them on parole. The economic status of over 95 percent of admissions was "dependent" or "marginal," (DMH 1941), and poor families were reluctant to take their children back from the institutions. High unemployment drastically reduced opportunities for placement in industrial colonies and increased labor union opposition to them (Trent 1994). Even farm colonies were increasingly providing food for the institutions rather than operating in the local rural economies.

World War II and the Impact on Services

World War II had enormous and long-lasting consequences for New York's institutions. Some of these were sudden and drastic changes brought about by the war, others were accelerations of trends that had begun during the Depression, and still others were important coincidences. The transfer of Willowbrook to the army, changes in the residents and employees of the institutions, and the death of Charles Bernstein were important and pivotal changes.

Transfer of Willowbrook to the Army and the Moratorium on Construction

The Department's *Annual Report* for 1940 stated, "Satisfactory progress was made in the construction of a new State school at Willowbrook, Staten Island, and it is expected that the first unit of this institution will be ready for occupancy in 1941" (DMH 1940, 63). The enthusiasm about the anticipated opening of Willowbrook was dashed with the exigencies of the war. The *Annual Report* for 1942 explained that, in response to a request from the Secretary of War, on September 23, 1942, this "hospital-school of modern design and equipment, erected on Staten Island at a cost of over $12,000,000, to provide accommodations for 3,000 mental defectives, was transferred to the United States Army for its use as Halloran General Hospital for the duration of the war emergency" (DMH 1942).

The transfer of Willowbrook had enormous consequences for the institution system and the organization of services for the remainder of the century and beyond. It was the most salient but not the only major problem for the state's institutions. In addition to the loss of 3,000 anticipated beds at Willowbrook, construction of additions and major repairs to other facilities virtually halted as expenditures for capital construction plummeted. From $5.1 million in 1941, annual capital construction expenditures dropped to $3.9 million in 1942, to $1.0 million in 1943, to $275,000 in 1944, and finally to $15,000 in 1945 (DMH 1943–1946).

Accelerating Changes in New Admissions and Institution Census

The cumulative effect of the Depression and the entry of the United States into World War II accelerated changes in the makeup of the residents of the state schools. The census in the institutions increased from 16,047 in 1941 to 16,375 in 1945, and overall overcrowding increased to 21.7 percent over capacity. The relatively small increase in the overall census reflected the drop in admissions. First admissions to the state schools dropped from 1,655 in 1941 to 1,380 in 1945 (DMH 1945, 294). A moratorium on construction not only left nothing in the pipeline for new facilities, but the much lower rates of admission during the war contributed to a backlog and pressure for admissions after the war. Had the rate of admissions remained at the 1941 level of 12.2 per 100,000 during the war years rather than dropping to 9.9 per 100,000 in 1945, approximately 1,365 additional admissions would have occurred.

Two other important changes in the population of the state schools also began to accelerate during the war. The percentage of first admissions classified as "idiot" (the most disabled) jumped from 7.8 percent in 1941 to 12.9 percent in 1945. The percentage of first admissions to the state schools of individuals under the age of ten leaped from 24.8 percent of first admissions in 1941 to 32.8 percent in 1945. It was apparent that the state schools were beginning to serve a much younger and more disabled population before the formal change in policy in 1945, and this compounded the problems of shortages in staff and facilities.

One other characteristic of first admissions that indicates the shift in the role of state institutions was their economic condition. The institutions traditionally served a poor and economically marginal population as first admissions in the dependent and marginal categories were typically over 95 percent throughout the 1930s. In 1941, the economic conditions of first admissions to the state schools were classified as: 70.4 percent dependent; 26.2 percent marginal; and 3.4 percent comfortable (DMH 1941, 322). In 1945, the economic conditions of first admissions to the state schools were classified as: 38.8 percent dependent; 43.0 percent marginal; and 6.2 percent comfortable (DMH 1945, 301). This shift was due in large measure to the exigencies of the war. Fathers off to the armed services, mothers working, and housing shortages placed additional strains on families with a child with mental retardation. This shift toward placement in state schools of children from more middle-class circumstances was also an early indication of the large-scale attitudinal, social, and economic changes that would emerge following the war.

Closing Colonies and Contracting Family Care

Charles Bernstein, the director of Rome State School and the most ardent proponent of colonies, died in 1942. Both a change in philosophy of care and the war resulted in the rapid closing of colonies. From 1941 to 1945, the total number of individuals in colonies dropped from 1,659 to 1,265 (DMH 1946).

Family Care placements increased slightly through the war years from 527 in 1941 to 621 in 1945, creating revised expectations about the need for institutions. The *Annual Report* for 1942 pointed out, "It has become evident that the growth of Family Care will lessen the necessity for additional institution capacity. The ultimate saving in construction costs will amount to many million dollars" (DMH 1942, 70). The numbers of individuals on Parole declined over the war years from 2,254 in 1941 to 2,059 in 1945. By 1945, the percentage of individuals "on the books" of the state schools who were now in the institution proper had climbed to over 80 percent (DMH 1946).

Loss of Employees

In addition to the growing crisis in physical plant capacity, the state institution system experienced many of the problems of labor shortages brought on by the war, exacerbating the problems existing before the war. As Lend Lease and other pre-war expansion programs drew more people into factories, and into the armed forces with the war, employment in the state schools stagnated and dropped. In 1942, the number of employees dropped to 3,297, in 1943 to 2,935, in 1944 to 2,800, and by 1945 the of employees in the schools dropped to 2,611, the lowest number of employees since 1936. In 1945, there were 1,403 vacancies in the overall authorization of 4,014 employees, and 25 of the 63 medical officer positions were vacant (DMH 1946).

Public Institutions in State and National Politics

The conditions in the state's institutions remained largely invisible to the general public until unforeseen events thrust the institutions into the state and national political scene.

Temporary Commission on State Hospital Problems

The growth in the population of the state's mental institutions was a major concern for the state administration, and in 1940, Governor Herbert Lehman appointed a Temporary Commission on State Hospital Problems "to study the possibility of diminishing the rate of growth of the State Hospitals for the mentally ill" (Temporary State Commission 1942). The primary focus of the Commission was not overcrowding but the cost of care. The Commission's 1942 Progress Report calculated the annual census increases from 1930 through 1942 and concluded, "There has been nothing like this in the history of the New York State Hospitals during the past fifty years. The fiscal implications of the above figures are substantial" (Temporary Commission, 1942, 3). The report then analyzed the savings in food, clothing and maintenance that could be realized if patient populations were reduced by greater use of parole and family care. The report pointed out that the cost of construction of new beds ("before it became impossible to build them at all") for the 3,710 patients exceeding the existing capacity could be postponed, or avoided indefinitely, with the reduction of the census.

While the Temporary Commission was focused on lessening the costs of care, the effects of overcrowding were gaining public attention. Photojournalism played its first in a long series of roles in bringing the worsening conditions in the state schools to public attention when, in 1941, Arnold Genthe did a photographic series on Letchworth Village for *US Camera* that exposed terrible conditions in what was supposed to be a model institution (Trent 1994). *Reader's Digest* published Edith Stern's exposé, "Our Ailing Mental Hospitals" in 1941. At the same time Albert Deutsch, the author of the landmark post-war indictment of the mental hospitals, *The Mentally Ill in America,* was attacking the New York administration and the recommendations of the Temporary Commission in articles for the newspaper, *PM* (Grob 1991).

Scandals in the Department of Mental Hygiene: An Election Issue

The revelations of poor conditions in the institutions took place during an election cycle, and this election was especially significant. In 1942, Thomas E. Dewey was elected Governor of New York, the first Republican elected to that office in over two decades. Dewey had lost the 1938 election to Governor Herbert Lehman but remained a national political force on his record as a crusading Manhattan District Attorney, losing a narrow race to Wendell Willke for the Republican presidential nomination in 1940.

In the 1942 campaign, Dewey charged that the Lehman administration was composed of men "who had gone soft in the deep ruts of comfortable routine" (Beyer 1979). There was nothing in Dewey's background that suggested a special interest in the state's care of people with mental disabilities, but the problems being uncovered in the Department of Mental Hygiene and the state's institutions provided Dewey with a prime example of the failures of the previous Democrat administrations.

When Dewey took office in 1943, he attacked what he had called "twenty years of dry rot" (Beyer 1979). Dewey's view of the many years of Democrat administration was also intensified by a national political ambition and the view that state governments' roles needed to be enhanced to reverse the nationalizing effects of the New Deal. Dewey saw strengthening the state's administrative capacity as crucial to increasing the importance of state government.

Moreland Act Commissions: Findings and Recommendations

The problems of overcrowding and the controversies surrounding the work and recommendations of the Temporary State Commission might have been sufficient cause to focus Dewey's prosecutorial zeal on the Department of Mental Hygiene. However, shortly after taking office in March 1943, the governor received information of a rapidly spreading outbreak of amoebic dysentery at Creedmoor State Hospital in Queens Village, New York City, and of the failure of the Superintendent of the hospital to take steps recommended by local health authorities to stop its spread (Moreland 1944). This new scandal in the Department of Mental Hygiene gave the new administration an excellent opportunity to demonstrate its approach to this issue.

Governor Dewey appointed a special Commission under the Moreland Act to investigate the affairs and management of Creedmoor State Hospital and the role of the Department of Mental Hygiene in handling the outbreak. The Moreland Act (Section 8 of the Executive Law) was Progressive Era legislation that gave a governor the authority and administrative machinery for independent, comprehensive, and speedy investigations and had been used by governors to conduct inquiries into a variety of matters (Missall 1946).

As the investigation began, Dr. William J. Tiffany, Commissioner of the Department of Mental Hygiene since 1937, resigned, and Dr. George W. Mills, superintendent of Creedmoor State Hospital since 1935, was retired. "The report of that investigation indicated that the lax handling of the outbreak of amoebic dysentery was merely a symptom of administrative incapacity at the hospital. The investigation further showed, as set forth in the report, "an administrative breakdown in the Department as a whole" (Moreland 1944, 7).

On May 26, 1943, Governor Dewey appointed a second commission under the Moreland Act, "to examine the management and affairs of the Department of Mental Hygiene and its institutions with a view toward making constructive recommendations to improve their administration" (DMH 1944, 13). Dewey named Archie O. Dawson, an attorney, who had led the investigation at Creedmoor to chair the new Commission with other members representing the state's medical society and superintendents of public and private hospitals. The staff of the Commission drew in a wide variety of national experts in psychiatry, nursing, nutrition, hospital administration, and accounting. The Commission also established several advisory committees on medical care, nursing, dietetics, social service, accounting, and hospital administration and other program areas.

Governor Dewey's new Director of the Budget, John Burton, formed a Research Unit in the Division of Budget. One of its first assignments was to begin an analysis of the Department of Mental Hygiene administration and operations. The analyses of the Division of Budget were coordinated with the work of the Moreland Act Commission. The Dewey administration was going to use the investigation of the Department of Mental Hygiene as a vehicle for demonstrating the errors of the previous administration and as a model for reorganizing and revitalizing state administration and operations.

The Commission, its staff, and members of the advisory committees visited each of the twenty-six institutions operated by the department in its comprehensive review of the agency. The Moreland Act Commission reported its findings in March 1944, and its report was an extensive evaluation of the department's organization and operations as well as a series of recommendations for a comprehensive overhaul of the Department of Mental Hygiene and its institutions. No major area was left unexamined: the professional care of patients, medical and nursing education, research, physical plant, procedures for admission, discharge and placement in family and convalescent care, financing of care, personnel and business office methods, and department and institution management.

The Moreland Act Commission report and recommendations are important to the history of public institutions in New York State for several reasons. They demonstrate that the appalling conditions of abuse and neglect that triggered the crisis at Willowbrook more than twenty-five years later were not new and unknown. They go beyond and below these problems to examine underlying elements of administration, finance, construction, and other key organizational issues contributing to poor care. Perhaps most importantly, confidence that the problems were identified, the solutions clearly outlined, and the political will and administrative frameworks necessary for successful implementation were in place permeated the report. It was a blueprint for reform that, thirty years later, at the end of another comprehensive review and plan, would leave representatives of parent groups again calling for "a new beginning."

Conditions in the Institutions

Accounts of appalling conditions in New York State's institutions form the core of the literature in this area (Blatt 1980; Grob 1991; Rothman and Rothman 1984), and the Commission found deficiencies in virtually every aspect of institutional life. The report on Craig Colony was typical of the conditions found in the institutions: severe overcrowding, residents sleeping on mattresses wherever space could be found, virtually no place to rest in the day rooms, residents wandering in various states of undress, people sitting in their own excrement, young boys "herded together" with older men "some admittedly sexual perverts," and every other atrocious condition that earned these places the label of "snake pit" (Ward 1946). One passage from the report on Craig, however, was an especially poignant commentary on what the Commission found:

> "The contrast between these crowded buildings and the cow barn, where the dairy herd of the institution is kept, is marked. The cows are kept in clean spacious quarters, well provided with fodder, while certain of the wards of the State in this institution have lived and slept under conditions which members of the Commission felt could never have existed in a civilized community" (Moreland 1944, 45).

With the exposure of terrible conditions in the institutions at the core, the findings of the Commission are remarkable for their assessment of the causes. The Commission found that many of these conditions were the result of various deficiencies in statute, regulation, policy, exercise of authority, organization, and administrative methods and practices.

Organization of Patient Care

In area after area of direct patient care: medicine, nursing, occupational therapy, social work, and nutrition, the Commission emphasized defects in statute, organizational structure, failures of executive direction, lack of managerial oversight, and inadequate and improper methods and procedures as the primary problems. The report stated, "War problems, however, are not permanent problems and the war is not an excuse for certain conditions which have existed for many years" (Moreland 1944, 15).

The Commission examined the managerial problems presented by the distance of colonies from their home institution. It found that, "Such distant units are difficult to supervise and expensive to operate. They have been established over the years without sufficient thought given to proper location" (Moreland 1944, 42). The Commission endorsed Commissioner MacCurdy's transfers of control of colonies to the nearest institution and the relocation of distant colonies closer to those institutions, which concentrated more care in the institutions proper.

Segregated education and the admission of infants were two important topics because of the long-term ramifications of the recommendations in these areas as well as for their indication of the prevailing public philosophy of a Commission composed of the most prominent professionals in the mental hygiene area. On education in the state schools, the Commission noted that while "higher grades" might benefit from vocational training and "become less burdensome," "Those at the lower end of the scale are practically without mentality, helpless, and unteachable" (41). The Commission raised the question "whether the teachable mental defectives should not be placed in separate schools and removed from contact with the low grade imbeciles and idiots" (41).

The Commission's observations on admission and care of children under the age of five were not lengthy. Nonetheless, the reference to the anomalies in the state's policy and practice not only presaged the seminal decision in 1945 to change the policy on this crucial issue but also provided a concise insight into the state's interest in the mentally retarded child in a family at this time.

> "More adequate provision should also be made for mentally defective infants in certain of the State schools. While an opinion of the Attorney General can be construed to mean that the State does not assume responsibility for mental defectives under the age of five years, as a practical matter the responsibility has been assumed but without corresponding accommodations being made available. A mentally defective child under five, particularly if of low grade, can be harmful to and disruptive of normal family life and it is to the interest of the State, as well as to the family, to have such a child cared for in a suitable institution. If they are to be accepted, however, adequate facilities must be provided for them" (41–42).

Reimbursement for Patient Care: Accounting Procedures

The Commission's position on family policy and the state's role also ran through its consideration of the problems of reimbursement for care. This lengthy section of the Commission's report opened with the stark reminder that, "The institutions in this Department are maintained "for the care and treatment of poor and indigent persons" (Mental Hygiene Law, Sec. 24-a)" (66). The Commission's investigations disclosed that only 11 percent of the patients in the institutions were paying, but if the statute were properly applied, reimbursement from the approximately 25 percent of patients with "relatives legally liable and with sufficient ability to pay" would result in additional reimbursements of $3,000,000 per year (Moreland 1944, 67). The report includes extensive analyses of the determination of a relative's ability to pay, failures of the department to establish uniform formulas for reimbursement, rates, and procedures for pursuing payments and enforcing judgments as well as recommendations in each of these areas. It is apparent from the length and detail of this portion of the report that while the Commission acknowledged that more infants would be admitted to the institutions, it was creating greater expectations that families would pay for their care. This was taking place at the same time that the economic status of the families of first admissions was shifting from "dependent" to "marginal," and "comfortable."

Physical Plant: Size and Design

The transfer of Willowbrook to the Army and the subsequent moratorium on construction dominated the discussion of the institutions' physical plants. Following the recommendation of the Temporary Commission on State Hospital Problems to expand the state institution capacity, Governor Lehman proposed a $50 million bond issue for construction, but by that point the conditions in the institutions had become politicized, and the Republican-controlled legislature did not approve the placement of the bond proposal on the ballot.

The Moreland Act Commission report was issued in this context, and it made some surprising observations about the size and design of the facilities that had long-term implications for public institutions in the state. The Commission pointed out that the older institutions grew without an overall guiding plan and often used buildings designed and built for other purposes. However, looking ahead to the expected postwar construction, the Commission report observed:

"There are good arguments from an economic point of view to support the value of such enormous institutions as those caring for 5,000 patients and more. There is little doubt, however, that size has an important bearing on the quality of medical care" (60).

The Commission also pointed out that high-rise buildings based on general hospital models did not allow patients to get out of doors, and the lack of interior enclosed space restricted exercise. The Commission not only found fault in the older facilities, but also in the design of the department's two newest facilities, Wassaic and Willowbrook.

"Wassaic State School, which was opened in 1930, has been built with an orderly arrangement of buildings but no protective passageways were provided between the dormitories and the dining halls. As a result, the thousands of mentally defective children who are patients of the school have to tramp three times a day through rain and snow for considerable distances from their residence buildings in order to get their meals. They frequently arrive at dining halls wet through and must eat in damp clothes and with wet feet and return in the same condition to their residence buildings before they can change their shoes or clothes" (61).

"Willowbrook State School, a still later example of planning, also was not provided with covered passageways to the dining halls. It is noteworthy, however, that as soon as the army took it over for use as Halloran General Hospital it erected covered passageways" (61).

The Commission noted that the twenty-six institutions of the Department represented an "investment by the State of New York of $18,000,000," and recommended that the department reorganize and address the needs for maintenance, fire prevention, and service equipment appropriate to an investment of this magnitude.

Large Budget Surpluses

The Commission's recommendations for addressing the need to protect the state's capital investment were made at a time when the state was experiencing a dramatic upturn in its finances. In his first *Executive Budget* for 1943–1944, Governor Dewey stated:

"The business boom associated with the launching and rapid development of the national defense program in 1941 and 1942, almost overnight restored the budget to balance. It unexpectedly rolled up for the State an accumulated surplus of more than $54 million—the first accumulated surplus of any size since 1931" (v).

In his 1944–1945 Executive Budget, Governor Dewey forecast a budget surplus of $148 million, but the actual surplus at the end of the fiscal year was $163 million (*Executive Budget* 1945–46, v). However, despite the surpluses, the amounts expended for capital construction in the state schools plummeted from $5.2 million in 1941 to an almost negligible $15,000 in 1945. In the context of relatively flat expenditures on maintenance of the facilities, large numbers of vacancies in staffing, and a moratorium on capital construction during the war, the Commission could make sweeping proposals for new programs on the assumption that lack of funding would not be a problem in the immediate postwar era. This assumption was echoed in the department's 1944 *Annual Report*: "Looking ahead to the increased demands expected during the postwar years, Commissioner MacCurdy is laying plans for a large

construction program for the development and expansion of institutional facilities" (17). The department expected to request the Postwar Public Works
Planning Commission to approve $50,000,000 in construction to expand and
modernize mental hygiene facilities "as rapidly as possible" after the war
(DMH 1944, 17).

Executive Leadership and Reorganization of the Department of Mental Hygiene

The Moreland Act Commission Report laid the blame for problems in the
institutions squarely on the leadership of the Department of Mental Hygiene.

> "The primary cause of the failure of the Department of Mental
> Hygiene to keep pace with progress in the care of the mentally ill
> in New York in the last few years was this weakness of leadership
> at the top. This weakness was not because of lack of authority, for
> the Mental Hygiene Law confers wide administrative and supervi-
> sory powers on the Commissioner. It appears to have been because
> of the failure of the former Commissioner to exercise his legal pow-
> ers and assume his legal responsibilities with necessary vigor" (97).

Shortly after the Moreland Act Commission began its studies, Governor
Dewey appointed Dr. Frederick MacCurdy, formerly of the Vanderbilt Clinic
of Columbia Presbyterian Hospital, as Commissioner of the Department of
Mental Hygiene. Commissioner MacCurdy replaced many administrators from
the previous administrations and began a comprehensive reorganization of the
department following the recommendations of the Commission and the Division of the Budget. The department's administrative structure was reorganized, and new bureaus were created for central supervision of professional
and clinical practice. Special attention was given to the reorganization of the
bureau of medical inspection, and additional medical inspectors were appointed. The department's business office procedures were modernized, and
offices were reorganized in anticipation of addressing postwar building needs.

The recommendations included a number of changes to the Mental Hygiene Law. Changes in terminology ("convalescent care" replacing "parole," for
example), changes in procedures for admissions (as well as detention and discharge), clarification of the role of Boards of Visitors, and enhanced powers to
the Commissioner of Mental Hygiene over licensing of psychologists were
among the statutory changes recommended and subsequently enacted.

The Commission's report paid particular attention to the problems of
staffing that had grown from the Depression through the war, especially
in medical and professional staff. It proposed a reclassification of ward

personnel, establishment of schools for practical nursing, increased dietetic personnel, and modernizing titles and pay in the institutions.

Fault Lines

The Moreland Act Commission's findings were dramatic, its indictments of past administrations and practices were damning, and its recommendations for reform were bold.

The recommendations, Governor Dewey's aggressive reorganization of the Department of Mental Hygiene, a large state budget surplus, and a revitalized department's plans for postwar construction and new programs all seemed to signal success in the new direction Commissioner MacCurdy predicted. However, the fundamental fault lines below the surface of this postwar enthusiasm remained.

Severe overcrowding was the most prominent feature of the state's institutions, and budget surpluses could not be spent for expanded and new civilian facilities during the war. Not only was new construction out of the question, the deferral of maintenance on existing facilities was a looming problem. No new construction in the pipeline and bold plans for postwar construction programs masked the fact that any renewed expansion would have to be from a standing start.

Admissions had been deferred, but a greater proportion of the individuals on the books of the state schools were living in the institutions proper. In the immediate postwar *Annual Reports*, the return of Willowbrook from the army as a solution to overcrowding took on mythical proportions, but the return would not address the demographic realities apparent from the department's own statistics. They showed that the admission of children under the age of five had been well underway at least four years before Commissioner MacCurdy's formal announcement of the change in policy. The full impact of caring for severely disabled infants was masked by the loss of staff to the armed services, the closing of colonies, and the wartime moratorium on construction. The kinds of services required by this new population, the staffing, and the configuration of the facilities was still not apparent. Moreover, the admission of infants was an early and subtle indication of enormous changes in society and social policy that would have substantial long-term consequences for the state's institutions.

The Moreland Act Commission report, the governor's budget messages, and the department's *Annual Reports* looked to the end of the war as bringing a return of employees to the institutions. They would be lured back by higher pay, promotion opportunities, more education and training, and the other reforms proposed and enacted during the early years of the Dewey administration. In the meantime, admittedly less capable employees were working alongside the more capable residents providing custodial care to a younger and more disabled population increasingly concentrated in the institutions as colonies closed and the numbers in Family and Convalescent Care stagnated. By 1945, the percentage of those on the books and living in the institution had risen to over 80 percent, and this was before Commissioner MacCurdy made the formal announcement that the state would admit infants.

The Moreland Act Commission report also carried important and complex messages about the responsibilities of families and the state in caring for children with disabilities. State government was taking a new view of families, couching its role in terms of relieving families of the burden of caring for a disabled child who would be "harmful to and disruptive of normal family life." The admission of individuals from less economically dependent families and the relatively constant and low capacity of private schools in the state were subtle signs of a shift from serving the poor and indigent to serving a more middle-class clientele and a signal of the state's role in positive social and family policy.

The Moreland Act Commission's report also contained traditional conservative messages of personal responsibility, especially in its treatment of families' obligations to pay their fair share for the care of their relatives in the institutions. A strong theme in the report was government's expanded role in education and training and medical research that would lay the bases for new and positive approaches to people with mental disabilities. But the report also advocated "triaging" (perhaps with the war experience in mind) education services for disabled children by segregating those "helpless and unteachable" from those "capable of rehabilitation."

The darker features of services for people with developmental disabilities were overshadowed by the confidence with which the state faced the postwar world. Radical changes, new and dynamic programs, reform, and the promises of education and science were eagerly anticipated, but the fault lines in institution capacity, resident characteristics, staffing, and expectations about the roles and responsibilities of families and state in the care of people with disabilities lay beneath this enthusiasm.

Chapter 2

Babies and Buildings: 1945 to 1959

If present trends continue, even after the construction of all the new mental hospitals facilities to be financed from bond funds, it is now estimated that there will still be a substantial shortage of facilities because of the continuing increase in the number of patients requiring hospital care.

—Executive Budget, 1955–56

"Snake pits" and the "Shame of the States" became the damning and enduring labels for institutions for people with mental disabilities in the post-World War II era (Ward 1946; Deutsch 1948). The New York State Department of Mental Hygiene's announcement of a *"radical departure"* in its policy on the admission of infants and children was intended as a progressive and optimistic solution to a growing problem. But as the Moreland Act Commission report described in extensive and painful detail, New York's public institutions had reached a state of crisis before the end of the war. It was a crisis that became a chronic condition.

World War II and the years following the war were marked by a number of broad and profound changes in American society, the economy, and politics, and these contributed to substantial increases in the size and number of the state's public institutions and changes in the characteristics of their residents and staff. Postwar optimism about solving the problem of overcrowding was overwhelmed by the state's inability—and unwillingness—to construct enough institutional capacity to meet ten years of pent-up demand. Delayed implementation of prewar construction plans produced models of institutional care that did not fit the needs of the younger and more disabled population that resulted from the state's radical departure in admission policy.

At the same time New York's public institutions were being overwhelmed by severely disabled infants, parents who did not institutionalize their children

41

struggled to create education and other services outside the institutions without the support of, and often in spite of opposition by, the state. The postwar emergence of parent-advocacy organizations providing services began the fundamental duality of institutional versus community approaches that added stress to the widening fault lines in the mental hygiene and developmental services arenas. Growing disparities in funding, approaches to services, administrative control, legislative and executive political cleavages, and interorganizational conflicts within the Department of Mental Hygiene built toward a series of political and organizational crises.

The Decision to Admit Infants

It is virtually impossible to exaggerate the long-term and profound importance of the decision to admit infants to the state schools. This decision accelerated the transformation of these institutions from providing custodial care for moderately retarded adults in a variety of residential settings to the concentration of large numbers of severely and profoundly disabled infants in overcrowded infirmaries. Relieving the burden on families was the rationale for the new policy. However, as important as the near-term consequences of this decision were for changing the state's institutions, this rationale also carried the germ of a another radical split over policy and practice: institution versus community services.

The announcement of the state's decision in the *Annual Report* for 1946 referred to the state assuming the responsibility that had been left to families and county and municipal authorities. At the time, the Deputy Commissioner of the New York State Department of Mental Hygiene responsible for mental retardation services argued in the leading journal in the field:

> "Mental hygiene education has been sufficiently widespread to create a greater demand for the removal of young idiot children from the family unit. Social workers recognizing them are prone to advise institutionalization, and in many instances it is undoubtedly a wise recommendation. Physicians, who now receive more psychiatric training, are also alert to the social implications of an idiot child in the home, and they, too, are urging institutional care. The response to this situation will depend on the attitude of legislatures as to whether these children are a family, a local community, or a state responsibility" (Pense 1945–1946).

Prominent professionals in the field such as Dr. Donovan J. McCune of the Vanderbilt Clinic in New York City proposed infant institutionalization and new facilities, noting that, "families are being demoralized and institutions for sick children overcrowded and disorganized by the presence of these unfortunate children" (Lerner 1972, 30). The *Annual Reports* of the department in the postwar years repeat the refrain, "Careful consideration is being given to the admission of infants and young children where such admissions alleviate exceptionally difficult home situations" (DMH 1947, 219); and "A policy of admitting such patients [very young first admissions] has been adopted in order to relieve conditions in homes where such defectives create a very serious problem" (DMH 1948, 200).

Trent (1994) describes "the confessional literature" that emerged after the war in which such prominent individuals as Pearl Buck, Roy Rogers, and Dale Evans revealed the birth and institutionalization of children with mental retardation. He also cites many professionals and medical experts such as Dr. Benjamin Spock urging parents in popular magazines and books to put their retarded children away and forget about them (Trent 1994, 241). Reformers such as Alfred Deutsch (1948) described the horrors of institutions but also argued that the lack of "proper institutions" and the inability of thousands of families to get their children admitted to them was one of the most heartbreaking situations in American life, leading to a great toll of family breakdown" (123). The Department of Mental Hygiene's position was carried by Dr. Henry C. Storrs, the Director of Letchworth Village State School writing in the 1945–1946 *American Journal of Mental Deficiency*, in which he urged professionals to recommend immediate institutional care to parents (Storrs, 1945–1946).

In the background of this concern for the toll of family breakdown lay the increases in survival rates of disabled infants attributed to the new "wonder drugs" and surgical-medical procedures that grew out of the wartime experience. Constraints on housing that began during the war and continued for several years after, the increased mobility of American families, women's changing expectations for careers and family, as well as a postwar society that emphasized education, opportunity, and prosperity were other aspects of the culture that rationalized institutionalization of mentally retarded infants. Institutionalization also involved therapeutic and educational justifications as plans were made for the construction of "infirmaries" for "patients," and formal classes in the state schools were expanded. After the war, new government programs in medicine, science, and education provided a basis for middle-class families to rely more on public institutions. The state schools became less like poor houses as the proportion of admissions of individuals from "dependent" and "marginal" circumstances dropped (DMH 1946, 1950). New York's radical policy departure was intended to meet the needs of families, and construction of new facilities was to be the primary instrument of that policy.

State Schools: "Perpetual Building" and Overcrowding

The vigor and enthusiasm of the postwar era were echoed in *Annual Reports* of the revamped Department of Mental Hygiene and the Budget Messages of Governor Dewey as he grasped the reins of the state administration and looked toward national possibilities. The *Annual Report* for 1946 featured plans for postwar construction that had been "under continuous and intensive study by the department for the past two years" and included additional facilities for "problem children" and special buildings at the state schools for mentally defective infants and children (DMH 1946, 17). In the shadow of the Moreland Act Commission findings at Craig Colony, the 1946 *Annual Report* announced that work had already begun on construction of a new 200-bed infirmary at that institution. The department also reported:

> "There was a marked increase in 1945–1946 of first admissions less than 5 years old. This was due to a relaxation of the rules respecting the admissions of infants and very young children to the state schools, in order to relieve the very difficult home situations involving the care of such children (DMH 1946, 225–226)."

In the first year of the relaxation of the rules, the admission of children under the age of ten leaped from 32.8 percent in 1945 to 36.6 percent in 1946, with 8.2 percent of those admissions under the age of five. This marked increase was more startling at Craig Colony where 31.7 percent of the individuals admitted in 1946 were under the age of ten, and 15.3 percent were under the age of five (DMH 1946, 279, 324). These younger first admissions continued the trend of also being more disabled as the *Annual Report* detailed the rise in the percent of first admissions classified as "idiot" at 14.1 percent of state school first admissions and 19.0 percent of first admissions at Craig, a 5 percent leap from the previous year (DMH 1946, 285, 326). First admissions to the state schools also continued to come less from dependent and economically marginal families and more from those in more comfortable economic circumstances (DMH 1946).

Willowbrook

The admission of larger numbers of younger and more disabled individuals began to overwhelm the department's plans for new facilities, and the state looked to the return of Willowbrook from the federal government as the solution to this problem. As soon as the federal government took over the newly completed Willowbrook State School and converted it into Halloran General Hospital in 1942, *Annual Reports* of the department included plans for its return to the state. However, at the end of the war, the federal government transferred the hospital from the Army to the Veterans Administration that refused to return it. Governor Dewey beseeched the Veterans Administration to return the facility. He pointed out that there were 800 to 900 infants on the waiting list for admission, severe overcrowding in other state schools as a result of the continuing unavailability of the 3,000 beds at Willowbrook, and parents unable to provide the constant care these infants required nor able to afford to place them in private institutions. Dewey suggested that the Veterans Administration purchase Willowbrook if it was not going to return it so the state could use the funds for construction of a new state school in the New York City metropolitan area (Lerner 1972). However, Dewey undoubtedly knew that funds were not going to solve the problem. The state budget had a record surplus, and even in the absence of postwar constraints on construction, the state would not have been able to plan and build a replacement for Willowbrook for several years.

Dewey's efforts to regain Willowbrook were made in the shadow of the findings and recommendations of the Moreland Act Commission. Having made a major issue of the failures of the prior Democrat administrations in this area, Dewey did not want those problems to rebound on his administration's plans for reform. The Democrats apparently sensed Dewey's predicament and introduced a bill to set up a temporary commission to study the problems of delinquent, mentally ill, and mentally defective children (Lerner 1972). Dewey and the Department of Mental Hygiene countered by playing on the failure of the Democrat administration in Washington to return Willowbrook to the state and the waiting parents.

"A large growth in population had been expected with the completion of the Willowbrook State School. However, this school was used as an army hospital during the war, which caused a postponement of the date when the beds will be available to mentally defective patients" (DMH 1946, 286).

Willowbrook went from being the solution to the explanation for overcrowding in state institutions.

In 1947, the federal government agreed to formally return Willowbrook to New York State on the condition that the state immediately lease "part of its facilities" back to the Veterans Administration for continued occupation as a hospital until a new veterans hospital in Brooklyn could be completed (DMH 1948, 38). "Part of its facilities" was a generous phrase in light of the fact that only fifty-eight patients from state schools were in the Willowbrook "part" on March 31, 1948 (DMH 1948, 189).

The fiction that Willowbrook had been returned to the State continued as the *Annual Report* for 1949 reported on the increase in the state school census. "The increase in 1948–1949 resulted from the opening of part of Willowbrook State School. There will be a further growth in population when the facilities of the latter institution [Willowbrook] become fully available" (DMH 1949, 205). At the end of 1949, there were 454 patients with mental retardation in the state's "part" of Willowbrook, and the Department of Mental Hygiene reported for 1950, "In the last 2 years the rate of growth [in the census] has been accelerated as a result of the opening of Willowbrook State School" (DMH 1950, 209). Despite this optimistic report, at the end of the 1950 fiscal year, there were 973 patients in Willowbrook, an institution with a capacity of 3,000.

The overcrowding in the state hospitals and the Korean War also rebounded on Willowbrook. In 1948, the Department of Mental Hygiene took over part of the Sampson Naval Training Base on Seneca Lake in upstate New York to be operated as a unit of Willard State Hospital for the care and treatment of elderly patients (*Executive Budget* 1948–49, 367). At the outbreak of the Korean War, the Sampson Unit was taken over by the Air Force, and 500 elderly mental patients formerly housed at Sampson were moved to Willowbrook (*Executive Budget* 1952–53, 424). It was not until the 1955–56 fiscal year that the remaining 250 mental patients, transferred from Sampson to Willowbrook, were again transferred to an annex of St. Lawrence State Hospital in Malone (*Executive Budget* 1955–56, 375). It was virtually the end of the postwar era before Willowbrook served the population for which it was built.

Constraints on Construction and Overcrowding in the State Schools

The federal government's failure to return Willowbrook was featured as the excuse for overcrowding. However, the more significant reason for overcrowding was that construction was severely constrained after the war, and new and expanded facilities for "mental defectives" were not high in the priorities for scarce building resources. Despite the yearly report of plans for construction, the rated capacity in the state schools in 1950 was exactly that in 1945—11,712 (DMH 1951). In its *Annual Report* for 1948, the department finally conceded that the promised postwar construction would not occur:

"Toward the end of the last fiscal year it was considered best not to place any more contracts for the preparation of building plans until building conditions had improved."

"Spiraling building costs as well as the postwar shortages of material and labor have prevented any appreciable progress in actual construction up to the present time. Planning has been far-sighted and thorough, however, and it is expected that building can proceed immediately when the industry returns to an even keel" (DMH 1948, 39, 40).

In the five years from 1946 to 1950, overcrowding in the state schools went from 27.2 percent to 37.5 percent over capacity with state schools housing 4,392 patients in excess of their rated capacity (DMH 1950, 319).

Overcrowding was compounded by concentration of residents in the institutions. In 1945, the percentage of those "on the books" actually living in the institutions reached 80 percent of the total. By 1950, those in the institutions proper were 86.1 percent of the total on the books (DMH 1951). A 100 person increase in Family Care over the five years (621 to 722) was offset by large drops in the numbers in Colonies and Convalescent Care (1,265 to 884 and 2,059 to 1,506). Although the department expected that Family Care would greatly lessen the need for new and expanded institutions, the 722 people in Family Care in 1950 was approaching the historic high for this program and would never be a significant factor in construction plans. Similarly, the numbers in Convalescent Care were reaching their historic peaks, and the number and census in Colonies continued to decline. By 1950, state services for people with mental retardation were virtually synonymous with care inside large institutions.

Overcrowding as a Partisan Issue

Although Newark was 47.2 percent over capacity and Rome 50.3 percent over capacity, the partisan focus on overcrowding turned on Letchworth State School (only 36.3 percent over capacity). Governor Dewey did note the overcrowding problem in his 1947 Budget Message request for additional funds for the department, but was dismayed that Democrats used the issue against him in the 1950 gubernatorial campaign.

The Democrat candidate for governor, Congressman Walter A. Lynch, repeated a complaint made by the Director of Letchworth State School that 500 patients were sleeping on mattresses on the floor because of the overcrowding. The Director of Letchworth replied that only 250 children were sleeping on mattresses on the floors and claimed that this figure was dropping as patients were transferred to Willowbrook. Governor Dewey said that no children were sleeping on the floor and blamed the overcrowding on the federal government's refusal to return Willowbrook to the state (Lerner 1972).

Earlier in the year, the state suffered another setback on Willowbrook. The Veterans Administration had agreed to return Willowbrook to the state by June 1950. However, protests from veterans' groups forced the VA to rescind its offer of full return, and the federal government announced that it would retain more than 250 beds at the facility until the new VA hospitals were completed (Lerner 1972).

Outdated Plans

New construction was again featured in the *Annual Report* for 1949, when the Department of Mental Hygiene announced that the wartime shortages of material had eased, and activity in veterans' housing, which had been given priority, had reached sufficient levels to allow construction of facilities for mental patients. However, the department pointed out that the cost estimates for the various state facilities that had been held in abeyance were based on 1940 figures, and construction costs had doubled since then. Moreover, the plans had not been updated, and "the plans now being perfected for the many units of the new building program will be expressions of the best architectural thought of the day, coordinating the new ideas proposed by many associates from various parts of the state with ideas of the State Architect, grown out of long experience with public building" (DMH 1949, 53). The department's *Annual Report* warned that the approval of plans and allowing contractors to make their bids were both time-consuming processes (DMH 1949, 54). These failures to update plans or cost estimates became irrelevant with the outbreak of the Korean War. In his *Message to the Legislature* delivering the *Executive Budget* for 1952–1953, Governor Dewey conceded, "In the past year, the State's construction program has been slowed somewhat by shortages of steel and personnel" (19).

Overcrowding: A "Perpetual" Problem

The opening lines of the *Annual Report* for 1951 suggest that the Department of Mental Hygiene was beginning to operate with a fatalistic philosophy that overcrowding was an intractable historical phenomenon.

> "Overcrowding has been a continuous problem ever since New York State more than a century ago first undertook to provide institutions for the mentally disabled. Even while gaining in the scientific knowledge which brought improvement in care and treatment, the state lost ground steadily in a race to keep up with demand for more facilities" (DMH 1950, 1).

The state had embarked on "a practically perpetual building program," but this was being further undermined by, "the trend toward a smaller family housing unit making home care difficult or impossible, plus the increased span of life which is of course reflected in the patient population as in the community outside" (DMH 1950, 1). Along with reminders that the federal government had expropriated Willowbrook, the *Annual Reports* in the 1950s continued to argue that wartime building restrictions and postwar shortages also caused "facilities filled far beyond their capacities to convert their dayrooms and corridors into bed wards."

Trying to Catch Up: Construction in the 1950s

The Department of Mental Hygiene began the 1950s with the state schools and Craig Colony housing an excess of 4,383 individuals over their rated capacity (DMH 1950, 319). The sections of the department's *Annual Reports* devoted to services for people with mental retardation were full of plans for expansion and laments about continuing overcrowding—and the costs of overcrowding to the state. The *Annual Report* for 1950 included a statement of alarm from Governor Dewey that mental illness was costing the state more than one-third of its operating budget (DMH 1950, 17). Additions to existing state schools were announced every year, and in the *Annual Report*, for 1952, the department announced that:

> "On a long range basis the only solution to overcrowding lies in the construction of new hospitals and new schools. In planning new institutions, the location of adequate land space is equally as important as the appropriation of funds. This, however, often is one of the main obstacles to new construction, particularly in large metropolitan areas like New York City where available property is limited" (DMH 1952, 66).

The department's belief that construction of new facilities was the "only solution" and construction in New York City would be "one of the main obstacles" were unintended prophesies of an impending rupture along two major fault lines of policy and practice in New York.

Construction Bond Issue

Despite the reports of increased costs of new construction, the 1953 Legislature substantially lowered the amounts for new construction in the Department of Mental Hygiene budget (DMH 1953, 66). However, the 1954 State Legislature authorized a $350 million bond issue for construction of new facilities. In its *Annual Report* for 1954, the Department of Mental Hygiene stated:

> "The mental health construction bond act was passed unanimously by both houses and signed by the Governor, but it must be submitted

to the people at the November 1954 election. In his annual message to the legislature Governor Dewey emphasized the imperative need for new facilities to take care of the state's mentally ill. Despite large-scale construction now in progress, he pointed out the mental institutions are, and will continue to be, overcrowded unless an expanded building program is undertaken immediately" (DMH 1954, 17).

Governor Dewey was referring to the New York State constitutional requirement that bond acts be passed by two separately elected Legislatures (two-year terms) and approved by the voters in the subsequent general election. The mental health construction bond act was approved by a five-to-one margin in the November 1954 election.

Construction of New Facilities in the Harriman Administration

In the 1954 election, Averell Harriman was elected governor, the first Democrat since 1944, and he began his administration with an indictment of the Dewey administration for overcrowding in Department of Mental Hygiene facilities and lack of funding for new construction. In the first budget submitted by Harriman, the governor noted that he had inherited a substantial cash surplus from the previous administration. He charged that this was due to the failure to allocate sufficient current funds to capital construction. Although Dewey and the Department of Mental Hygiene had argued that post-World War II and then Korean War shortages explained the lack of construction of mental hygiene and other facilities, Harriman pointed out in his first *Message to the Legislature* that "the completed cost of the Thruway as estimated by the Thruway Authority will nearly equal total State capital expenditures for all purposes over the past decade" (23). This Thruway construction proceeded despite the fact that in the mental hygiene area "needs have been growing in geometric proportions" (*Executive Budget 1955–56*, 23). Harriman charged that Dewey's "pay-as-you-go" policy was actually a "pay-from-reserve" policy that necessitated the bond issue passed in 1954. Despite the passage of the bond issue, Harriman concluded:

> "The State has permitted the continuing of the overcrowded situation in our mental institutions to become increasingly worse since World War II. Although the capacities of existing institutions have been somewhat enlarged, no new ones have been built since the War. Neglect of this emerging need led to the absolute necessity of the bond issue that was approved last year. But the bond issue will only

alleviate—it will not solve the problem. **If present trends continue, even after the construction of all the new mental hospitals facilities to be financed from bond funds, it is now estimated that there will still be a substantial shortage of facilities because of the continuing increase in the number of patients requiring hospital care**" (23). [Bold in original.]

In his next *Executive Budget*, Harriman reported accelerated planning and awarding of $40 million in contracts for construction of mental hygiene facilities. He also stated, "This year we have made a fresh appraisal of needs and redirected the construction program to take account of new thinking about the type and size of mental institutions that will best serve our needs." This new thinking and fresh appraisal was primarily focused on the community mental health approach that was becoming more prominent in the mental health field. Services for people with mental retardation and the situation in the state schools continued to deteriorate, and in his *Executive Budget* for 1957–58, Harriman was forced to concede:

"The Department of Mental Hygiene has had an exceedingly large number of requests from families and social agencies to admit children under five years of age. In the downstate area, because of overcrowding at Wassaic and Letchworth State Schools, these children have been admitted chiefly to the Willowbrook State School. Facilities for these children, who are mostly crib cases, are overcrowded by 50 percent or more. A similar situation exists in the upstate area.

In view of the serious physical and social problems involved, funds totaling $300,000 are recommended for the rental and maintenance of facilities for the care of additional children during the ensuing year" (396–7).

Reorganization

Following the 1954 gubernatorial election, Dr. Paul Hoch, a noted researcher from the New York State Psychiatric Institute, was named Commissioner of Mental Hygiene. The *Annual Report* for 1955 announced a reorganization of the department "to keep pace with the increasing scope and complexity of its services" (4). The impact on mental retardation services was minimal as Dr. Arthur Pense, who had headed the Mental Retardation Division since the early 1940s, remained Deputy Commissioner. Plans for construction of new facilities continued to be featured in the *Annual Reports* of the department, but discussion of education and delinquency in the state institutions mirrored the attention these topics were receiving in the community.

With the influx of greater numbers of children, more attention was given to education, and the *Annual Reports* announced the creation of additional classes in the state schools and the creation of experimental classes for severely retarded children in public schools. However, to the increasing consternation of advocacy groups (which will be discussed in more detail later), the department spent a great deal of effort studying the problems. In its *Annual Report* for 1956, the department announced that,

> "Considerable progress has been made in the department's efforts to acquire much-needed information regarding the education of mentally retarded children both in institutions and in the community. Five separate studies are under way dealing with the prevalence of mental retardation, special classes for severely retarded children, a census of trainable children, children who have been in classes for severely retarded in New York City, and the programs for severely retarded in other states" (DMH 1956, 12).

Mental retardation, however, was not a major priority in the Department of Mental Hygiene. After several years of major reorganizations on the mental health side of the agency, primarily in community mental health, research, and training, it was not until Harriman's last budget for 1958–1959 that the administration proposed a very modest reorganization for mental retardation services and plans for new classes and occupational training programs.

More Plans for Construction: Overcrowding and Waiting Lists

The 1955 Legislature appropriated $32 million from the bond act for the addition of 3,554 new beds in eight of the department's institutions, including buildings at Rome and Willowbrook. The *Annual Report* for 1955 noted the appointment of a special subcommittee of the Mental Hygiene Council to advise the Commissioner on the development of new state schools. While the additions to existing facilities increased the rated capacity of the state schools and Craig Colony to 17,859 beds, the numbers in excess of capacity had climbed to 4,595 (DMH 1955).

The *Annual Report* for 1956 announced plans for a new state schools at West Seneca in Erie County and in Brooklyn, two of four new institutions planned as a result of the construction bond act. The new state school at West Seneca incorporated the department's new organization of its institutions into geographic catchment areas and designated the counties from which the new school would take admissions. The plans for the new state school in Brooklyn, however, continued the notion of a mission-specific organization of other state schools (e.g., "educables" at Syracuse; epileptics at Craig Colony), with a focus on psychiatric and vocational services.

The *Annual Reports* also signaled an awareness of the cumulative impact of the state's postwar policies on admissions and its lagging construction program. The *Annual Report* for 1957 provided a realistic assessment of what had become of the state schools.

"The influx of younger and more severely retarded children over the past few years has been effecting a significant change in the population of these institutions. Because of the intensive medical and nursing care required by these largely helpless patients, the state schools have in fact become hospitals in the nature of the services they are called upon to render" (DMH 1957, 15).

The characterization of state schools as "hospitals" hid the fact that great numbers of these "young helpless patients" were dying within a year of admission, and those that survived were living longer. In 1935, the average age of death (including those on parole) was 21.7 years, and the average time in the institution prior to death was 6.9 years. By 1955, the percentage of patients dying less than one year after admission had risen to 36.9 percent of total deaths (DMH 1955, 133). By 1959, the average age of death of all patients was 33 years of age, and the average time in the institution prior to death was 15 years (DMH 1960,158).

The 1957 *Annual Report* announced the dedication of four new infirmary buildings at Newark and the awarding of contracts for an 800-bed infants' building at Willowbrook. It also pointed out that the 1957–1958 budget for the department included $300,000 for the rental and operation of a facility [Gouverneur Hospital] to care for an additional 150 mentally retarded children under 5 years of age. The report stated, "At present time state schools are accommodating as many patients as possible but a substantial demand exists for those under 5" (17). By the end of the 1950s, the Department of Mental Hygiene's *Annual Reports* on construction and overcrowding read as though they were reprinted from earlier reports.

Harriman's first *Executive Budget* for 1955–56 contained an indictment of the Dewey administration for its failure to solve the overcrowding problem. In what would be Harriman's final *Executive Budget*, for 1958–59, he was able to begin by pointing out, "The continuing reduction in the population of our State's mental hygiene hospitals is an exciting fact (18)." However, for the state schools, he was forced to report:

"Due to overcrowding in the state schools (33 percent—October 1957) and the mounting requests for admission of children under five years of age, the Department of Mental Hygiene found it necessary to revise admission procedures. An investigative or screening unit has been established to determine the medical and social aspects of all applications. Children in need of institutional care are placed on a waiting list for admission as vacancies occur. This procedure is the only equitable way to cope with the situation. Funds are again recommended for the rental of temporary facilities to care for these children. To date, the Department of Mental Hygiene has been unable to locate a suitable facility" (388).

Neither new construction, conversion of unused facilities, or rental of space brought down the waiting lists. In 1959, legislation was passed permitting the Commissioner to defer admissions to state schools "when overcrowding became so great that adequate care could not be provided if any additional patients were admitted" (DMH 1959, 8). The legislation provided some legal rationalization for delaying admissions, but waiting lists had been officially proclaimed since the 1940s and the definition of "adequate care" now included hallways crowded with cots and occupation of World War II Quonset huts. The Association for the Help of Retarded Children (AHRC) supported a bill that would pay for private placement of children on the waiting list, but it was not passed until 1962 (Lerner, 1972).

Services in Communities: 1945 to 1959

"To mothers of Retarded Children, Ages 4 to 8: Are you interested in helping start a day nursery for your children?"

The Emergence of Community Advocacy Organizations

This advertisement placed by two mothers in the *New York Post* in 1948 was the faint *döppleganger* of the state's postwar enthusiasm for construction of new and expanded institutions (NYSARC 1989). These words led to the founding of the Association for the Help of Retarded Children (AHRC) and the creation of the framework for parent cooperation, political advocacy, and community services that would ultimately redefine institutions and the organization of developmental services in New York State. The advertisement drew ten parents to a meeting in a Bronx home, and although the nursery was not established, a series of meetings began which drew larger numbers of parents (NYSARC 1989). By early 1949, more than three hundred parents met at the National Hospital for Speech Disorders, and the Association to Help Retarded Children of New York City was formed. Shortly after, chapters were established in Sullivan, Westchester, and Long Island (NYSARC 1989).

Formal advocacy organizations for people with mental retardation had already emerged in the 1930s and grew out of parent support groups that were first oriented toward lobbying school systems for special education classes (Scheerenberger 1987). Parent groups also formed around public institutions, and in New York, the Welfare League for Retarded Children was created in 1939 by parents of children at Letchworth Village State School. A Sunshine League was formed at Newark State School. The Benevolent Society for Retarded Children was formed by parents when Willowbrook State School opened in 1949, and the Sunshine League for the Retarded Children of Western New York at Wassaic State School was formed in 1952 to join an already existing Community Society at that institution (Lerner 1972). The primary focus of these groups was to provide amenities such as gifts and recreational programs that the institutions were not supplying, but they also began to lobby the state legislature on behalf of the institution administrations for improvements in those facilities.

The creation of the AHRC was not only a manifestation of the lack of attention to children who remained with their families but involved socioeconomic, ethnic, and organizational tensions that ultimately had important consequences for developmental services in New York in the last quarter of the century. Lerner (1972) points out, "The New York State Association for Retarded Citizens has from its inception been a creature of middle-class concerns, and its leadership was largely professionals, business executives and their wives" (12).

Another important difference between the AHRC and the institution-based parent groups was that immediately after its founding in New York City, the AHRC pursued an aggressive policy of expansion throughout the state, one focused on counties rather than institutions. By 1952, the AHRC had grown to fifteen county chapters spanning the state from Suffolk to Erie Counties that focused largely on special education, clinics, and workshops in the community (NYSARC 1989). In 1952, parent organizations at the state institutions formed the New York State Council for Retarded Children, and the AHRC agreed to work with those organizations to discuss "better care and training in the institutions" (NYSARC 1989). However, the primary attention of AHRC political advocacy remained squarely on educational, vocational, and other day services in communities.

Urging Parents to Keep Children at Home

The main features of the "confessional literature" of the late 1940s and 1950s were parents' explanations of and professionals' support for the institutionalizing of disabled children (Trent 1994). In the face of state schools bursting at the seams, new construction immediately filling to capacity and more, and a relentless search for vacant space no matter how unsuitable, the state opened a campaign to encourage parents to keep their children at home.

Dr. Stanley Davies, who would later be hired to head the department's mental retardation planning office, prepared a study for the New York State Association for Mental Health in 1959 that argued that the retarded should be institutionalized only as a last resort. Davies' study was featured in the department's publications (Lerner 1972, 137; *Mental Hygiene News, XXX*, 3 [Nov. 1959], 1). In May, 1959, Drs. Slobody and Scanlon, spokesmen for the American Association on Mental Deficiency, warned against early institutionalization of the mentally retarded child, arguing that it was, "too often ill-considered and unnecessary and frequently has serious emotional consequences for the child and family." The Department of Mental Hygiene reprinted the article in full in its February 1960 issue of *Mental Hygiene News* and sent copies of the article to all 26,000 general physicians in New York State (Lerner 1972). The complete turn-about in the state's position in such as short time may have been influenced by the community mental health approach, but is more likely that the cost of caring for this large and growing population in the state schools was a crucial factor. The state's new position on institutionalization could not have been based on the availability of services for people with mental retardation in communities.

Day Services: Clinics, Special Education, and Sheltered Workshops

The advertisement in the *New York Post* soliciting interest in a day nursery was prompted by the fact that although New York City had some special education classes, there were no public programs for children under seven years. There were Child Guidance Clinics operated by the Department of Mental Hygiene since the 1920s. These weekly outpatient clinics staffed by department psychiatrists and psychologists played an important role in diagnosing mental retardation as well as mental illness. In 1941 (their peak in the prewar years), 4,885 cases were seen, and 43.8 percent of these cases had IQ's of less than 79 (DMH 1941, 95). As a result of the loss of professional staff to the armed services, there was a severe curtailment in this service during the war, and the department recommended that, "local community groups must come to this realization now and make plans for the development and operation of their own clinic programs" (DMH 1941, 101). By 1950, the overall caseloads of the clinics climbed back to almost prewar levels, but the percentage of new cases with mental retardation and related disorders had dropped from 43.8 to slightly more than 30 percent of total cases (DMH 1941, 1950). This was yet another sign of emerging cleavages between mental health and mental retardation services in both institution and community services.

One of the first activities of the newly formed AHRC was a fund drive to establish a child guidance bureau with educational programs for parents. Private donors financed diagnostic clinics at Flower-Fifth Avenue and Brooklyn Jewish Hospitals, and by 1950 the AHRC had also started a speech clinic, a play therapy class, a social activities program for children, summer camp scholarships, and a vocational training program (Lerner 1972).

The lack of day services for children and families was the initial impetus for the founding of the AHRC, but the new organization quickly turned to lobbying the state and its municipalities to expand special education classes in the public schools. Trent (1994) estimated that before the federal Education of All Handicapped Children Act (PL 94-142) passed in 1975, only about fifteen percent of mentally retarded children living with parents or relatives were receiving special education. In the late 1940s and early 1950s, New York State statute required public school classes for children with IQs between 50 and 75, with chronological ages of seven and mental ages of five, and approximately 11,000 children in these ranges were in New York City public schools and about 6,000 in public schools in the rest of the state (Lerner 1972, 67). Public schools often used questionable judgments about mental-chronological age, failures to take censuses of eligible children, claims that they lacked teachers and other resources, or simple refusals to serve otherwise eligible children as excuses for not meeting statutory mandates.

In 1953, the AHRC called for state legislation to require more adequate facilities and increased state aid for children in the mandated ranges, public school programs for children with IQs between 25 and 50, a differential pay for special education teachers; home teaching where necessary, and a mandated school board census of mentally retarded children similar to that required for physically handicapped children (Lerner 1972, 68). The bill backed by the AHRC was killed in committee because of opposition by both the state Departments of Education and Mental Hygiene who argued that these issues should await the results of a study being done by the Department of Mental Hygiene of the entire problem of mental retardation (Lerner 1972). In 1954, the AHRC, with the support of the New York State Federation of Women's Clubs and the New York State Teacher's Association were successful in getting the Dewey administration to back a small number of experimental public school programs for severely retarded children, but half of the funds appropriated went to an evaluation of the program by the Mental Health Commission (Lerner 1972). At the local level, some AHRC chapters were able to convince municipalities to give them space to operate their own schools and special education classes, although the AHRC's request for available space in a public school was denied by the New York City Board of Education because it did not want to establish a precedent for such programs (NYSARC 1989). The 1953 and 1954 legislative sessions were typical of the state's relationship with the AHRC and other advocates for education for children with mental disabilities during the 1950s: opposition to expansion of eligibility and school programs, small experiments, and further study of the problem.

Sheltered workshops for adults with mental retardation became another important concern for parent groups. In 1953, the AHRC opened a "Training and Sheltered Workshop" in Brooklyn, the first facility of its kind, for twenty-three workers, followed shortly by a second training center in Manhattan (NYSARC 1989). By the mid-1950s, several chapters of the AHRC established sheltered workshops, taking advantage of federal grants authorized through the Vocational Rehabilitation Act of 1954.

The AHRC continued its rapid expansion of chapters as well as expansion of workshops, clinics, and its own special education classes. In 1956, the Association changed its name to the New York State Association for Retarded Children, Inc., and the AHRC reverted to its role as the New York City chapter (NYSARC 1989). In 1958, the Welfare League at Letchworth Village State School and the Community League at Wassaic State School joined the ARC, and the Benevolent Society at Willowbrook joined in 1959. By the end of the 1950s, the Association for Retarded Children (ARC) was a county-based, statewide organization that had largely subsumed the institution-based advocacy groups. By 1959, there were chapters in three quarters of the counties in the state and over 2,000 individual members (NYSARC 1989). The ARC and related parent organizations had established almost all the basic elements that would form the framework of developmental services in New York for the rest of the century: a state-wide network of parent advocacy organizations, clinics and other day services, sheltered workshops, and special education classes. Government funding for these services was unevenly spread among programs, as municipalities, school districts, the state, and the federal government contributed relatively small amounts often in grants for pilot and experimental programs. Nonetheless, as Lerner (1972) points out, this dual role of advocating for as well as operating government-funded services was unusual for advocacy organizations, and it would become a critical factor for the strategic change in direction New York would take in the 1970s.

The AHRC and Political Advocacy

Advocacy for a Separate State Agency for Mental Retardation

The dual role of advocacy and operation of programs was important, but the ARC had begun and continued a strong adversarial relationship with the state agencies that would lead to another crucial conflict affecting the state's and other developmental services—a separate state agency for mental retardation. The social context of the postwar era was important in shaping the adversarial nature of the politics of mental retardation. Professionals, celebrities, reformers and the state were not only arguing that placing a disabled child in an institution was "a wise recommendation for the family," they were virtually indicting those who chose to keep a disabled child at home. Choosing to keep a disabled child at home was virtually an act of rebellion against the prevailing professional and political forces of the day, and was not an act that parents could expect to be rewarded for or supported by the state.

The parent-advocacy groups that emerged around the institutions in the late 1930s operated in concert with institution administrations to lobby the legislature and state administration for improvements as well as to provide ameliorative supplements not funded by the state. The initial impetus of the AHRC was the desire of parents to band together to provide day services for their children and expanded special education classes in public schools. The founding leadership of AHRC, composed of business people and professionals, were familiar with and not reluctant to employ political activism (Lerner 1972). Most notably, Joseph T. (Jerry) Weingold, an energetic attorney, became the first president of the newly formed ARC, its Executive Director from 1949 to 1980, and the driving force in the organizational expansion and political activities of the group.

Weingold and the ARC put together a political agenda that challenged local school boards, counties and other municipalities, and the agencies of state government to provide and expand education and community programs for disabled children living at home. The state Department of Education generally opposed the objectives of the ARC, and the state Department of Mental Hygiene was preoccupied with expanding institutional capacity. Community programs such as colonies and convalescent care were being abandoned as clients and services concentrated in the institutions. The Department of Mental Hygiene, by statute headed by a psychiatrist routinely opposed the ARC's proposals for new and expanded community services, promised studies of the problem, and reluctantly approved small numbers of pilot or experimental projects with time-limited funding.

The ARC's promotion of a separate state agency for mental retardation services began as a proposal in 1950 for a Commission on Mental Retardation, separate and distinct from the Mental Health Commission that was created in 1949 under the aegis of the Department of Mental Hygiene that was the vehicle for postwar comprehensive planning in the field. The commission was empowered to "initiate, formulate, and co-ordinate a master plan for the promotion of mental health programs" in recruitment and training of professional and other staff for psychiatric work, development of psychiatric facilities in general hospitals and a variety of outpatient clinics, state-aid for local mental health programs, and development of research programs into the causes, diagnoses, prevention and cure of mental illness (DMH 1949, 43). *Annual Reports* of the department featured aspects of the work of the commission, and consistent with its initial charge, there were almost no references to issues directly affecting people with mental retardation. The state, on the other hand, referred to the commission's "studies" when opposing or seeking deferral of demands made by the ARC and other advocates (Lerner 1972).

The ARC argued for a separate commission, charging that mental retardation issues were not being adequately addressed by the Mental Health Commission. The Department of Mental Hygiene opposed the legislation, and the demand for a separate state agency quickly became a core element of the organization's political agenda and indicative of the adversarial relationship between the organization and the state agency.

A Platform for Advocacy: The Joint Legislative Committee

The state legislature used the vehicle of Joint Legislative Committees to devote special and long-term attention to policy issues and areas not easily encompassed within the regular committee structure of the two houses. The legislature had already established a Joint Legislative Committee on Cerebral Palsy, and, while increasing its lobbying of the Departments of Education and Mental Hygiene, the ARC turned more of its efforts toward establishing a permanent legislative platform for its work, first proposing a Joint Legislative Committee in 1951. The proposal was opposed by the Department of Mental Hygiene which argued that the problem of mental retardation should be studied by the Mental Health Commission. However, by 1955 the Mental Health Commission had not issued any reports on the topic. In 1955, the state legislature established a Joint Legislative Committee on Mental Retardation to "investigate and study the extent and scope of mental retardation, wherever it may exist in this state, and the social, educational, economic, mental and physical problems arising therefrom" (Lerner 1972, 88). With its own budget for staff, which later included Jerry Weingold as Counsel, the ability to issue reports and be a continuing presence in the state legislature, the Joint Legislative Committee became an important organizational feature of political advocacy.

Institutions and Mental Retardation Services at the End of the Postwar Era

Averell Harriman was an able, but quiet, executive whose skills seemed more suited to the world of diplomacy from which he had come. His one term as governor of New York was unremarkable, and he was defeated in his bid for reelection by Nelson A. Rockefeller. The end of his administration was the end of the postwar era for institutions and mental retardation services in the state.

Babies and Buildings

Harriman's administration brought little immediate change in the mental retardation area. With more than ten years having passed since the institution scandals uncovered by the Moreland Act Commission, and with the promise of tranquillizing drugs as the silver bullet solution to overcrowding in the state psychiatric hospitals, the Department of Mental Hygiene had successfully cultivated a progressive, professional, and apolitical reputation (Hevesi 1975).

The post-war *Annual Reports* exuded an aura of optimism with features and photographs on nutrition, social service, training, and recreation programs. Advances and hopes in medical treatment and research, including lobotomies, insulin shock therapy, and group therapy were highlighted, but services for people with mental retardation were rarely mentioned with the same enthusiasm and lengthy description. The state administration continued to use the Mental Health Commission as a vehicle for deflecting the demands of the mental retardation advocates by promising to direct the commission to study the problem. Promised studies rarely materialized, and requests for a separate commission on mental retardation were denied. In 1957, the legislature passed a bill calling for the creation of the Institute for Basic Research in Mental Retardation, but did not appropriate funds for construction. At the same time New York was initiating the first innovative community mental health programs, the state administration was resisting efforts by the ARC to expand state funding for clinics, workshops, and other day services in communities.

The state's "first of its kind" 1954 Community Mental Health Act was "designed to foster the development of local psychiatric services" (DMH 1955, 5). It established a system of state reimbursement to localities, primarily counties, for the following "eligible services: outpatient psychiatric clinics, inpatient psychiatric clinics in general hospitals, psychiatric rehabilitation services, and consultant and educational services to schools, courts, health and welfare agencies" (DMH 1955, 5). Advocates for and agencies providing services for people with mental retardation were even more handicapped in their efforts to get funding from the county-based Community Mental Health Boards that were created to fund, operate, and administer the services authorized by the legislation.

The state's Community Mental Health Services Act of 1954 was trumpeted as a model for the country, and "substantial expansions" of community programs were announced in each *Annual Report*. The opening of the *Annual Report* for 1956 was especially important.

"The year 1955–56 will be a significant one historically in the field of mental health since it marked the first real break in the rising trend of mental hospital populations during a century of recorded statistics" (DMH 1956, 3).

On March 31, 1956, there were 500 fewer patients in the hospitals than the year before. The number of admissions was about the same, but tranquillizing drugs allowed for the release of 2,600 more patients than the previous year (DMH 1956, 3). The promises of tranquillizing drugs, aftercare clinics, day hospitals, research, and reorganized treatment teams seemed to be paying dividends.

In contrast to the promise of improvements in treatment of mental illness, the Department of Mental Hygiene also had to announce that, "The population trend of the state schools for the retarded was not affected by the forces operating in the hospitals" (DMH 1956, 3). It would be eleven more years before the department could announce a drop in the census of the state schools.

By the end of the Harriman administration, reductions in the population in the psychiatric hospitals were characterized as "exciting" improvements. However, the governor reported, "The problem of mental retardation has become one of the major concerns not only in this State but throughout the nation" (*Executive Budget 1958–59*, 388). As in the case of the need for a "perpetual building program," mental retardation was a problem "throughout the nation" which implied that, unlike the improvements in mental health, it was somehow beyond the capacity of the Department of Mental Hygiene and the state to solve. Perhaps in reaction to the ARC's call for a separate agency or as the reflexive tactic of an administration dealing with a seemingly intractable problem, the governor announced another reorganization and further study of the problem of mental retardation. Harriman proposed the creation of "a new administrative unit headed by a staff officer, directly responsible to the Commissioner of Mental Hygiene, who will be empowered to explore the need for the development and expansion of services and facilities and the coordination of ancillary services for the mentally retarded" (*Executive Budget 1958–59*, 388). In the same *Executive Budget*, the Governor also announced other measures being taken to deal with the problem: a new admission screening unit, a waiting list, and a search for temporary rental facilities.

By the end of the 1950s, the deterioration of services in the state schools seemed to have become an embarrassment in the otherwise optimistic reports of the Department of Mental Hygiene—holding little promise of fulfilling the plans for improvement that were central to the community mental hygiene movement of the era. The problem of mental retardation was also an increasing fiscal burden for the state.

Costs of Institutional Care

In the 1945–46 fiscal year, the total appropriations for the Department of Mental Hygiene were $48.0 million—6.6 percent of the total state appropriation of $726.3 million (*Executive Budget* 1946–47). By the 1950–51 fiscal year, appropriations for the Department of Mental Hygiene had climbed to 12.3 percent of total state appropriations. By the 1959–60 fiscal year, the Department of Mental Hygiene's total appropriation of $256.4 million was 14.2 percent of the total state appropriation of $1.8 billion (*Executive Budget* 1960–61). Community mental health was being promoted as not only better care for people with mental disabilities, but less expensive care. The continued growth in the census of state schools was not only a contrast with the declining census in the state hospitals, but it was contributing to the growing fiscal burden that would reach crisis proportions in the Rockefeller Administration.

In 1945, with the findings and recommendations of the Moreland Act Commission still fresh and the department's announcements of bold plans for reform, the per capita costs of care in the state schools was 85.4 percent of that of care in state hospitals—$421 versus $493 (DMH 1946). By 1950, the per capita expenditures in state schools had climbed to $880 per year, 92 percent of the $957 spent per capita in state hospitals (DMH 1950, 298, 293). In 1955, it had risen to $1,164, 96.5 percent of that in state hospitals (DMH 1955, 190), and in 1959, those expenditures increased to $1,523 although dropping back to 91.5 percent of per capita expenditures in the state hospitals (DMH 1959, 204–206).

The cost of care was primarily in the cost of staff. The state was unable to secure the return of Willowbrook or add new beds to its other facilities until the early 1950s. It was, however, able to address the problems of shortages of employees. From the low point of 2,611 employees in the state schools and Craig Colony in 1945, the number rose quickly to 3,019 in 1946 as employees who had been in the armed services or wartime occupations returned to their positions. The administration recommended higher salaries in order to recruit more and better personnel, and the postwar *Annual Reports* were replete with plans for various professional training programs.

The overwhelming majority (approximately 2,600) of the 3,019 total positions were in ward service, grounds, power plant, laundry, food service and similar titles. Only 275 were in professional-clinical positions such as medical officers, dentists, occupational and physical therapy, or social work. About 140 positions were in the administrative and business office areas. At the beginning of the postwar era, the staff of the state institutions resembled flat pyramids: a handful of managers and clinicians overseeing thousands of attendants, grounds keepers, and other employees in largely custodial roles (DMH 1947).

By 1950, there were 4,491 employees in the state schools (a ratio of 1:4.3 employees to residents (DMH 1951, 315). By 1955, the number of employees had risen to 5,596 (a 1:4 ratio of staff to residents), and while attendants still formed the base of the nonprofessional pyramid, the number of nursing positions rose to 176 (DMH 1956, 220). In 1959, there were 7,507 employees in the state schools (a 1:3.7 ratio of staff to residents). The 1959 *Annual Report* does not provide a breakdown of employees in the state schools and hospitals, but the total number of nurses in the Department of Mental Hygiene institutions had risen more than 30 percent to 2, 010 from 1950 (DMH 1960, 223).

Defective Delinquents

The primary emphasis of the postwar expansion of admissions was on relieving the burden defective infants placed on the family, but juvenile delinquency was an issue that continued to percolate below the surface. It reemerged in the 1950s (Trent 1992). The *Annual Report* for 1956 also announced that:

> "A special study was made of the educational program of the Wassaic State School, where a high percentage of delinquent and predelinquent adolescents were adding to the problems of academic education and training."
>
> "On recommendation of the Commissioner, a new type of mental hygiene institution was proposed by Governor Harriman to accommodate emotionally disturbed and semidelinquent adolescent mental defectives now being committed to the state schools for the mentally retarded" (DMH 1956, 12–13).

From 1935, the only attention given to the issue of delinquency was the statistical summary in each *Annual Report* showing the numbers of defective delinquents in the state's training schools for defective delinquents operated by the Department of Corrections and loosely monitored by the Department of Mental Hygiene. In 1935, there were 1,223 residents in those two (briefly three) facilities for male and female defective delinquents. The peak census was reached in 1939 with 2,080, and with steady declines in subsequent years, the census in the Department of Corrections facilities dropped to 1,189 in 1955 (DMH 1955). By 1959, there were only 892 "defective delinquents" left in Naponoch and Albion. Defective delinquents were finding their way into the state schools.

Institutions and Mental Retardation Services at the End of the Postwar Era

Fifteen years after the Moreland Act Commission, the state schools had become overcrowded hospitals filled with younger and more severely disabled people. Services were concentrated in the institutions, and severe overcrowding and growing waiting lists guaranteed that the planned new schools would not solve the problem, especially since six years after their authorization none was approaching completion. By the end of the 1950s, the state administration was portraying the problems in the state schools as a virtually intractable problem, reflecting inexorable historical forces.

The problems in the state schools exasperated the state administration because they stood in stark contrast to the increasing optimism about the decline in the census of state hospitals and the promises of the community mental health movement in which New York claimed national leadership. Minor administrative reorganizations, more studies of the problems, and patience until more large institutions could be built were the main remedies proposed by the state administration through this entire period. But, the politics of mental retardation would change irrevocably in this era. First, the ARC, from its inception, was fundamentally oriented toward community services. Although the ARC subsumed institution-based organizations within its umbrella and, most notably at Willowbrook, advocated for better conditions in the institutions, the first feature of the political cleavage that emerged was the community *versus* the institution. This cleavage was exacerbated as the state encouraged parents to keep children at home but provided little support and considerable opposition to funding adequate community services.

The second cleavage was mental retardation *versus* mental health. From the creation of the Department of Mental Hygiene in 1927 through the 1930s and early 1940s, state services for people with mental retardation and epilepsy and services for people with mental illnesses operated on two, virtually parallel, tracks. It was not until the postwar era and the creation of the Mental Health Commission in 1948 and the passage of the state's Community Mental Health Act in 1954 that the advocates perceived, and began to argue in the political arena, that mental retardation was the stepchild in the Department of Mental Hygiene. Although the gap between expenditures on state hospitals and state schools narrowed in this period, there was still a substantial difference in the amounts expended in the two fields. The psychiatrist-dominated Department of Mental Hygiene reported increases in the state school census as blots on the otherwise glowing plans for progress.

A legislative *versus* executive dimension also emerged in the politics of mental retardation in the postwar era. The creation of the Joint Legislative Committee on Mental Retardation in 1955, and the appointment of ARC Executive Director Joseph Weingold as Counsel, provided the ARC semiofficial status. It was a small but legitimate base from which it could counter the routine opposition from the Department of Mental Hygiene, the Department of Education, and the Executive Office to almost all their major proposals. The JLC could commission and issue reports, lobby legislators and state administrators, and lend governmental authority to the demands of the ARC.

Three new and important features of the economics of mental retardation also emerged in the postwar era. First, the costs of delivering mental retardation services became a major concern as its proportion of the state budget grew. The problems of increases in state school censuses, large and growing waiting lists, the cumulative impact of admitting younger and more disabled people, and the construction costs in the "perpetual building program" that emerged after the war remained unresolved at the end of the postwar period.

The number of employees in the state schools grew substantially in the postwar era, and this would become a significant element in the economics of mental retardation. The state was unable to solve the overcrowding in the institutions, but it did provide larger numbers of employees to care for the residents. Even with many new employees, state schools personnel were still arrayed in flat pyramids of a few physician-administrators overseeing thousands of direct care and support staff. Nonetheless, the exigencies of operating infirmaries for younger and more disabled patients required an exponential increase in the number of nurses working in the institutions. State schools were emerging as potent economic factors in local economies, especially in the rural areas where most of the institutions were located.

The operation of clinics, education programs, sheltered workshops, and other day services by the AHRC, and later ARC, began virtually by default as municipalities, school districts, and the state refused to serve certain people. The AHRC's willingness to step into that vacuum and run the programs itself was controversial when it began in the late 1940s. By the end of the postwar era, the chapters of the statewide organization were operating scores of these programs, most notably sheltered workshops. The operational, organizational, and political ramifications of those early postwar decisions did not become clear until decades later. However, the foundations of what became known by the 1980s as "the industry" were clearly laid out in the postwar era.

At the end of the postwar era, services for people with mental retardation in New York had deteriorated in several important respects. State services became increasingly concentrated in larger institutions as colonies atrophied and other programs outside institutions stagnated and were ill suited to the younger and more disabled people being admitted. Ranks of cribs in infant infirmaries became the norm at Willowbrook and other state schools. New buildings were immediately filled to overcapacity as waiting lists grew. Even as the costs of care in the state schools grew, people with mental retardation did not seem to fit the Department of Mental Hygiene's vision of community mental health. These institutional factors would ultimately contribute to significant changes in the ways services would be provided in New York State. The advocacy of the ARC and its operation of community programs would provide the catalyst for and the basis of a solution to the crises that were on the horizon.

Chapter 3

Planning: The Rhetoric of Public Institutions and Community Services

> There should be a new beginning based on what we have learned in the past fifty years.
>
> —Leo Fixler, Minority Report, *Comprehensive Plan,* 1965

Plans, plans, and more plans. There was no activity more ubiquitous in the early years of the administration of Governor Nelson A. Rockefeller than planning—and nothing that had so little impact on the future of public institutions and other services for people with developmental disabilities. Leo Fixler's call for a new beginning in his Minority Report to the Task Force on Mental Retardation and the Law was expressing the profound pessimism of the mental retardation constituency at the conclusion of the most visible of several planning efforts at that time.

This was a pivotal period in the history of services for people with mental retardation. The failure of comprehensive and master plans to explain the subsequent direction of developmental services in New York provides crucial insights into what other factors influenced the future of institutions and other developmental services. The plans were undertaken against the backdrop of President John F. Kennedy's plans for mental retardation services that signaled a new role for the federal government in this area. The success of Kennedy's plans with their rapid completion and enactment into legislation contrasted with confusion, delay, and contention in New York, and was one more element fueling the political rivalry between Rockefeller and the Kennedys. The multiple and overlapping state plans contained glaring contradictions within and between plans, and had virtually no relationship to what types of public institutions were constructed, where they were located, and how they were connected to community services. The various plan processes involved virtually every interested party in the mental retardation constituency and managed to disappoint and alienate them all. For these participants, fundamental problems were left unresolved, a few long-standing and hard-fought victories were reopened, and their proposals for an alternate future were voted down. The plan processes, with the mental retardation constituencies variously excluded, in a minority or ignored, explain why the state and these interests clashed so violently in the following years and why Leo Fixler's call for a new beginning pointed toward the confrontation at Willowbrook.

Fire, Ready, Aim: Planning in the Rockefeller Administration

In 1956 Rockefeller was appointed Chairman of the Temporary Commission on the Constitutional Convention. This was a joint appointment from Governor Averell Harriman, who Rockefeller would defeat in 1958, and Senate Majority Leader Walter Mahoney and Assembly Speaker Oswald D. Heck, both of whom Rockefeller would defeat for the Republican nomination for Governor. With the assistance of William Ronan, his chief aide, as Executive Secretary of the Commission, Rockefeller used the Temporary Commission as a political launching pad. The extensive plans for new programs and reorganization of New York State government were not only elements in a political platform but a blueprint for what Rockefeller expected to accomplish after his election.

Competing and Parallel Plans in the First Rockefeller Administration

In Rockefeller's first, fiscally constrained administration, the governor's initiatives in the mental retardation arena were largely confined to a reorganization of the Department of Mental Hygiene in which Dr. Pense was once again named as head of the mental retardation division. It was not until the last year of his first administration that the governor, in January 1962, in a special message to the legislature, announced, "a broad plan developed by [Commissioner] Dr. Hoch" (Master Plan 1962). In the mental retardation area, the five-year plan called for intensified application of modern treatment methods, expanded and intensified research, and development of coordinated community services.

> "Also stressed will be expansion of state school facilities for the retarded; better care, food and clothing for state school patients; strengthened central administrative direction of programs for the retarded; expanded research programs; strengthened recruitment and training of personnel; expanded and coordinated community programs with increased state aid looking toward the removal of the per

capita ceiling; and a comprehensive study to modernize admission procedures" (Master Plan 1962, 3).

The major elements of what became known as "the master plan" had not only been laid out without an explicit, formal planning process, but this "master plan" exacerbated a rift between the mental retardation constituency and the administration and added to a distrust of planning on the part of these groups.

An Interdepartmental Health and Hospital Council was originally established during the Harriman administration as the Interdepartmental Health Resources Board with an advisory committee on mental retardation. When the Council was reestablished as the Interdepartmental Health and Hospital Council in the Rockefeller administration, according to Lerner, a "protracted, behind-the-scenes struggle" broke out among the ARC, the Department of Mental Hygiene, the state Departments of Health, Education, and Social Welfare, and the governor's office over whether an advisory committee would be appointed and what its relationship would be to the Department of Mental Hygiene, the Governor's office, and the Interdepartmental Council (1972, 179). This caused a delay that fueled the mental retardation constituency's resentment of the department's determination to maintain hegemony over this arena.

In his January 1962 *Message to the Legislature* announcing the department's master plan, the governor also announced that he would appoint a Citizens Committee on Mental Retardation to advise in the formulation and implementation of the state's programs for the mentally retarded (Lerner 1972). According to Lerner, the committee was never appointed because of opposing pressure from the psychiatry-dominated Department of Mental Hygiene. These episodes did not contribute to an investment by the mental retardation constituents in the state planning process.

Planning at the Federal Level

At the time New York's plans in the mental retardation area were closely held and delayed, federal plans in this area were off to a fast and public start. In October 1961, nine months after his inauguration, President John F. Kennedy appointed a special President's Panel on Mental Retardation. The panel included a wide range of academic, clinical, and other professional experts in the mental retardation area. It also employed a series of task forces and advisors and held public hearings as well as site visits in England and several Scandinavian countries (Scheerenberger 1987). Normalization, a concept that had gained currency in Denmark and Sweden, found an important vehicle into American thinking in the mental retardation field through the work of the President's Panel. Extensive reviews of the growing professional literature and exemplary practice were another important feature of the work of the Panel.

The President's Panel completed its work in an astonishingly rapid manner and submitted its report, *A Proposed Program for National Action to Combat Mental Retardation*, to the President in a little over a year (President's Panel 1982). This was an emphatic demonstration of the consensus in the academic-professional ranks around the key elements of the panel's report: research, prevention, education, comprehensive clinical and social services, emphasis on local and community facilities of care, staffing, new legal and social concepts of mental retardation, and public information and awareness. The report, issued in October 1962, was followed by President Kennedy's address to Congress in early 1963, the first time mental retardation issues had been given such an important forum. Shortly after, the passage of the Maternal and Child Health and Mental Retardation Planning Amendments of 1963 as well as the Mental Retardation Facilities and Community Mental Health Centers Construction Act of 1963 were remarkable for the speed of the process and its significant statutory outcomes (Scheerenberger 1987).

The *Proposed Program for National Action to Combat Mental Retardation* was one of the first expressions of what would become typical approaches to social problems in the 1960s. The format of the report, opening with sections on Research, Prevention, and Education, demonstrated the confidence that problems such as mental retardation, like poverty, could be solved with "wars" that employed the weapons of science, planning, and coordination. The report also laid out several concepts about the organization of developmental services that would find their way into the planning documents of the Rockefeller administration and the prevailing approach to services. They included the notion of a "continuum of care," purchase of care from private institutions and voluntary agencies, the 1,000-bed ceiling for public institutions, and area mental retardation centers linking services in a locale or region (President's Panel 1962).

The President's Panel, its report, and subsequent legislation had special significance for New York. It initiated a federal government involvement in what had been an exclusively state government policy area. New York and other states would no longer be able to operate programs for people with mental retardation without taking into account the framework and incentives established through these federal government efforts. This had a particularly important impact on New York because it had created the Mental Health Commission in 1948 to study many of these issues and passed its own Community Mental Health Act in 1954. While New York could claim a pioneering role, its advocates for people with mental retardation could point to the state's lack of attention and progress on virtually every one of the elements of the President's Panel's recommendations after many more years of study. The federal plan and legislation began to lay the foundation for a significant federal role in this area, a role that would have important political, fiscal, and organizational consequences for institutional and community services in New York.

The federal plan also added fuel to the partisan political differences between Rockefeller and the leadership of the ARC, and it established mental retardation as a forum in the national political rivalry between Nelson Rockefeller and, first, President John F. Kennedy and, later, Senator Robert F. Kennedy. It is not clear whether and to what extent Kennedy's appointment of a President's Panel stimulated Rockefeller's announcement of a master plan, but it is highly unlikely that Rockefeller's presidential ambitions and his great sensitivity to New York's presumed role as a national leader in the area of mental disabilities were not challenged by Kennedy's early and bold federal initiative. New York's ARC, with its New York City-based, Democrat-leaning leadership, which Rockefeller had suspected of thinly veiled support of his opponent in the 1958 gubernatorial election, could now add the example of a broad-based and open planning process at the federal level to its list of complaints about the Rockefeller administration's efforts. The controversy over the federal plan was an opening skirmish in a Rockefeller-Kennedy, federal-state, parent-professional battle that would culminate a decade later in *ARC v. Rockefeller*—the parents' suit in federal court against the state.

New York State Planning in the Second Rockefeller Administration

The federally funded *Comprehensive Plan* process reopened many of the hostilities between the mental retardation constituency and the Department of Mental Hygiene. By the time New York applied for the U.S. Public Health Service grants for comprehensive planning in mental health and mental retardation provided by the new federal legislation, the state was already laying out key features of its state school construction program, establishing the new financing mechanisms, and implementing other elements of its own five-year master plan. In the spring of 1963, the Department of Mental Hygiene appointed a Mental Health Section of the State Planning Committee to undertake New York's comprehensive plan. However, it was not until the summer of 1964 that the Commissioner of Mental Hygiene appointed a Mental Retardation Section of that committee (*Comprehensive Plan* 1965, Report, 1965, I).

This issue of a separate committee for mental retardation had a contentious history that clouded subsequent planning efforts. The initial federal funding for planning presumed a unified mental disorders approach, and New York's Department of Mental Hygiene strongly supported this approach. When federal legislation authorized funding for mental retardation planning, New York subsumed that effort within its original *comprehensive* approach. The Assistant Commissioner of the Department of Mental Hygiene who was in charge of the planning process, told the 1963 Annual Conference of Community Mental Health Boards:

> "It's no secret to tell you Dr. Hoch feels this kind of separation is, first, wrong from a practical point of view, second, wrong from the interests of the mentally retarded" (quoted in Lerner 1972, 175).

The mental retardation constituency joined the comprehensive planning initiative with grave reservations.

The death of Commissioner Paul Hoch in 1964 created an important hiatus in the plan process. The administration began a national search for a new commissioner, and it was rumored that several potential candidates for the position declined because the governor's office had already made key decisions about reorganization and construction that would predetermine the major policy directions for a new commissioner. After two years of national searching, the administration offered the commissioner position to one of the department's assistant commissioners, Dr. Alan Miller, who headed the small Division of Community Services. Miller had been playing a role in the *Comprehensive Plan* process, but by the time of his appointment in 1966, the process had been completed.

Process as the Problem

The *Comprehensive Plan* process was important because (in contrast to the closely held master plan developed by the Department of Mental Hygiene), virtually everyone in the state involved or interested in mental health or mental retardation services served as a member or consultant to one or more of the myriad committees. The New York State Planning Committee on Mental Disorders was organized into two sections, Mental Health and Mental Retardation, each with dozens of members and consultants. There were ten regional committees that were organized into numerous subcommittees and task forces. The New York City regional committee had sixty-three members representing different agencies dealing with mental disorders, twelve individual members, and scores of "Additional subcommittee members invited to serve by the Subcommittee chairman," as well as myriad consultants (*Comprehensive Plan* 1965 Vol. II, xi–xvi). The pattern was repeated throughout the state.

In addition to the statewide sections and regional committees, there was a series of issue-oriented Task Forces. In the Mental Retardation Section these included: Finance, Education, Training of Professional Personnel, Prevention, Social Welfare, Vocational Rehabilitation and Employment Services, Parent and Volunteer Groups and Community Organizations, Research and Demonstration Projects, Clinics and Hospitals, Mental Retardation and the

Law, and Facilities Construction. Hundreds of members from the Mental Retardation Section as well as additional members and consultants served on these task forces.

There were several reasons why the planning process had few direct consequences for the shape and direction of mental retardation services. The first problem was that despite the fact that the terms *comprehensive, integrated, systematic,* and *statewide* littered virtually every other page of the plans of the era, the Rockefeller administration had several plans dealing with mental retardation services—and there was often little agreement among them on critical issues. The seven volume *A Plan for a Comprehensive Mental Health and Mental Retardation Program for New York State* issued by the New York State Planning Committee on Mental Disorders in 1965 constantly refers to "the department's plan," which was the "master plan" announced by Governor Rockefeller in 1962. The department's master plan was distinct from the construction plans already being implemented by the semi-independent Mental Hygiene Facilities Improvement Fund. Indeed, the existence of several comprehensive and master plans for mental retardation services initiated at virtually the same time by agencies with overlapping responsibilities in the area made a mockery of the notion of planning. The large and growing numbers of comprehensive plans, new and reconstituted planning agencies, task forces, interagency coordinating bodies, and various committees appointed to study and report on virtually every aspect of state policy were so numerous that a large Office of Planning Coordination was established in the Executive Office to oversee the scores of statewide and regional committees.

The multiple and competing plans were also demonstrations of the substantial cleavages that existed in this area, between the new role of the federal government and the traditional role of state governments, between the state government and local governments, between mental retardation and mental health interests, and between mental retardation and other disability interests. Each of the several plan processes had its biases.

New York's mental retardation constituency believed that it was being punished for its Democrat leanings and tacit support of Averell Harriman against Nelson Rockefeller by the revocation of its formal advisory role in the Interdepartmental Health and Hospital Council plan process. The mental retardation constituency felt vindicated by President Kennedy's highlighting of mental retardation as a separate focus in the new and prominent federal planning, and the New York advocates highlighted the contrast between President Kennedy's early and vigorous attention to mental retardation and Governor Rockefeller's comparative indifference to this distinct area.

The mental retardation interests were excluded from involvement in developing the Department of Mental Hygiene's "master plan," and the mistrust and hostilities carried over into the *Comprehensive Plan* process in the initial opposition to a separate mental retardation section and the belated naming of a section and committees. Even the regional planning processes that were subsets of and constituted much of the 1965 *Comprehensive Plan* exacerbated the long-standing hostilities between mental retardation interests and local governments in New York. By 1965, the mental retardation constituencies had reason to feel excluded and disadvantaged in one way or another in each of New York's interdepartmental, master, local, and comprehensive plans. As each of the many processes unfolded, the mental retardation constituency was reminded, in subtle and pointed ways, of its secondary role in the mental hygiene, health, education, and social welfare policy and administrative arenas in New York.

Although hundreds of key members of the mental retardation constituency were eventually brought into deliberations, key features of the *Comprehensive Plan* framework and processes foreordained the outcomes. On several crucial issues, the proposals of local or mental retardation committees became minority opinions in the statewide reports where they were outvoted by the larger and prevailing mental health makeup of the combined task forces. The statewide reports show hardened veterans of decades-long policy wrangles going along with the process with a skeptical view of its outcome. However, a process that included hundreds of knowledgeable and interested people across the state, that was mirrored by a prominent new initiative by the federal government, and that yielded hundreds of recommendations for new and improved mental retardation services (albeit not adopted in the final reports) created new and rekindled old expectations which created the danger of a backlash if those expectations were not met. The testimony of key mental retardation advocates in the process showed that they understood that crucial decisions on finance, facilities construction, and the roles of respective levels of government and administrative agencies had already been made or were being made elsewhere.

Issues in the Plan: Conflict and Confusion

Despite the numerous flaws in the background and processes of planning, the *Comprehensive Plan* is important. It provided a description of the major issues in the field at the time, although perhaps the most important issue— the construction of new institutions—was already being implemented and was discussed with either vague allusions or analytic contortions. It is especially significant because the *Comprehensive Plan* documents the enormous differences between what virtually the entire mental retardation constituency and its professional allies believed should be the future of services on key issues and what actually happened.

Who pays the costs of mental retardation services?

The report of the Task Force on Financing was the shortest of the twelve task force reports in the 1965 *Comprehensive Plan*, but its opening lines were the most succinct statement of issues in the seven volumes.

> "When all the smoke is cleared in our planning efforts, two questions will emerge, the answers to which may mean that our efforts will be either exercises in futility or a meaningful blueprint for a better life for the mentally retarded and their families. These questions are: How much will it cost? Where is the money coming from?" (*Comprehensive Plan* 1965, V, 10).

A review of the various plans shows that the answer was not clear except for the consensus that the costs were large and growing. The question of where is the money coming from was addressed in the plans although long unresolved disputes were often obscured in the subtext of the analyses and recommendations. In the mid-1960s, the issue was staked out largely along two dimensions. How much of the costs of care were family members expected to bear? How would the public costs be shared among the local, state, and federal governments?

The question of family responsibility for the costs of care in the state's institutions (and for the costs of a disabled child's education) was a long-standing source of contention between parents of disabled children and the state. The issue of parental fees became increasingly problematic as admissions of younger and more disabled children from middle-class families replaced a largely indigent resident population. In considering how much families could be expected to pay, the plan participants had to contend with the fact that New York's institutional care fees were the highest in the nation, and the state was proposing to earmark fees for dedicated purposes such as the creation of a research fund rather than direct services (Lerner 1972, 110, 215). The ARC clearly understood that parental fees were linked to the repayment of forty-year construction bonds, an understanding underscored by Governor Rockefeller's veto message of the bill limiting family liability that confirmed "the guarantee to the bondholders." While the battle over parental fees was carried on largely outside the plan process, the Mental Retardation Section of the State Planning Committee did address the fee-bond issue.

> "The consensus of the Mental Retardation Section of the State Planning Committee is that the practice of utilizing fees paid for those in State institutions as a financial base for the Mental Hygiene Facilities Improvement Fund represents a wrong principle" (*Comprehensive Plan* 1965, I, 99).

However, no formal recommendation was made on this "consensus."

The second dimension of the question of who will pay revolved around the relative share of the costs to be borne by local governments (including school districts), the state, and the federal government. It rekindled rather than resolved a century-old dispute that had three main features: local government responsibility for costs of state institutional care, the costs of special education, and the costs of community programs. An additional, although not yet major, feature was the role of federal government financing of services.

On the issue of a local government share of institutional costs, the Task Force on Financing stirred a smoldering fire when it pointed out that "local governments find it easy to escape the responsibility for providing facilities by relegating the retarded to state institutions since the state assumes total financial responsibility for such services" and recommended, "That local governments (county and city) share with the state, on an equal basis, the difference between the fees received and the total cost of care, treatment and education of the mentally retarded in state schools" (*Comprehensive Plan* 1965, V, 13). The localities operated on the assumption that the county poor house-state asylum issue had been settled in 1890 when the state passed the New York Care Act which made financial responsibility for the chronic care of people with mental disabilities a state responsibility. In *A Proposal for the Future Development of State Schools for the Retarded*, Volume VII of the Comprehensive Plan, the issue was not only reopened but reversed in the proposal that:

> "Primary responsibility for the mentally ill and the mentally retarded should be returned to local government and communities. The state should share in the fiscal support of the community programs and establish and maintain standards. Operational responsibility should be assigned to the localities" (*Comprehensive Plan* 1965, VII, 39).

These recommendations that local governments take *primary* responsibility and the state's role would be to *share* in the fiscal support put local governments in a hostile defensive posture at the same time other plan task forces were painting a glowing picture of a future of community services and state and local cooperation.

The Task Force on Financing rekindled another controversy when it charged that many school districts were not meeting their obligations to the retarded. It recommended that additional weighting be given to pupils in special education classes in the state education aid formula and that school districts be mandated (with state aid) to reimburse parents for tuition and expenses incurred in placing mentally retarded children in private schools when no public school classes are available (*Comprehensive Plan* 1965, V,

10, 11). These issues were central to long-standing disputes between advocates, school districts, and the state. In 1962, the state had revised the education law to eliminate both special state aid for special classes for the handicapped and the previous rate of increase in funding for special classes.

The third dimension of the dispute over local-state government share of costs revolved around community programs. Since the passage of the Community Mental Health Act of 1954, New York regarded itself as a pioneer in community mental health programs. The ARC and advocates for people with mental retardation repeatedly pointed out that the overwhelming majority of the funds allocated by Community Mental Health Boards went to programs for people with mental illness. Day training, clinics, education and other programs for people with mental retardation were rarely funded and then only at token amounts. As Lerner (1972) points out, "Even where counties were contracting with local chapters of NYSARC for service programs, . . . the local governments were contributing little more than 8% of the local share (284)." Overall, local governments were contributing miserly amounts to community programs, and mental retardation services were getting minuscule proportions of those funds.

The Task Force on Financing noted the recommendations of several regional task forces for separate local mental retardation boards (which mirrored the ARC's long-standing position), but took no official position. It did recommend an increase in the rate of state participation in costs (from 50 percent to 75 percent) for services for the mentally retarded through the local mental health boards and estimated that while costs would rise, this would "at least double or triple existing day training centers" (*Comprehensive Plan* 1965, V). In the view of the mental retardation constituencies, this was typical of the chasm between rhetoric and reality on community programs throughout the *Comprehensive Plan*. Localities that had not contributed significant amounts to community programs (and less to mental retardation services) and school districts that had not met mandates for special classes would be expected to be linchpins in a new era of community programs.

The final intergovernmental dimension of the question of who will pay was the role of the federal government. The vague outlines of a federal role in financing mental health and mental retardation services were only beginning to be seen by the mid-1960s and played only a peripheral role in the plans of the era. Of course, the *Comprehensive Plan* process was largely financed with newly available federal funds, but the federal role and the status of mental retardation vis-à-vis mental health constituents contributed to existing tensions in the area. The Task Force on Financing did note that the federal Construction of Mental Retardation Facilities Act (PL 88-164) would provide $4 million in matching funds for construction. It recommended changes in legislation to empower the Mental Hygiene Facilities Improvement Fund to receive the federal funds. Although federal funds were available, the respective federal, state, and local shares would be 37.67 percent, 31.16 percent, and 31.16 percent, still requiring a substantial local fiscal commitment. The state was already foregoing federal funds for vocational rehabilitation programs because the state was not appropriating matching funds (*Comprehensive Plan* 1965, V, 14). Medicaid, although recently passed as an obscure rider to Medicare, was not yet on the map of state planners for a federal role in financing services.

Administrative Roles and Responsibilities of State and Local Governments

The issue of the respective roles in managing programs for people with mental disabilities was closely related to the financing issue, but there were features of the *Comprehensive Plan* on this topic that had a distinct impact on the direction of services for people with mental retardation. The mental retardation interests on the plan committees and task forces hammered on their bitter disappointment in the record of county-controlled Community Mental Health Boards to fund mental retardation services. Nonetheless, the recommendations of the larger Joint Task Forces on Coordination, Continued Planning, and Evaluation "agreed that at the present time a single agency for each local government would provide the best organizational structure within which mental health and mental retardation programs could be developed and provided" (*Comprehensive Plan* 1965, V, 2). In *A Proposal for the Future Development of State Schools for the Retarded*, Volume VII of the *Comprehensive Plan*, the anticipated role of local government was made even more specific, "Consistent with both the above themes is the recognition that primary responsibility for the mentally ill and the mentally retarded should be returned to local government and the communities" (39). The *Comprehensive Plan* discussion of regional organizations overseeing services did little but contribute to the long-standing tension between local governments and the state over funding and fueled the frustration of the mental retardation constituency with both the state and Community Mental Health Boards.

Role of Private Organizations in the Delivery of Services

The role of private organizations in the delivery of services was another area in which the plan process and its reports exacerbated rather than closed long-standing cleavages. Private social welfare agencies, general and psychiatric hospitals, and nursing homes were inventoried as local resources in various task force reports. The Task Force on Parent Groups, Community, Civic, Volunteer, Groups, Recreation, and Public Education did make a "preliminary report" which noted the existence of many voluntary agencies programs (including those run by the ARC). However, little attention was given to the arguments by the mental retardation representatives on the various committees about the chronic underfunding by local governments and Community Mental Health Boards of the sheltered workshops, clinics, education, and other programs they operated. More disturbing was the report of the Task Force on Clinics and Hospitals, which had no mental retardation representative,

> "Day care centers, in some cases, are presently run by volunteer organizations (AHRC). Experience of one of our task force members indicates that volunteer agencies are not always necessarily best equipped to run such centers and may prove incapable of dealing with problems of administration, budgeting, staff planning, etc. Perhaps day care centers are best operated by a child care agency" (*Comprehensive Plan* 1965, V, 120).

Role of State Schools in the Comprehensive Service System

In 1965, state schools were still virtually the only state-operated model of services for people with mental retardation. It would seem that an extensive consideration of their number, size, and role in the future of services would be central to a *Comprehensive Plan*. However, by the time the *Comprehensive Plan* process got underway, Governor Rockefeller had already announced a five-year, $138 million state schools construction program as part of a more than $500 million mental hygiene construction plan. The five-year construction plan was ostensibly based on the "preliminary findings" of the task forces at work on the *Comprehensive Plan*, but the reports of those task forces referred back to the construction plan. For example, the Task Force on Construction of Facilities in the *Comprehensive Plan* process reported, "The findings and recommendations of this task force must be regarded as tentative and very limited due to a variety of circumstances, among which was the time factor" (*Comprehensive Plan* 1965, V, 163). Of course, among this "variety of circumstances" was the fact that the construction plan was largely completed, the financing and administrative mechanisms (that will be described later) were in place, and construction was underway. The fact that these crucial issues were only dealt with tangentially, in reference to other plans, or in oblique allusions to what everyone knew was already underway is another reason why the planning process and its recommendations exacerbated tensions.

The construction plan and its implementation had an enormous impact on the future shape and direction of mental retardation services in New York, and its immediate and long-term consequences will be discussed in the next chapter. Nonetheless, while the construction of new institutions had little or no relationship to the analyses, guidelines, and recommendations of the comprehensive plans, it is important to examine them because they help explain why the cleavages between the state and the mental retardation constituencies widened, why public institutions remained in contrast to community service models, and why these gaps had to be bridged.

Models of Community Services for People with Mental Retardation

The *Comprehensive Plan* Task Force on Financing described the crux of the problem of institutional *versus* community services:

> "The statistics available clearly indicate that in New York State more than 95% of the mentally retarded live in the community. Yet we spend on community services but a minuscule fraction of the total expenditure by the state on mental retardation. In the year 1963–64, the state spent $50 some odd million dollars on patient care in the state schools for the mentally retarded (without construction), but only a little over $330,000 on community services for the mentally retarded (other than public education or vocational rehabilitation for which statistics are not available). These $330,000 include state aid to the clinics and day training centers, etc., all operated by units of the Association for Retarded Children."
>
> "The Governor's program for the mentally retarded for the next five years includes $138 million for construction of institution beds for the mentally retarded as well as several million dollars for improved patient care and staffing new facilities. There are no comparable expenditures proposed at this time for the 95% of the mentally retarded not in institutions" (V, 10).

The lack of funding for community programs and the absence of community mental retardation facilities in the construction plan were major issues overhanging the discussion of community mental retardation services. There were, however, discussions that indicated aspirations and plans that would eventually influence the shape and direction of mental retardation services. For example, the importance of vocational rehabilitation for adults was emphasized in several task force reports. The Task Force on Financing argued:

> "The very keystone of services for the retarded adult is the provision of work. Without participation in the world of work, he is not a whole man. In fact, the attrition of idleness is a corrosive on all family relations and the retarded's personality. It leads, almost inevitably, to institutionalization" (*Comprehensive Plan* 1965, V, 13).

Despite this picture of the dire consequences of idleness, this task force noted that the New York State Division of Vocational Rehabilitation had not used even the small amounts appropriated under a 1963 amendment to the Education Law for staffing sheltered workshops for the severely handicapped because of a State Education Department "administrative interpretation," and the state was losing $2 million a year in federal funds through the failure of the legislature to appropriate matching funds (V, 14).

The Task Force on Vocational Rehabilitation and Employment Services repeated some of the criticisms of the Task Force on Financing with respect to the lack of funding of sheltered workshops. It also addressed another important issue that lurked below the surface of funding and would have important consequences for the future shape of developmental services—specialized or comprehensive services. The task force came down strongly on both sides of the issue.

"The task force agreed that the past neglect of the mentally retarded now presents us with the need for developing programs for a very large number of individuals and that, therefore, there is an urgent need for specialized programs and facilities just for the mentally retarded" (V, 78).

However, the task force split on whether services should be for a variety of handicapped or otherwise disadvantaged individuals or limited to individuals with mental retardation. The majority of the task force urged integration of the retarded into programs serving others but recognized that the severely retarded might need separate facilities, and specialized facilities would cost more.

Having dodged a stance on specialized facilities, the Task Force on Vocational Rehabilitation and Employment Services noted the "huge gap between the needs and existing programs for rehabilitation services and facilities," and launched into an extensive discussion of how "coordinated," "flexible," and "comprehensive" programs would address these problems. Although noting that some regional reports recommended establishing facilities on a county basis while others urged centralized programs, the task force described a concept of a rehabilitation program encompassing both the comprehensive community mental retardation center (CCMRC) and the state institutions. The task force proposed that the individual could move among these CCMRCs and the "intermediate facilities" (in the primary, intermediate, and satellite scheme proposed elsewhere) as well as prevocational school programs, and "occupational day centers" (modeled on the *one* existing center operated by the New York City Board of Education). Here, as in other significant elements of the comprehensive plans, the analyses and recommendations ignored decades of inaction on key issues, rested on assumptions that vast new networks of hitherto nonexistent programs and facilities would quickly materialize, and presumed that a new era of coordination and cooperation would dawn.

Community Residential Services

Community residential service models were dealt with in vague generalizations in most of the *Comprehensive Plan* task force reports. "Residence facilities to help the retarded remain in the community, including short term residences for all ages as well as group living for adults who may work in the community but need social supervision their families can no longer provide," was one expression of the framework for community residential models (*Comprehensive Plan* 1965, V, 10). The need for "generic services," the notion of a "continuum of care," and the proposal for Community Mental Retardation Centers, intermediate centers, and satellite centers were other concepts that floated in the various task force reports, although the conflict over state and local government shares of the cost of local as well as state institutional costs was never far from the discussions.

The *Comprehensive Plan* Task Force on Social Welfare report was the most thorough of the twelve reports. It covered a wide range of topics, brought in the results of current research, and took cognizance of the work and background of the President's Panel in its analyses and recommendations. It was this task force that pointed to the relationship between lower socioeconomic status, diagnoses of mental retardation, and institution admissions (*Comprehensive Plan* VII, 65). The task force recommended broadening day as well as residential programs and discussed foster family boarding homes for up to six children; private agency operated boarding homes for up to six children; private agency-owned group homes for up to twelve children, and private agency-owned group residences for up to twenty-five children (VII, 70).

The Task Force on Vocational Rehabilitation, Employment, and Workshops recommended that "Halfway Houses" for twenty to twenty-five residents be established as "an intermediate program base" in a "complex" of long-term residential facilities and rehabilitation workshops (V, 82). The task force acknowledged that this type of facility was "practically non-existent," and there has been too little experience for determining the length of residence required to accomplish its aims most effectively," but it was nonetheless "clear that a large number of these facilities will be required and there is a need to begin establishment of the programs on a broad scale as soon as possible" (V, 82). The Task Force on Clinics and Hospitals also noted the handful of existing halfway houses, briefly mentioned "hostels" as another model of "inpatient community center," and recommended an extension of the "colony system which has worked advantageously in some upstate regions" (V, 121–122).

The various task force reports that dealt with community residential models seemed unanimous in their observation that virtually none of these models existed. However, there was almost no discussion and analysis of what the various models would entail and no agreement (or consensus in the overall *Comprehensive Plan*) as to what approach would be taken among the hodge-podge of Community Mental Retardation Centers, intermediate and satellite centers, vocational rehabilitation halfway houses, boarding homes, group homes, hostels, colonies, and other options that were mentioned.

Some of these discussions took a prescient look at the importance of work force issues in these various program models. Most often, these were *pro forma* observations that more staff would be needed. Many of the reports also contained extended discussions of the need for special education teachers, psychologists, occupational and physical therapists, and other professional staff.

Two aspects of the staffing issue with long-term consequences for public institutions and the organization of developmental services were also touched on in the task force reports. The Task Force on Clinics and Hospitals argued that while smaller residential centers should be established, "it is not feasible to abandon the larger state institutions now harboring the bulk of the resident population of retardates" (*Comprehensive Plan* 1965, V, 121). However, the task force pointed out that in staffing these smaller facilities, "One of the problems in New York State is the eight-hour day" (V, 121). It suggested that this problem could be met by having couples take care of these individuals in smaller semi-independent units following the model of the housefather and housemother of the colonies," (V, 121) presaging a debate that would take place a decade or more later on the basic model of community residential services.

The Task Force on Clinics and Hospitals also took on another issue ignored by the task forces and committees on work force and those dealing directly with state schools when it pointed out:

"A particular problem to which we wish to draw attention is the de-crease in the relative proportion of mildly retarded patients in state institutions. At the present time mildly retarded patients perform much of the manual labor in institutions. It is well known that sometimes state schools tend to retain patients who could be rehabilitated because they are needed in the institution. It is essential for budget directors to recognize that as the census of mildly retarded adolescents and adults is reduced, it is inevitable that the numbers of maintenance and service personnel will have to be substantially increased" (V, 122).

This was another issue with long-term implications for institutions and community services that received only this passing, albeit pointed, mention.

Demographic Analyses and Planning: Reading the Menu from Right to Right

At this critical juncture—despite research on the epidemiology of mental retardation, assessments of the needs of people with mental retardation, and analyses of past and (then) current service utilization made by the many experts involved in the *Comprehensive Plan*—virtually all the critical projections in the plan were wildly off the mark. The 1965 *Comprehensive Plan* used an estimated 1963 state population of 17,371,907 as the basis for calculations of service utilization and projected a 43 percent increase in the state population for estimates of need in 1975 and 1990. Instead of a 43 percent increase from 1960 to 1990, the state's population grew by a little over 7 percent. Embedded in this demographic miscalculation were optimistic assumptions about the positive direction of the state's economy which had short and long-term consequences for the direction of mental retardation and other public services in New York. The errors in estimating the numbers of people with mental disabilities and their projected use of services were not unique to New York's planners. There had been little relationship among these figures since the federal government began including the number of people with mental disability in the census in 1840 (Scheerenberger 1987). Virtually every other plan at the time made the same assumptions about the state's population growth and many of the projections of future utilization, including those for the new State University system, proved to be wrong. However, analysts and planners working on the *Comprehensive Plan* faced two unique challenges that ensured that their projections would be erroneous—and would be yet another source of contention for plan participants.

First, they had to work with the realization that the state school construction program *already underway* bore almost no relationship to any systematic analyses of population distribution, current utilization, or projected need. Second, the analyses and projections had to be shoe-horned into to a preexisting and elaborate scheme of comprehensive regional networks within which "primary" 1,000-bed institutions would be linked to "intermediate" and "satellite" centers embedded in an array of locally supported community services—where none existed, were being built, or even planned.

Planners were trapped between the *realpolitik* of the ongoing construction, other plans, and a fantastical alternate reality of comprehensive regional networks of services. The estimates and projections of need and utilization that filled a separate volume of the *Comprehensive Plan (Source Documents and Data: The Foundations for Planning, Volume VII)* and permeated other volumes reflected these fundamental flaws. The estimates of incidence and prevalence were consistent with those made at the time and twenty years later (Conley 1973; Kiernan and Bruninks 1986). However, even simple calculations of the projections of the need for specialized services and *planned* new facilities and programs left hundreds of thousands of individuals with severe mental retardation unaccounted for.

The problem was not that the experts and planners were wrong. The problem was that everyone knew it. In report after report in the multivolume plan, representatives of the mental retardation interests pointed out the glaring discrepancies. How construction of new and expanded institutions was actually implemented, where new facilities were built, why, and what the mental retardation interests did are issues discussed in the next chapter. The basic problem with the planning process for new construction was that it threw another log on the fire. In many other areas in the plan, the mental retardation interests were ignored or outvoted. On this central issue, for the hundreds of key actors drawn into the planning process, the Department of Mental Hygiene challenged their ability to add and subtract.

Reaction of the Mental Retardation Constituency to the Plan

The bitter dispute over a separate state mental retardation agency that the ARC had been proposing for years finally surfaced in the last report in the plan in a "minority view" formally submitted by one of the ARC representatives on the Task Force on Mental Retardation and the Law. The report of that task force was the longest of the task force reports in the *Comprehensive Plan*. It summarized the statutes that dealt with persons with mental retardation and made a number of recommendations for changes, including new definitions of mental retardation (including functional criteria), safeguards in institutional care, guardianship, employment, and protections in the criminal justice system. This task force report was the only one that included a formal minority view, that of Leo Fixler, an ARC member. Mr. Fixler's minority report repeated the long-standing position of the ARC on a separate state agency.

> "In line with our suggestion that retardates should be treated independently, we lean to the view that in order to adequately and properly follow this theory of independence, a new agency on a state level should be initiated separate and distinct from the Department of Mental Hygiene" (*Comprehensive Plan* 1965 V, 158).

The concluding paragraph of the minority report, however, was the most succinct expression of the mental retardation constituency's frustrations with the many plans, task forces, and experience with the New York State Department of Mental Hygiene.

> "All agree that there must be a revision of the present laws but unfortunately, changing the law will not, in and of itself, remedy the evils or provide the needed protection and supervision. There should be a new beginning based on what we have learned in the past fifty

years. A new law setting up a new state agency given the power and authority to do all the things suggested in the recommendations of all involved in the task force operation, is to this writer, a present need" (V, 159).

The mental retardation interests who labored through the numerous task forces and committees of the 1965 *Comprehensive Plan* were miserably disappointed and wanted a *new beginning*.

Impact of Planning on Public Institutions and Community Services

Leo Fixler's call for a new beginning was an implicit but clear answer to the question of what was the impact of the plans of the Rockefeller era on the direction of developmental services. The Rockefeller plans, as imperfect as they were, laid out a vision of the future of services, but the mental retardation constituency saw that blueprint as an extension of the neglect of its interests and a continuation of its subservient role in policy making at the state and local levels. "Comprehensive" was not benign plan-speak to the mental retardation constituency who understood that term and its companions—*coordinated* and *integrated*—as code words for the continued absorption and submission of mental retardation under the mental hygiene-psychiatry umbrella. The rancor over the issue of separate and specialized mental retardation services lurked below the planners' rhapsodies about the benefits of comprehensive, coordinated, and integrated services. The vision of "community services" repeated as a mantra in virtually every one of the reports was a reminder of the failure of local governments, school districts, and Community Mental Health Boards to provide adequate services for people with mental retardation despite the so-called pioneering efforts of the state more than a decade earlier. There was virtually no discussion of what, other than innumerable calls for public awareness and similarly soft recommendations, was going to fill the enormous gap between need and existing community capacity that every report acknowledged.

The decisions about new and expanded state schools were central to plans for the future, but it was obvious that these decisions had already been made elsewhere and had not involved those who were participating in the *Comprehensive Plan* process. Even the size of the new state schools, which planners used as a standard, was an epi-phenomenon of the 1,000-bed hospital concept for psychiatric hospitals.

So, what was the importance of these plans? They highlighted the deepseated and long-term problems in developmental services at the time. The

Comprehensive Plan demonstrated the vast difference between the vision about the future of small public institutions and extensive community services of the mental retardation constituency and that of the Department of Mental Hygiene and the administration that wrote the final reports. The vision of the department was more akin to an hallucination with its descriptions of primary, intermediate, and satellite centers with no linkages to budgets or operational capacity; projections of populations, need, and institution size that simply did not add up, references to crucial but nonexistent community services, and plans for phantom institutions. Nonetheless, the plans were important because they demonstrated that what happened subsequent to them could not be attributed to a lack of attention and awareness of the wide range of issues and problems in the area. What happened was the implementation of *another* plan. That was the long-standing construction plan of the Department of Mental Hygiene—financed with moral obligation bonds, backed by patient fees, and administered by a public authority.

Leo Fixler's minority report showed that the plans represented a watershed in the thinking of the mental retardation constituency in New York State. They had reluctantly but fully participated in the plan processes, but at the conclusion they recognized that a "new beginning" meant going a separate way and not proceeding under the delusion that the plans of the state were going to improve services for people with mental retardation.

Part 2

Sweeping Away the Old Order

Chapter 4

Bonding and Construction:
The Foundations of Public Institutions

I'm not sure we know exactly what kind of hospitals we want to build,
what their programs should be, or how they should be working with local
programs.

—Alan Miller, Commissioner of Mental Hygiene

The fifteen-year administration of Governor Nelson A. Rockefeller was marked
by large and long-lasting changes in state government, politics, and the state's
economy. The Rockefeller era also saw a geometric expansion in the state's
physical infrastructure. A State University system was created from a string
of teacher colleges, vast state office complexes were constructed, an environ-
mental bond issue financed water and sewage treatment plants throughout the
state, low and middle income housing projects mushroomed, drug treatment
facilities were built, and new state schools and psychiatric centers were constructed, expanded, and modernized.

The state schools that were built had important and enduring consequences
for institutional and community developmental services, but the most important
and enduring legacy of the Rockefeller era was the fiscal foundations on which
those buildings rested. The two major components of that foundation were
moral obligation bonds that financed their construction and, later, federal
Medicaid reimbursement that replaced patient fees and state tax dollars to pay
bondholders and finance the bulk of developmental services in the state.

The incoming Rockefeller administration inherited the legacy of overcrowded state schools and was forced to scour the state for additional space
as the Department of Mental Hygiene's construction program continued to
lag and newly constructed facilities were immediately filled from long waiting lists. Governor Rockefeller also inherited a severe fiscal crisis that ham-
pered his ability to launch the plans for the new programs he had developed

in his role in planning for a constitutional convention before becoming governor. Fiscal constraints, frustration with the slow pace of government operations, and a political and organizational pragmatism led to an expanded use of public authorities and the use of a new financial instrument—the moral obligation bond—as the centerpieces in the administration's strategy.

Fiscal Crisis, Moral Obligation Bonding, Public Authorities, and State Institutions

"The State of New York today is faced with the most serious fiscal problem in more than a generation. This budget reflects the critical condition" (*Executive Budget Message* 1959, 7). These were the opening words of Governor Nelson A. Rockefeller's first budget. No one had ever been elected Governor of New York with more extensive and detailed plans for new programs than Nelson Rockefeller. Financing his plans was the major problem facing Rockefeller on his inauguration.

The Problem: The State Constitution

The New York State Constitution (Article VII, Section 11) articulated Rockefeller's problem in clear and unmistakable terms:

> "No debts shall be hereafter contracted by or in behalf of the State, unless such debt shall be authorized by law for some single work or purpose, to be distinctly specified therein. No such law shall take effect until it shall, at a general election, have been submitted to the people, and have received a majority of all the votes cast."

Bonds authorized through this constitutionally mandated process were backed by the full faith and credit of the State of New York. This created for bondholders the assurance that courts would uphold the constitutional obligation of the state to repay the bonds, in fact giving bonds priority over other obligations such as contracts and appropriations. The process was lengthy, cumbersome, and highly uncertain. The process would have to be repeated for each specific bond, and even as the state's fiscal condition improved, the voters rejected a number of the full faith and credit proposals sent to them.

The governor could not open his first *Executive Budget Message* with the statement, "The State of New York today is faced with the most serious fiscal problem in more than a generation," and expect that the legislature and electorate would back new massive bonding for public works projects. A major theme in Rockefeller's campaign to unseat Averell Harriman was the "reckless financing" that led to a deficit of $850 million (Benjamin and Hurd 1984,

196). Rockefeller's initial fiscal objectives were to use a minimum of bond financing and the reestablishment of sound fiscal policies based on the principle of "pay-as-you-go." Moreover, the 1954 legislature had already authorized, and the voters had approved, a $350 million bond issue for construction of mental hygiene facilities, and tens of millions of dollars remained available when Rockefeller took office.

The regular capital construction budget process was another financing vehicle that was potentially open to the Rockefeller administration. However, the governor's advisors argued that the formal capital construction budget process would not have yielded more than a million or two dollars a year (Benjamin and Hurd 1984). Moreover, the state commissioners were used to a slow and incremental process. Construction of Department of Mental Hygiene facilities was carried out by the Department of Public Works operating with plans drawn and approved by the State Architect and contracts with builders that met extensive legal requirements for competitive bidding and other statutory and regulatory strictures. The pace of construction appalled Rockefeller, according to William Ronan, now Rockefeller's chief of staff (Benjamin and Hurd 1984, 270).

The Solution: Public Authorities and Moral Obligation Bonds

Rockefeller addressed these financial and organizational hurdles in the bold and pragmatic manner that would become characteristic of his administrations: expanding on existing mechanisms, going outside state government, and going outside the state.

Public authorities were a major component of the solution to Rockefeller's dilemma. Luther Gulick's classic definition of public authorities and public benefit corporations was, " a government business corporation set up outside the normal structure of traditional government so that it can give continuity, business efficiency, and elastic management to the construction or operation of a self-supporting or revenue-producing public enterprise" (Axelrod 1992,14). These limited-purpose public benefit corporations ranged from local government housing authorities, to state power authorities, to such federal agencies as the Federal Deposit Insurance Corporation and the Tennessee Valley Authority. Fortunately for Rockefeller, New York already had a plethora of public authorities that could be used as frameworks for his plans and their financing. He also had a model of bold use of the public authority vehicle. Robert Moses, using the Triborough Bridge and Tunnel Authority as the keystone of an interlocked set of public authorities, had transformed large parts of the New York metropolitan area with use of the organizational and financial power of public authorities (Caro 1974). Despite the rivalry between Rockefeller and Moses, one that would eventually see Moses ousted in a bitter battle, the governor and his aides recognized that an expansive use of existing, interlocked, and new public authorities could be a cornerstone of the strategy. As plans in each area (State University, Mental Hygiene, Pure Waters) were developed, Rockefeller, with legislative support, added twenty-three public authorities to the twenty-six already in existence in New York (Axelrod 1992; McClelland and Magdovitz 1981).

Public authorities in New York had an enormous range and power that appealed to Rockefeller. However, as one long-time observer and advisor in this area pointed out, "New York's Constitution does not permit the State government or any general-purpose local government to issue honest-to-goodness revenue bonds; only authorities can do so, but authorities are limited in other ways. For example, an authority has no taxing power, so it can't pledge an earmarked tax to a revenue bond. To authorize outright revenue bond financing by the State itself requires amending the Constitution, a slow and uncertain process" (Benjamin and Hurd 1984, 225).

The solution to that central problem and the other cornerstone of Rockefeller's strategy was the creation of moral obligation bonds. Rockefeller and his aides wanted to augment the funds available for middle income housing, but were stymied by the full faith and credit strictures on bonding in the state constitution. After several false starts, Rockefeller and his advisors took the advice of Edward Logue who had been recruited from a successful career in building public housing in Massachusetts and Connecticut to head the Urban Development Corporation (a new public authority). Logue suggested using a variation of a bonding scheme used for low and middle income housing in Connecticut. With Logue's advice, Rockefeller's aides went back to a model used by the New York City Housing Authority which financed a program of housing without cash subsidies from New York City using revenue bonds that did not require the full faith and credit of the state. The debt service was paid by the rents. This enabled the authority to sell bond anticipation notes that allowed the authority to proceed immediately with construction. George Wood, a Rockefeller friend and former Chairman of the World Bank, explained how the World Bank had used dual bonding techniques such as those being proposed by Logue.

Rockefeller also turned to John A. Mitchell, an eminent bond counsel for the law firm Nixon, Rose, and Mudge, who would later become Richard Nixon's Attorney General, on the legal feasibility of this scheme. Mitchell elaborated on the notion of using a public authority to issue tax-exempt bonds that it could pay off with fees and rents charged for its services. It was Mitchell who is credited with the idea of calling the bonds issued "moral obligation" rather than "full faith and credit" bonds (Axelrod 1992, 5; McCelland and Magdovitz 1981; Benjamin and Hurd 1984).

These bonds had to have the moral obligation of the state to repay them because, outside the framework of constitutionally mandated bonds, there was no obligation for the state to repay bondholders should the issuing public authority default. The innovative use of public authorities and the designation of "moral obligation" were creative uses of existing mechanisms, but several other important hurdles had to be overcome to guarantee the success of Rockefeller's scheme.

The first was the willingness of investors to purchase moral obligation bonds. Almost every person who has written about Nelson Rockefeller emphasized his extraordinary powers of persuasion, and those qualities undoubtedly came into play (Benjamin and Hurd 1984). There can be no doubt that Rockefeller's ties to the banking community, which included his brother David as Chairman of the Chase Manhattan Bank, were enormously important in convincing investors to purchase the moral obligation bonds issued by these public authorities. In addition to the premium public authorities paid over full faith and credit bonds, the tax-exempt status of these moral obligation bonds was crucial to their attractiveness to investors. At that time, New York had the highest personal income tax rate in the country. With the federal deductibility of state and local income taxes on the high marginal rates typically paid by bond purchasers, expanding the market for tax-exempt bonds paying a premium over full faith and credit bonds was an attractive way to satisfy this constituency and effectively off-load some of the cost to the federal government. However, in order to retain this tax-exempt status, the bonds had to meet federal tax code standards that required specificity of purpose and use of the bonds. As the Rockefeller administration employed an increasingly aggressive and expansive strategy in using these bonds, Logue argued that Rockefeller was able to influence the federal Secretary of the Treasury, David Kennedy, to take a broad view of the uses of housing bonds, leaving their tax exempt status intact (Benjamin and Hurd 1984). There can be little doubt that Rockefeller's moral obligation bonding strategy rested in large measure on his influence in the banking and investment communities.

A Web of Innovative Fiscal Mechanisms

Despite the creative use of public authorities and moral obligation bonds, the issuance of these bonds required the prior approval of the separately elected Comptroller of the State of New York, Arthur Levitt, a Democrat. Moreover, while public authorities and moral obligation bonding were the two pillars of this new financing edifice, implementation and operation depended on other fiscal mechanisms that required approval by the legislature. In these spheres, Rockefeller demonstrated his enormous political talents.

Comptroller Arthur Levitt loathed the idea of moral obligation bonds and spoke with great fervor about their negative effects on the soundness of the state's fiscal condition. However, while Levitt had the legal authority to disapprove the issuance of the moral obligation bonds, he was persuaded to approve them when he got to review the projects that would be financed by them (Benjamin and Hurd 1984, 209). In the years Levitt was Comptroller, predating and postdating Rockefeller's governorship, he approved the issuance of every single moral obligation bond. Rockefeller, in dealing with Levitt, the Democrats who controlled one or both houses of the legislature at various times, conservative Republicans who distrusted the governor, and local government and business leaders, was willing and adept at trading convention centers, civic auditoriums, and whatever else was necessary to get the interim financing he needed for the projects (Benjamin and Hurd 1984).

Other financing mechanisms were also creatively employed to underpin the use of moral obligation bonds and public authorities. First instance appropriations, a little-used (to that point) budget mechanism, were vastly expanded and used as bridge loans to the various state authorities issuing moral obligation bonds. Lease-purchase agreements were used on a grand scale to undergird the larger financing and construction schemes. For example, in financing the South Mall, Rockefeller's enormous office complex in Albany, Rockefeller, Albany Mayor Erastus Corning, and Comptroller Levitt (Democrats) agreed to an arrangement in which the general obligation bonding authority of Albany County would be vastly increased. This allowed the county to act as the front in building the South Mall with the state repaying the county through lease-purchase agreements. To circumvent the constitutional limits on local government bonded indebtedness, Comptroller Levitt exempted the county from the limit on the assertion that the bonds were self-liquidating. All the parties ignored the "executory clause" of the state constitution that placed a one-year legal limitation on lease obligations. The bond purchasers were told that although the forty-year Albany County bonds were backed by the state's lease-purchase agreements, these agreements were a year-to-year obligation by the state with the state assuming a moral obligation to pay a county general obligation bond.

Rockefeller's program goals, those of legislative leaders from both parties, and those of local government executives from both parties, became increasingly embedded in complex financing schemes. These schemes involved a variety of political trade-offs, tied state government objectives to often disparate local government plans, relied on public authorities that had only tangential accountability to state and local governments, and had bond purchasers as the ultimate constituents.

Mental Hygiene Facilities Improvement Fund

The public authority-moral obligation bonding framework for construction of facilities in the Department of Mental Hygiene was created in 1963 when Governor Rockefeller submitted and the legislature passed a bill creating the

Mental Hygiene Facilities Improvement Fund (MHFIF)—a public benefit corporation (virtually identical to a public authority) whose role was to expedite construction and rehabilitation of state hospitals and state schools. Under the statute creating "the Fund" (as the MHFIF became known), all Department of Mental Hygiene facilities were transferred to MHFIF. The property and buildings of the psychiatric hospitals and state schools would no longer be owned by the State of New York but by the public benefit corporation. The Fund would finance construction of the facilities by the sale of bonds and through first instance and capital construction funds allocated by the state. After January 1, 1964, the Fund would receive all reimbursement monies collected by the state for the care, maintenance, and treatment of patients in state mental facilities.

The legislation also authorized the Housing Finance Agency (another public authority) to issue bonds and notes secured by rent payments from the Mental Hygiene Facilities Improvement Fund and from reserves established from reimbursement revenues. The Fund would turn back to the state those funds not required for the repayment of the moral obligation bonds sold for the construction and rehabilitation of the facilities. The Department of Mental Hygiene regarded this change as great news because it created an earmarked reimbursement fund for mental hygiene. Those funds not required for repayment of the bonds would eventually be transferred to the state's general fund, but the two-step process created a fiscal mechanism that took the department's budget partially off-line.

With new and multiple public authorities involved, a new type of bonding, the transfer of property and facilities, and interchanges in the state budget among new fund categories the funding processes were complex and, some argued, purposely obscure. One observer of the Rockefeller administration characterized these arrangements as "stealth"—so intricate as to be not clear to most people, or what Alton G. Marshall, former secretary of Governor Rockefeller, called a "no worry" bond (Benjamin and Hurd 1984, 219). Nonetheless, the essence was that with this act New York mortgaged the residents of its state schools and other mental hygiene institutions to the holders of the bonds. From this point, generating the revenues necessary to repay those bonds became a major objective of public policy in the mental disabilities arena.

Importance of Patient Fees

The central importance of fees to financing repayment of the bonds for state schools and other mental hygiene facilities exacerbated the conflict between the Rockefeller administration and the ARC. Resident fees had been a problem for many years. The Mental Hygiene Law stipulated that the institutions of the Department of Mental Hygiene are maintained "for the care and treatment of poor and indigent persons. The Commissioner may, however, permit persons who are neither poor nor indigent to be received and maintained in an institution conditioned upon prompt and regular payment for their care and treatment" (Mental Hygiene Law, Sec. 24-a).

The Moreland Act Commission devoted an extensive portion of its final report to the necessity of increasing reimbursement from "relatives legally liable and with sufficient ability to pay" (Moreland 1944). This issue became a continuing bone of contention between parents and the state, especially as the state schools admitted larger numbers of children from middle class families able to pay. Elimination of parental fees was a perennial plank in the ARC legislative platform, and the ARC recognized the impact of the legislation creating the MHFIF on fees. The ARC strongly opposed the establishment of the MHFIF because the fees it hoped to have eliminated were now to be earmarked to pay for forty-year construction bonds. New York was assailed in an editorial in the ARC news letter *Our Children's Voice* for charging the highest rate per month in the nation for the retarded in its state schools and also for forcing the afflicted to pay for construction of facilities both for themselves and for future patients by making them pay interest on loans taken to construct new facilities for future patients (Lerner 1972, 215).

Rockefeller was unmoved by the ARC's position for several reasons. The first was financial. Rockefeller and his aides had not gone through the complex arrangements to create public authorities and sell moral obligation bonds backed by resident fees only to immediately exempt users from those fees. The impact on the investment community would have been devastating to the state's and the authorities' credibility. The second reason was a tenet of Rockefeller's political philosophy that users of government services should pay at least a portion of their costs. Rockefeller applied this philosophy in a number of areas, and fees charged to residents were not anomalies but consistent with the direction Rockefeller was moving (Benjamin and Hurd 1984). The third reason was fiscal. Rockefeller had run for reelection in 1962 on the pledge to not raise taxes. Faced with a looming deficit after the election, he embarked on an aggressive and highly unpopular campaign to raise fees. Every fee the state charged, from driver to barber licenses, were raised to close the budget gap. The state needed the money, and there was no inclination, especially in light of the other reasons, to eliminate fees for residents of state institutions.

In 1965, the ARC was successful in getting the legislature to pass a bill eliminating fees, a legislature undoubtedly secure in the realization that the governor would veto the bill. In his veto message, Governor Rockefeller pointed out that the fees from patients had to be maintained as guarantee to the bondholders of the Mental Hygiene Facilities Improvement Fund and that the basis for payments of interest and principal to them would not be changed or in any way impaired (Lerner 1972).

Lerner argued that the ARC understood this to mean that to keep the interest monies available for the bonds, the governor would also have to keep the institutions full, in contrast to the planning efforts striving for more community care (Lerner 1972, 215). In 1965, with overcrowding still heading toward its peak, it would have been difficult to imagine emptying institutions in the face of worries about whether resident fees would be sufficient to pay the bond holders. From the inception of the Mental Hygiene Facilities Improvement Fund in 1963, fees from the residents of state schools became even more critical sources of revenue.

Establishing a Legacy of Creative Financing

There was another very important long-term impact of the innovations in finance during the Rockefeller administration. According to Milton Musicus, the first director of the Mental Hygiene Facilities Improvement Fund, the schemes created during the Rockefeller administration forced an entirely new way of thinking about financing programs (Benjamin and Hurd 1984). The creative use of bonding, public authorities, revenue maximization, special purpose funding, and a variety of other techniques were elements in a strategic approach to public finance that permeated New York government during the Rockefeller administration.

The fiscal structures created during the Rockefeller era were the outcomes of pragmatic problem solving: pulling together a wide variety of resources, making creative use of instruments often designed for other purposes, and taking a flexible approach to process and structure. These initiatives were carried out by the large number of professionals recruited into New York State government during that era, in the many public authorities and the agencies that underwent exponential growth at that time. Those individuals who learned and employed these techniques remained long after Rockefeller left. Many rose to senior policymaking and administrative roles and refined and amplified these strategies during the 1980s and 1990s. The Rockefeller era left a programmatic and public finance legacy in New York that had a substantial impact on the financing and organization of developmental services in the state.

Inheriting a Legacy of Overcrowding and Slow Construction

In each of the years of Rockefeller's first administration, the Department of Mental Hygiene reported the opening of new facilities: five new dormitories and an infant building at Willowbrook, and four infirmaries at Rome. However, the facilities filled as soon as they opened, and new construction was taking too long. In 1961, the department announced the opening of the administration building at the new West Seneca State School, an institution that had been on the drawing boards since 1953 and would not take in residents until 1963. As a supplement to new construction, the state began to acquire other facilities to house its burgeoning state school population. Funds had been appropriated to allow the Department of Mental Hygiene to lease temporary quarters to relieve overcrowding, but as Rockefeller's first term opened, the department had been unable to locate satisfactory space. As the search continued, other public facilities were pressed into service. The hospital at Sampson Air Force Base on Seneca Lake had been used by the department at various times since 1948, and it was expanded to take transfers from overcrowded state schools. The Mount McGregor Veterans Rest at Wilton in Saratoga County was converted into a division of the severely overcrowded Rome State School. The J. N. Adam annex, the former state tuberculosis hospital on the grounds of Gowanda State Hospital, was taken over and converted to a state school. In August 1961, the state took over five floors of Gouverneur, a hospital New York City no longer used for inpatient care, and used it to house nonambulatory children from Willowbrook. The notion that state schools would expand along the lines of "comprehensive" and "master" plans was undermined by frenetic acquisitions of Quonset huts, an abandoned TB hospital, a veterans' rest home, and a derelict municipal hospital. In fact, Gouverneur would arguably have more long-term consequences for public institutions and developmental services in New York than any of the plans.

Which Plan? Competing Guidelines for State School Construction

In 1965 there were three separate plans (Master, Comprehensive, and Construction) bearing on the future of state schools and community developmental services as well as a series of proposals and position papers on state school construction made by the ARC. As the description of the *Comprehensive Plan* process showed, the Rockefeller administration and the mental retardation constituency were deeply divided on almost every key issue. Compounding this divide was the fact that there were critical differences between the *Comprehensive Plan* and the administration's construction plan. The decisions made and concrete actions taken on the size of new state schools, the role they would play, their design, their location, and the financing of their construction set the direction for institutions and the organization of developmental services for decades.

    The Rockefeller administration's five-year construction plan was ostensibly based on the preliminary findings of the task forces at work on the *Comprehensive Plan*. The reports of these task forces, however, referred back to the already existing construction plan. Despite the confusion and cross-cutting endorsements, the Task Force on Construction report in the *Comprehensive Plan* did specify guidelines for construction of new facilities.

1. New facilities and major remodeling or additions to existing facilities should be jointly financed out of public, federal, state, local, and/or private funds.

2. New construction and major remodeling should be done in those areas, regions, or communities where the greatest needs exist.

3. Any new state school facility should not be more than 1,000 beds.

4. Effort should be made to check the trend of placing more responsibility on the state by providing more adequate local community treatment facilities.

5. Primary community retardation centers should be related to medical schools near teaching and research hospitals wherever possible.

6. Those responsible for approving plans and specifications for primary community centers should think not only of the services to be rendered directly to the mentally retarded, but should think also in terms of the values which may be derived from such centers in the training of personnel and in the conduct of research.

7. Plant facilities should afford equal opportunities for the care and development of the mentally retarded regardless of their location or socioeconomic status.

8. New state facilities should be located near the centers of the population to be served.

9. Plans and specifications for new construction should give attention to the principle of flexibility in construction to accommodate new developments in the field as well as to provide most adequately for the needs of those to be served now.

10. Standards are to be adhered to, especially those spelled out in codes pertaining to public buildings while at the same time, providing opportunity for encouraging local initiative in planning for new construction. (163)

The construction plan was not a new plan as much as an acceleration of long-standing Department of Mental Hygiene plans. Its objectives were to relieve overcrowding, modernize facilities, locate facilities close to the people they are to serve, and achieve timely construction at a reasonable cost (LCER 1973, 3). The construction plan included the following facilities:

Syracuse	(Replacement of existing school)	1,000 beds
Oswald D. Heck	(Schenectady County)	1,000 beds
Wilton	(Saratoga County)	1,000 beds
Brooklyn		1,000 beds
Queens		1,000 beds
Bronx		1,000 beds
Manhattan		1,000 beds

As the Rockefeller construction plan was being formulated, the ARC proposed its own seven-point plan to relieve overcrowding. Its major points were:

1. Setting a new pattern of residential care by developing smaller facilities, for between 50 to 150 retardates, near their current place of residence.

2. Expansion of family care programs, including raising rates paid to families to take mentally retarded persons from the institutions.

3. Subsidies to community hospitals and nursing homes to take total care and senile retardates.

4. Transfer of total care patients to state hospitals.

5. Expansion of colony or halfway house programs.

6. Preadmission counseling and study of patients on waiting lists to determine the necessity of institutionalization.

7. Short-stay care in the state schools to relieve crisis situations. (Lerner 1972, 201)

The ARC proposals were reiterated and expanded in Executive Director Weingold's budget hearing testimony in 1965 and in a series of position papers that detailed the association's positions and attacked the Rockefeller administration's construction plan. In the context of Governor Rockefeller's just-released construction plan for seven 1,000-bed state schools, it is not surprising that the Department of Mental Hygiene dismissed the proposals. On the issue of short-stay care, for example, Lerner states that the directors of the state schools were opposed on the grounds that it was difficult to determine real family emergencies, and they did not want to become temporary "baby-sitters" for families on vacation (Lerner 1972, 201).

Role of State Schools in Developmental Services

The administration's construction plan embodied a relatively narrow view of the role of the new state schools: relieve overcrowding, modernize facilities, locate facilities close to the people they are to serve, and achieve timely construction at a reasonable cost. Although the *Comprehensive Plan* proffered a scheme of state schools as integral to regional networks of primary, intermediate, and satellite centers, the ARC viewed the governor's construction program "with consternation and alarm" because community services were not considered at all in relation to these new proposed institutions (Lerner 1972).

In its 1965 position papers, the ARC argued that the new state schools would replicate the "psychomedical" approach that had not achieved adequate physical care. One paper pointed out that 1,000-bed models were proposed with no input from the mental retardation planning committees in the *Comprehensive Plan* process and that the 1,000-bed model was the application of the psychiatric center model to the state schools with virtually no independent consideration of differences. The ARC recommended that rather than seven 1,000-bed institutions, the state should construct thirty new smaller treatment centers along with a network of regional diagnostic, counseling, and service centers that would be operated under contract with local agencies and would be alternatives to institutionalization (Lerner 1972). The 1964 ARC proposals to the Department of Mental Hygiene had already called for preadmission counseling and short-stay care, subsidies to community hospitals and nursing homes for care of aged and senile individuals, and expansion of colonies and halfway houses. The ARC proposals more closely reflected the thrust of the *Comprehensive Plan* guidelines and the community services rhetoric of the Department of Mental Hygiene. Indeed, the most damning assessment of the role of the new facilities was made by Commissioner Miller, who said that when he and Governor Rockefeller discussed the fact that the 1,000-bed hospitals that were planned to be built around the state were at least a year behind schedule, Miller said that maybe it wasn't a bad thing. He told the governor, "I'm not sure we know exactly what kind of hospitals we want to build, what their programs should be, or how they should be working with local programs" (Benjamin and Hurd 1984, 34).

Location of State Schools

The ARC proposals, the *Comprehensive Plan*, and the construction plan all had explicit or implicit guidelines calling for the location of new state schools near centers of population and specialized and generic community services. The implementation of the construction plan did not follow these guidelines. A new state school planned and designed for Nassau County never made it into the formal construction plan because of community opposition (LCER 1973). The proposed new school for Queens was quickly canceled, and the proposed new Manhattan school was never built. The Brooklyn school was constructed on a site at the farthest reaches of that borough, and the Bronx school was constructed on the grounds of a psychiatric hospital hemmed in by parkways. Of the six new state schools in the original construction plan, only two of the four proposed for New York City (where the greatest need existed) were built, and only O.D. Heck (built between Albany and Schenectady) was located near existing communities.

Architectural and Functional Design of State Schools

Governor Rockefeller's chief aide, William Ronan, said that, "He [Rockefeller] himself said, more than once, that he was a frustrated architect," and "He was equally aghast at the ugliness of state buildings in the post-war era," and ridiculed the buildings designed by the State Architect's Office as "public works renaissance" or "budget bureau baroque" (Benjamin and Hurd 1984, 270). According to Ronan, this was an important feature in the creation of various construction authorities that increased architectural fees and engaged some of the world's leading architects on state projects. Rockefeller was not content to hire leading architects on state projects; he wanted to be the *de facto* architect for the South Mall and play a part in the design of other projects. Even after the plans were ostensibly complete, one Rockefeller aide reported that the governor kept an architectural model of the South Mall in a room adjoining his office and drove planners, architects, and budget advisors to despair with his expensive fiddling and repositioning of buildings.

Rockefeller's desire to ape the "grand style of Versailles or Brasilia," according to architectural historian Samuel Bleecker, was most apparent in state office complexes and university buildings (Benjamin and Hurd 1984). There is, however, little evidence that he paid any attention to how these buildings worked. The Bronx Developmental Center won awards from architectural associations but was repeatedly cited by quality assurance agencies for the serious health, safety, and functional inadequacies created by its design. Rockefeller's penchant for monumental repetitiveness, according to the art critic Robert Hughes (1991), appeared in the overall design and size of the program and living spaces within those buildings. The 1,000-bed size proposed for each and every new state hospital was carried over to each and every new state school in the original construction program. The proposed flexibility in construction of the facilities was also belied by "functional plans" that applied identical formats throughout and among facilities and bore no relationship to existing and future variations of resident characteristics and needs.

Size and Financing of State Schools

In its 1964 proposals, the ARC had recommended that facilities for 50 to 150 people be built near individuals' current place of residence. When this was rejected, a 1965 ARC position paper called for building 30 treatment facilities with 250 beds linked to supporting community services instead of the 1,000-

bed state schools (Lerner 1972). In his budget hearing testimony in 1965, ARC Executive Director Weingold pointed to California's proposed new 500-bed state schools as an example of smaller facilities. Moreover, the experts on the demographics of mental retardation who participated in the *Comprehensive Plan* process conceded that there was little solid evidence on which to estimate the number of beds a population needed. Although the size of the new state schools were eventually scaled back to several hundred beds, it was evident in 1965 that the state was never going to be able to build adequate facilities "near centers of population to be served" (especially in New York City) using a 1,000-bed model.

After the reorganization of the Department of Mental Hygiene and the installation of a number of progressive outsiders in the leadership of the Division of Mental Retardation, there was more disagreement over the size of state schools under construction. In the mental retardation section of the department's *Annual Report* for 1968, the report states that, "About one-third of the residents of State schools are capable of living in the community" (15). There were 27,352 residents of state schools at the time, so it seemed that the department's mental retardation leadership was estimating a long-term requirement for approximately 18,000 beds (DMH 1969). This appeared to be more of an educated guess and commitment to community services than careful demographic and clinical analysis, but, as seen in the projections of utilization in the *Comprehensive Plan*, it was another indication of the changing and uncertain bases of plans for construction of facilities that were bonded for forty years.

The issue of the size of the new state schools was much more than one of location, design or functional programming. It represented a fundamental concern about the implications of the financing of state schools with moral obligation bonds. Public authorities were a "hidden world" and a "shadow government" (Axelrod 1992), and moral obligation bonds were called "stealth bonds" by one of Rockefeller's chief aides (Benjamin and Hurd 1984). There was, however, no question in the minds of the ARC leadership that the 1,000-bed facilities, replicated in a cookie-cutter fashion across state hospitals and state schools, had much more to do with numbers of residents paying the fees needed for reimbursement to bond holders than any functional program. The ARC opposed the creation of the Mental Hygiene Facilities Improvement Fund and, in its 1965 position papers, demanded its abolition and an end to earmarking patients' and relatives' fees for interest and amortization payments toward construction of these new institutions.

Construction of New and Expanded State Schools

Despite the fact that the ARC was bitterly opposed to the use of public authorities and moral obligation bonding for construction of new and expanded state schools, they and others in the mental retardation community supported the construction of new facilities to relieve the severe overcrowding and long waiting lists. The Rockefeller administration promised that public authorities would speed the process that had lagged so badly. "Timely construction of facilities at a reasonable cost," was the first goal of the governor's 1965 construction plan, and the plan called for completion of them in five years. By September 1972, only Syracuse State School (an already existing facility) was operating, but well below its planned capacity (LCER 1973). The new state schools at Brooklyn, Wilton, O.D. Heck, Broome, and Monroe were not open, and the Bronx State School was still in design. Construction was substantially behind schedule, and the costs of the new facilities had escalated to an average of 86 percent more than the initial estimates (LCER 1973). The problem of huge cost overruns was endemic. Managers in public authorities overseeing construction of state schools and psychiatric centers, state universities, state office buildings, and other public facilities (often in the same locale) found themselves competing for scarce contractors who had little difficulty naming their own prices.

On the objective of relieving overcrowding, a Legislative Commission on Expenditure Review (LCER) audit concluded, "After many years and the expenditure of many millions of dollars, and despite population declines, New York State institutions still suffer from severe overcrowding (LCER, 1973, S-7). By 1972, the initial 1,000-bed size of each new facility had been scaled back by more than 40 percent, and while the reductions in size did not approach those recommended by the ARC in the mid-1960s, new construction would produce 2,880 less beds than in the original plan. The LCER projected that even with new facilities on line, state school populations would still be 40 percent over program capacity by 1977 (LCER 1972, S-7). As for the objective of locating of state schools "close to the people to be served," the cancellation of plans for new state schools in New York City (Manhattan and Queens), Nassau County, and Westchester County greatly exacerbated the already enormous gap between population centers and these planned facilities.

Mothballing New State Schools

By 1972, the state school construction program was lagging badly. No new state schools had opened. The existing state schools were overcrowded by approximately 2,000 residents, and the Department of Mental Hygiene had instituted "an orderly waiting list and an increase in screening activities," pointing out that, "Careful screening of applicants for admission will keep those retardates in the community who do not require in-institution care" (Executive Budget 1971–72, 540). Hiring freezes, reduced overtime, and the abolition of positions had worsened the problems in the existing state schools, but in his Budget Message for the 1972–73 fiscal year, Governor Rockefeller was forced to take even more drastic measures and announced that:

"Funds for the operations of the following new State school facilities to relieve overcrowding are not recommended [Wilton, Kings County (Brooklyn), Oswald D. Heck, Manhattan, Monroe]. However, $656,170 is recommended to establish 66 new positions to provide for necessary minimum maintenance and security measures, and heat and other plant maintenance activities. If the Department is able to transfer staff from existing facilities during 1972–73, some partial program operation might be possible. The new Syracuse State School with a 744 bed capacity, will be opened to the extent necessary to accommodate its present resident population. No additional positions are recommended for this facility" (*Executive Budget* 1972–73, 441).

The new state schools that were the centerpieces of the master and comprehensive plans were mothballed, empty shells patrolled by security staff and maintained by power plant operators keeping the pipes from freezing. Ironically, the mothballing and continuing budget crises that delayed the opening of these new facilities gave some reform-minded administrators another opportunity to revisit the use of these institutions that were scaled-down imitations of psychiatric centers with identical functional programs that bore little relationship to diverse service needs. Much of the construction was poor, and some of the new buildings were inherently dangerous.

New Foundations for Conflict

The Rockefeller administration's construction program, trapped by attempts to catch up with overcrowding, made a number of critical choices on the location, size, and design of new institutions that shaped the organization of developmental services for decades. They were not the result of a consensus, and they cannot be rationalized as representing the best thinking of the time that has since proven to be faulty. Planning, the most ubiquitous of activities in the early years of the Rockefeller era, had almost no impact on the shape and direction of public institutions and community services. Substantially different approaches to state school construction were not mere academic proposals from Scandinavian reformers removed from New York's political arena. They were proposals made by the ARC and reinforced by alternate and progressive experience in other states.

Moral obligation bonding had an enormous impact on the future of state institutions. It and the related mechanisms and approaches on which it rested also created a framework within which the still-emerging possibilities of Medicaid financing would fit. New state schools were being built (or not built) with new financing approaches that had as much long-term consequences as the buildings themselves. The conflict in this arena had moved beyond the acrimonious debates in planning forums. The inherent contradictions and diverging directions between the state and advocates were now concrete and moving toward a climax.

Chapter 5

The New Politics of Mental Retardation

Medicaid was a political decision. It was not some deep-rooted emotional humanitarian drive.

—Alton Marshall, Secretary to Governor Nelson A. Rockefeller

The state school construction program was creating a widening gap between the state administration and a broad consensus among professionals in the field and the mental retardation community. Cracks were also appearing along other lines as cleavages within the state administration grew wider, disagreements arose within and among the mental retardation interest groups, and clashing national political ambitions once again played out in this arena. Fiscal crises became chronic. The state's economy was showing evidence of a long-term structural deterioration, labor turmoil was growing, and a new politics of mental retardation was emerging.

Rhetoric and Reality of Community Programs: 1965 to 1972

"All but four percent of the retarded remain in the community and of those who do require residential care, a substantial proportion return to the community and need aftercare services supplemented by various other special services in the community" (DMH 1966, 9).

Community services were featured in the *Comprehensive Plan* and were a central concept in the rhetoric of the Department of Mental Hygiene ever since the 1954 Community Mental Health Services Act and the creation of Community Mental Health Boards. From the mid- to late 1960s, the *Annual Reports* of the Department of Mental Hygiene highlighted efforts to relieve the severe overcrowding in the state schools, described acquisition of additional space to house the overflow, and trumpeted the progress in community services. The *Annual Report* for 1966 stated,

> "The growth of community services throughout the State has enabled many retarded children to live at home while receiving the treatment they need" (10).

The report referred to thirty comprehensive mental retardation complexes that would maintain close ties with the state schools and provide a variety of preventive, emergency, diagnostic, outpatient, inpatient, and rehabilitative services (DMH 1966). The problem was that the department had made no budget request for these thirty comprehensive mental retardation complexes.

This confusion between rhetoric and reality became characteristic of the years from the promulgation of the *Comprehensive Plan* to the *ARC v. Rockefeller* suit at Willowbrook. A few steps were taken to create new community services, and while they seemed inadequate to the mental retardation constituency, some were important in laying the groundwork for a greater expansion in the 1970s. However, in the increasingly grandiose rhetoric of the Rockefeller administration and the Department of Mental Hygiene, the mental retardation constituency was forced to read about the growth of community services throughout the state when these services barely existed. They saw plans for comprehensive mental retardation complexes that had no budgetary, legislative, or programmatic bases. Plans for construction of state schools near population centers evaporated. The construction that was underway was falling years behind schedule. Key elements of community services were continuing problems, not triumphs.

Private Schools

For most of its history, the ARC battled local school districts and the state Department of Education over expansion of special education classes, and sought access and mandates to cover broader segments of children with mental retardation. While these battles were fought, ARC chapters struggled to operate their preschool and school programs, day services, and sheltered workshops with private fund-raising, federal grants, demonstration project funding, and a variety of other tenuous sources of support. Almost none came from Community Mental Health Boards.

In 1966, legislation amending Section 4707 of the Education Law was passed that allowed the state to subsidize private schools within and outside the state where no suitable public school facilities were available. The law, originally intended for a few multiply handicapped children with cerebral palsy, provided that where there were no facilities (public or private) within the state for the education and training of brain injured and physically handicapped children, the state would subsidize the education and training of these children outside the state (Lerner 1972, 261).

In 1967, the Division of Handicapped Children in the state Education Department approved more than 1200 applications by parents for funds to send their children to private facilities under Section 4407. ARC chapters operated a large number of these schools. This direct, increased, and regular funding of ARC chapter-operated education and training programs was an enormous victory and very important to stabilizing funding for ARC chapters (Lerner 1972).

Hostel Program

Hostels were homes in the community operated by house parents who lived with the residents and had been promoted by the ARC for a number of years. However, it was not until 1966 that legislation provided $1 million for the construction or acquisition of hostels that the Department of Mental Hygiene could contract with community agencies to operate. The legislation provided for grants of one-third the costs of acquisition and construction and 50 percent of operating costs, and the Mental Hygiene Facilities Improvement Fund was empowered to assist Community Mental Health Boards in planning and building local facilities (DMH 1967). The Department of Mental Hygiene announced the appointment of an assistant commissioner whose major responsibility was the development of the hostel program.

The ARC was pleased that the framework was created, but the bulk of responsibility for funding hostels still fell on the local chapters. They charged that the Community Mental Health Boards and the Mental Hygiene Facilities Improvement Fund were not providing their share of funding or operational support. Moreover, after creating the framework for construction of hostels (and winning reelection), Governor Rockefeller vetoed a bill passed in 1967 that would permit construction loans to private voluntary agencies to build mental retardation facilities. The veto came at the same time the governor signed legislation permitting the Housing Finance Agency to advance funds for construction and planning of nursing homes (Lerner 1972). In the 1966 election, the voters did approve a constitutional amendment that allowed state aid to private organizations for mental retardation and mental health services, and this paved the way for state aid to ARC chapters.

The *Annual Reports* of the Department of Mental Hygiene from 1966 repeated descriptions of the intent of the hostel program and announced locations of hostels "slated to open." It was not until April 1968 that the department purchased a townhouse in Manhattan for the first hostel which was to be operated by the New York City chapter of the ARC (Lerner 1972, 303). The progress of hostels was painfully slow, especially in light of the construction of institutions and the rhetoric of the Department's *Annual Reports*. As late as 1972, the Department of Mental Hygiene had only opened 19 hostels with a "capacity" of 190 individuals (Executive Budget 1972–73).

Halfway Houses

Among the resolutions passed at the ARC state convention in 1959 was one requesting the Department of Mental Hygiene to establish "halfway houses" with social supervision for retarded adults in the community (Lerner 1972, 120). Creation of halfway houses did not begin until the mid-1960s, but the *Annual Reports* of the department described this new residential program and announced openings around the state. The problem was that halfway houses were not in the community but typically located in old staff housing on the perimeter of the campuses of state schools, and the great majority of the residents never moved any further than these houses. Some critics argued that as the state changed its practice of providing on-campus housing for large numbers of staff, halfway houses were simply convenient locations for relief of overcrowding. The distance from a ward in the institution to a house on the edge of the campus was not halfway to anywhere, but the *Annual Reports* continued to include these facilities as part of the development of community programs.

Declining Residential Capacity

The census in the state schools began to decline after reaching its peak in 1967 at 27,554 residents (DMH 1968). In its *Annual Report* for 1968, the Department of Mental Hygiene pointed out that, "A significant reduction in overcrowding at State schools occurred during the year—from 3,951 on December 31, 1967, to 3,060 on December 31, 1968. A major reason is that admissions to State schools are being screened more selectively so that the schools can better serve the retarded who have special needs—the severely and profoundly retarded who are totally dependent, the retarded with physical and emotional handicaps, and dependent retardates for whom no adequate home care is available" (12). The report for 1968 also stated, "Many State school residents are ready to return to the community but they cannot go because there is no place for them" (DMH 1968, 15). Declining capacity in the institutions and the absence of community residential alternatives increased the tension between the department and parents.

Day Programs in the Community

At the end of the 1963–1964 fiscal year, there were almost 32,000 people with mental retardation in various public and private residential facilities in New York State; 1,150 people receiving services in Day Training Centers, largely sheltered workshops operated by ARC chapters; and 1,800 people using Outpatient Clinics, also largely operated by private voluntary agencies (*Comprehensive Plan VII*, 256). Although schools operated by the ARC chapters were being stabilized with Section 4407 funding after 1966, the funding for sheltered workshops, clinics, and other day programs remained tenuous. In 1967, local governments were contributing less than 10 percent of Community Mental Health Board (CMHB) expenditures for mental retardation programs, and by 1968, their contributions to CMHB expenditures for those programs dropped to 5 percent (Lerner 1972, 307).

By 1968, local chapters of the ARC were operating thirteen sheltered workshops and thirty-one day training centers (NYSARC 1989). The chapters were losing money on sheltered workshops, and a bill to pay workshops directly for each worker was opposed by the administration and failed to get out of committee (Lerner 1972). The ARC continued to appeal to the department for relief from the decisions of Community Mental Health Boards that were still providing very small grants to workshops. The ARC chapters continued in their long-standing dissatisfaction over referrals with the Office of Vocational Rehabilitation (OVR) of the state Education Department. OVR maintained that increases in aid were going to workshops, but the ARC claimed that aid was being funneled to workshops serving people with mental illness and other handicapped persons. The ARC was adamantly opposed to vocational facilities with mixed clienteles (NYSARC 1989).

Cleavage and Conflict in the Mental Retardation Arena

The "growth" of community services was much smaller than the promise of the plans and the claims of the department's *Annual Reports*, but the creation of the framework of the hostel program, approval for direct funding of community agencies, and the inflow of large amounts of funds to ARC chapters through Section 4407 funding for private schools were important in the long run. However, there were also several developments that created more cleavages within the mental retardation policy arena that would also lead to greater conflict and confrontation.

Cleavages in the Rockefeller Administration

In 1966, the governor announced another "sweeping" reorganization of the Department of Mental Hygiene, and a large number of top administrators joined the department and the Division of Mental Retardation from outside the state. Dr. Frederic Grunberg of the Saskatchewan Department of Public Health was appointed to the post of Deputy Commissioner for Mental Retardation, and he recruited a number of associate and assistant commissioners from Canada and other states. Lerner (1972) argues that the reorganization seemed to increase the autonomy of the Division of Mental Retardation within the Department of Mental Hygiene, and the appointment of new administrators with progressive views tempered the hostility between the ARC and the administration. The new administrators did champion community programs, but they also contributed to the problem of the gap between rhetoric and reality.

Much of the dissonance was around the state school construction program where severe overcrowding and long waiting lists remained the center of attention. No matter how vigorously the ARC and other advocates argued for more community programs, they also demanded new facilities. By the late 1960s, it was apparent that the state was doing nothing (nor planned to do anything) to develop small community mental retardation centers. The handful of programs grafted onto medical center services would not approach the demand.

The ARC had lobbied for smaller than 1,000-bed institutions, but as plans for new centers in New York City and the metropolitan area disappeared, it became apparent that all the construction in the pipeline, now years behind schedule, would not resolve overcrowding and waiting lists. Plans for 1,000-bed state schools were scaled back to around 750 beds, but the new administrators brought into the department were arguing that those were much too large. Confidential plans (at the least unauthorized by the governor's office) circulating within the department discussed abandoning these new facilities or cutting their size even more radically. The estimate (in the *Annual Report* for 1968) that one-third of the 27,352 residents of the state schools were capable of living in the community appeared to be based on educated guesses and a commitment to normalization, but it was not clearly linked to the long-term consequences of the construction program. The new cadre of administrators found themselves at odds with the governor's office, the Mental Hygiene Facilities Improvement Fund, and the more traditional state school directors over the size and pace of state school construction.

Dissonance within the Mental Disability Constituency

While many in the mental retardation constituency were cheered by promotion of progressive community services positions from within the Department of Mental Hygiene, old and new cleavages in the mental retardation constituency emerged. Since its assumption of the state school chapters in the 1950s, the ARC had to balance its institutional and community membership interests, which had a regional dimension since most of the state schools were upstate. The ARC still wanted more state school beds to relieve overcrowding and waiting lists, but it was obvious that whatever new capacity was created—larger or smaller, sooner or later—was going to cement the regional imbalance of that institutional capacity for the foreseeable future. By the 1960s, the dominant forces within the ARC were primarily concerned with services in communities, and getting stable and adequate funding for these services was the main thrust of the ARC's lobbying campaigns. New progressive administrators were allies in arguing against larger state schools, but the concomitant community services they promoted remained promises and plans.

The issues of separateness and specialization were other hairline cracks that began to widen. Most of the attention on this issue revolved around a demand for a separate agency for mental retardation, with a liberation from the psychiatry establishment that dominated the Department of Mental Hygiene. Less salient was the strong desire for maintaining a focus on programs for people with *mental retardation*. There had been a long history of antagonism between the ARC and the United Cerebral Palsy Associations, and the mental retardation interests were still smarting from the inclusion of "Physical Handicap" in the scope of the Joint Legislative Committee in 1966. The ARC had long-standing battles with the state Education Department's Division of Vocational Rehabilitation as well as with Community Mental Health Boards over funding of workshops and other community programs serving only people with mental retardation. The new leadership in the department was also promoting serving people with "developmental disabilities" which went beyond the traditional mental retardation focus and included those with cerebral palsy, epilepsy, autism, and other neurological impairments.

Another cleavage within the ARC was over whether to continue to operate programs. The national ARC opposed the operation of programs by local chapters, but New York's ARC argued that its operation of programs was to demonstrate that such services were feasible and could be assumed by the government as soon as possible (Lerner 1972). However, the ARC had more than twenty years experience operating a growing number and variety of community programs, including schools, that went far beyond short-term demonstration projects to be turned over to the state. In fact, virtually none were.

The ARC leadership had a strong New York City-Democrat Party identity, and from its birth as a support group for parents with children at home, the bulk of the leadership was white professional middle-class parents who had kept their children at home. Willowbrook was the only state school in New York City, and almost three-quarters of its residents were poor, black, and Hispanic (Lerner 1972; Rothman and Rothman 1984). Institution versus community, upstate versus downstate, Democrat versus Republican, mental retardation versus developmental disabilities, operation versus advocacy, along with racial, ethnic, and class issues were widening cleavages. Most issues cut in a number of directions within the Rockefeller administration, the department, and the mental retardation constituency and required the maintenance of a delicate balance. However, as the conflict with the Rockefeller administration escalated, each of these factors exacerbated the tensions and contributed to the confrontation at Willowbrook.

New Politics of Mental Retardation

From 1935 to 2000, services for people with mental retardation became a partisan political issue at a few critical junctures. The first revolved around the investigations of the Moreland Act Commission that provided newly elected Governor Dewey a platform to launch a reorganization of the Department of Mental Hygiene and demonstrate the managerial as well as prosecutorial skills that would burnish his credentials for the next presidential election. For much of the next fifteen years, the field sunk back below the statewide political horizon as the emerging ARC dogged the state administration and various departments on a variety of issues that were important to the mental retardation constituency but did not have electoral significance.

Mental retardation reemerged as a partisan issue in the 1958 election when it became apparent that the Democrat Party-leaning leadership of the ARC was informally backing incumbent Governor Averell Harriman against the challenge of Nelson Rockefeller. The ARC's opposition to Rockefeller's election carried over into a series of rancorous policy differences in the early years of his first administration that took on an increasingly partisan cast. John F. Kennedy's election as President in 1960 put mental retardation on the national political agenda and added a federal-state dimension to partisanship. Advocates in New York pointed to the speedy and high-level attention being paid to mental retardation by the new Democrat administration in Washington while movement on the state planning process and a variety of other issues was stalled in New York.

Partisan politics surrounding mental retardation issues in New York State took on heightened importance in the mid-1960s. The 1964 landslide reelection of President Lyndon Johnson swept the Democrats into control of both houses of the New York State Legislature for the first time in thirty years, and Robert F. Kennedy was elected United State Senator from New York. In 1965, John Lindsay was elected Mayor of New York City, the first Republican in that office since Fiorello LaGuardia. At the time Nelson Rockefeller was launching his construction program, promulgating his *Comprehensive Plan*, and preparing to run for a third term as governor, he was confronted with a hostile legislature, a likely rival for the presidency in Robert F. Kennedy, and, in Lindsay, a popular Republican with a powerful base who did not conceal his ambition to vie for control of the state party.

The quality of services in state institutions, the planning and construction of new institutions, the use of moral obligation bonding, the aggressive use of Medicaid funding, the organization of local services, and the statewide administration of mental retardation services were issues in which Democrat and Republican political interests, the presidential ambitions of Rockefeller and Kennedy, and the interplay of national and state politics were enmeshed in complex and often peculiar alliances.

Senator Robert Kennedy's Visit to Willowbrook and Rome State Schools

Senator Kennedy launched mental retardation issues into presidential and statewide politics with his testimony before a hearing of the Joint Legislative Committee on Mental Retardation and Physical Handicap (JLC) in September 1965. Kennedy made his visits to Rome and Willowbrook State Schools the feature of his testimony. Kennedy described conditions of abuse and neglect at Rome and Willowbrook not heard since the Moreland Act Commission reports of the1940s, and he resurrected the term *snake pit* to characterize them.

Kennedy's testimony to the JLC was a dramatic attack on the Rockefeller administration's failures in this area. It also contained features that had subtle but important political meaning for the players who would remain after Kennedy moved on to other topics. First, Kennedy paid special attention to the severe shortage of professional staff at Willowbrook—an aspect of the care at Willowbrook that would reverberate several years later in the ARC suit. Second, Kennedy's proposals for reform largely reiterated those made by the ARC over the years. The skirmishing between an interest group and the administration now became an alliance between the ARC and Rockefeller's political rival. Third, in his testimony, Kennedy called for the release of a confidential report that had been presented to the JLC in 1964, when the JLC was still chaired by Republican Senator Conklin. The Joint Legislative Committee had provided a forum for the ARC over the years, and Conklin had prodded the administration on mental retardation issues, but Kennedy's call for the release of the report was likely an attempt to create more divisions in an already fractured Republican party.

Legislative and Executive Politics

Senator Kennedy's testimony and his call for the release of the confidential JLC report prompted the *New York Times* to do a follow-up investigation. The director of Willowbrook was forced to defend the department's administration in Albany while conceding that his requests for additional staffing and relief from new admissions to an already overcrowded facility had not been met. This resulted in protestations by the acting Commissioner of Mental Hygiene that conditions were bad, but not that bad, and that staffing problems were the fault of underfunding by the legislature. Regardless of what position was objectively correct, politically, the controversy carried echoes of the 1948 gubernatorial campaign in which the Director of Letchworth Village, the Commissioner of Mental Hygiene, and the Governor argued about whether and how many residents were sleeping on mattresses in hallways.

On the day that the administration issued its *Comprehensive Plan*, the new Democrat Chairman of the Joint Legislative Committee sent a telegram to Governor Rockefeller calling for priority action to increase staffing at Willowbrook. Rockefeller responded with the charge that the Democrat-controlled legislature had cut his appropriation requests for the Department of Mental Hygiene and Willowbrook. Charges, countercharges, editorials and press releases continued for a few weeks. New staffing was authorized for Willlowbrook, the administration trumpeted the opening of Sunmount State School (a converted TB asylum), and Governor Rockefeller made a series of visits to state schools including Willowbrook. New charges by Senator Kennedy ignited another round of telegrams and letters between the senator and the governor in which they called for a nonpartisan approach to resolving the problem while reminding each other that the Democrat-controlled legislature had cut funds and the Republican administration had failed to take advantage of available federal funding. A *New York Times* feature on the controversy pointed out that, "At stake, ultimately, is political control of New York State . . . And that control could be a potent weapon in future Presidential conventions (*New York Times* December 26, 1965, IV–V, 2).

Senator Kennedy did move on to other issues: Governor Rockefeller's proposed budget for the 1966–1967 fiscal year contained a large increase for mental retardation services, and the governor spent a great deal of energy promoting his construction program. The controversies over conditions and staffing in the state schools that lasted through the fall of 1965 cooled somewhat. However, it was now clear that the problems were so deep-seated and the divisions between the mental retardation constituency and the administration so long-lasting that a reignition would have enormous consequences. These were the opening skirmishes in what the Rothmans (1984) would call *The Willowbrook Wars*.

Passage of Medicaid

Medicaid plays such a large role in New York and most other states' disability and long-term care policy that it is hard to remember that it was virtually an afterthought in the protracted struggle to enact Medicare and barely registered on the radar screen of most policy makers in state government (Marmor 1970). Medicaid did not begin to have a significant impact on the financing and organization of developmental services until the early 1970s, and this will be examined in detail in the next chapter. However, the politics of New

York's Medicaid program were inherent from its inception, and the circumstances surrounding the drafting of New York's statute illustrate the importance of the political dimension of this program.

The final negotiations over the key elements of New York's Medicaid statute were conducted at the podium of the State Assembly—while it was in session—between Speaker Anthony Travia, Alton Marshall (the chief executive officer to Governor Rockefeller), and Senator Robert Kennedy by telephone. Alton Marshall later described the negotiations:

> "Medicaid was a political decision. It was not some deep-rooted emotional humanitarian drive. I stood on the podium of the Speaker of the Assembly and negotiated the number that we were going to set in respect to the level for Medicaid eligibility."
>
> "You will recall, and others will speak about it in more detail, that since we had been very generous in the State of New York over time, as opposed to other states, we had an eligibility level of $4,800 for a family of four, or something like that. The Federal law on Medicaid was interpreted so that we had to improve on what we had in existence in order to be eligible for the Federal program. Bob Kennedy was insisting, through Travia, on a new level of $6,000. I started at $5,000. We ended up at $5,600. Rockefeller didn't know what it was to cost. It was probably the biggest financial boo-boo that we had in the history of the administration, except perhaps for the South Mall" (Benjamin and Hurd 1984, 31–32).

The "political decision" Marshall referred to as part of these negotiations had several dimensions, including the upcoming gubernatorial election in November 1966. Rockefeller was planning an unprecedented run for a third term despite being behind in the polls against a variety of potential challengers, including some in his own party. Most prominent of these was the Mayor of New York City, John Lindsay. Rockefeller's agreement to an extraordinarily generous welfare program was astute positioning for the upcoming gubernatorial election.

Presidential politics were always on the agenda in New York politics at the time. During the fall of 1965, Senator Kennedy had lambasted Rockefeller for not pursuing federal funds that were available for health and mental health programs. Rockefeller's bold move to maximize New York's participation in this new federal program was intended to preempt criticism that he was not taking full advantage of federal funding. Key legislators, including Republicans, were dismayed by the lack of information about the costs of the proposed Medicaid program, but the Rockefeller administration insisted that delays in passage would cost the state $6 to $7 million a month in federal aid, and on April 20, 1966, after a brief one-day public hearing, New York's Medicaid bill passed both houses of the Legislature (Benjamin and Hurd 1984; Hevesi 1975).

In addition to an eligibility level that many claimed would cover one-third of the residents of the state, New York's Medicaid *State Plan* included all the seventeen optional services allowed in the federal legislation. Shortly after its passage, the Secretary of Health, Education, and Welfare estimated that New York's Medicaid program would cost $217 million a year, greatly exceeding the $155 million Congress had appropriated for all the states for 1966 (McClelland and Magdovitz 1981,188). An astounded Congress quickly passed restraints on eligibility levels and other aspects of the design of states' Title XIX (Medicaid) programs, but New York's "Oklahoma Sooner" approach to Medicaid had staked out a major claim on the federal program that it ferociously and successfully defended for the next thirty-five years.

The scale and scope of New York's Medicaid program also astounded New York's policy makers as the implications of the potential costs of the program became apparent. Despite some immediate tightening in eligibility levels, the still relatively high eligibility levels, high utilization rates, and cost increases due to inflation, pushed expenditures for Medicaid even higher. In 1967, New York's expenditures (approximately 50 percent of the total shared with the federal government) were $606.7 million, and by 1972, expenditures were approaching two billion dollars a year (McClelland and Magdovitz 1981, 189). Despite the early awareness of the unforeseen costs of Medicaid to the federal government and the state, it is unlikely that anyone at that time foresaw its extraordinarily important role for public institutions and developmental services in the state.

A Deteriorating Economy and Fiscal Crises

"The days of wine and roses are over." Governor Hugh Carey's opening line of his first inaugural address marked the end of the Rockefeller era. A look back at the vast expansion in almost every area of public programs that began during the Rockefeller years suggests an era of unprecedented prosperity. A closer examination reveals that structural changes in the state's economy, the fiscal policies of the Rockefeller administration, and similar approaches used by New York City, as well as important demographic shifts were important factors contributing to the political and fiscal crises of the early 1970s and the restructuring of developmental services in New York.

Structural Changes in New York's Economy

New York, the Empire State, began the post-World War II era as the richest and most populous state in the nation. The state had a high concentration of heavy industry along its Hudson and Mohawk River corridors with large automobile, steel, heavy equipment, and consumer and industrial electronics manufacturing plants in Buffalo, Rochester, Syracuse, Schenectady, and Yonkers. New York City's apparel, printing, and other medium and light industries were important complements to the city's publishing, banking, and other financial services sectors. New York prospered in the postwar economic boom, but its growth began to lag behind that in other states.

By the time Governor Hugh Carey made his famous remark in the midst of the collapse of the Urban Development Corporation and impending bankruptcy of New York City, editorial obituaries for the city and state along with academic analyses of their dire fiscal condition were rife. The financial crisis of the mid-1970s was not the result of a unique and sudden economic collapse. It was preceded by a state budget crisis in the early 1970s and, most importantly, by a long-term deterioration in the state and New York City economies.

McClelland and Magdovitz (1981) argue that there were a number of reasons for New York's growing relative disadvantage to other states. They look back to a "freeze" on the capital equipment of New York's manufacturing caused first by the Depression and second by the wartime economy and suggest that there were long-standing problems of deterioration and technological obsolescence in New York's manufacturing capacity as the postwar era began. Another important factor contributing to New York's relative decline was a growing shift of the country's population west and south and the concomitant following of market-oriented firms. Construction of interstate highways continued the federal government investment in infrastructure begun during the Depression with the building of hydroelectric plants—facilitating the movement of population and manufacturing out of New York and other northeastern states (financed with taxes that were disproportionately paid by those states). The higher cost of energy in New York, its high taxes relative to southern and western states, and its largely unionized work force were other factors that contributed to the shift of jobs and population out of the state.

The loss of manufacturing plants and the high paying jobs in those industries started a downward trend in the early 1950s and began to accelerate by the late 1960s (McClelland and Magdovitz 1981, 41). Whether the jobs went south or to newly competitive foreign manufacturers, the impact on the state was substantial. Of particular importance to the eventual role of public employment in the state's economy, upstate manufacturing jobs were highly concentrated in Buffalo, Rochester, and Syracuse, and these cities began losing jobs faster than the overall state rate of loss. By 1970, more than any other state in the country, New York's economy came to be dominated by a single metropolitan area, New York City, which was losing high paying manufacturing jobs and executives to its surrounding counties. In contrast to that phenomenon in other states, those surrounding counties were in New Jersey and Connecticut. Demographically, New York City was also gaining a larger number of poorer residents who were not offsetting the economic loss of middle class and executive jobs to the suburbs and were adding to the growing welfare burden for the city.

By 1970, the structural problems in New York's economy were manifested in its exaggerated reaction to downturns in the national economy: compared to national recessions, New York's began earlier, lasted longer, and disappeared more gradually (McClelland and Magdovitz 1981). However, through most of the 1960s, these underlying problems were masked by a state economy that had not reached a crisis (although its loss of relative position to other states was becoming more evident) and by a national economy fueled by the Great Society programs of the Johnson administration and spending on the war in Vietnam.

Fiscal Policies of the Rockefeller Administration

The state's economy continued to grow during the 1960s. However, its deterioration was masked by the impact of exponential increases in state expenditures. The rate of increase in the State Purposes portion of the state's budget did not grow at an appreciably higher rate than under the preceding Harriman and Dewey administrations, but overall expenditures from "All Operating Funds" (including federal aid to localities, expenditures from first instance appropriations, and debt service not from the General Fund) skyrocketed almost 300 percent from 1965 to 1972 (McCelland and Magdovitz 1981, 414).

The linkages among the national and state economies and the state budget are not always clear. These relationships became much less clear as the Rockefeller administration implemented wide use of bonding (especially moral obligation bonding), public authorities, and revenue schemes that removed large parts of revenues and expenditures from the regular state budget processes. As the underlying weaknesses in the state's economy intensified the impact of a recession in the national economy, the vulnerabilities inherent in the state's fiscal practices added to the overall crisis. By the end of his administration, New York's indebtedness levels in its public authorities alone was twice the total debt of California and ten times the average level of indebtedness of all other states (McClelland and Magdovitz 1981, 139).

Overall debt not only skyrocketed under the Rockefeller administration, but, as described earlier, it was concealed in a complex array of financial instruments that few, if any, understood. The Rockefeller administration did not abandon the traditional borrowing route, and full faith and credit debt tripled from $1.1 billion to $3.4 billion (McClelland and Magdovitz 1981,166). However, moral obligation bonding and the adaptation of public authorities as their financial and administrative framework were the hallmarks of the growth of indebtedness under Rockefeller. By the time Rockefeller left the governor's office in 1974, the moral obligation debt of 230 public authorities and public benefit corporations had grown to $13.3 billion—four times the full faith and credit debt of the state. The state and New York City also issued Bond Anticipation Notes and Revenue Anticipation Notes. These debt instruments had long been used to raise relatively small amounts of funding in anticipation of near-term revenues. By the end of the Rockefeller administration, hundreds of millions of dollars of these short-term instruments were being rolled-over to cover long-term, regular expenditures. Lease-purchase agreements and first instance appropriations were among other fiscal mechanisms that had traditionally been used for small, short-term, and special purposes that were woven into an enormous and complex pattern of debt.

What was the long-term impact of the shift to debt financing on public institutions for people with mental retardation? The answer was clear to the mental retardation constituency from the start. Early in the Rockefeller administration the ARC had opposed the creation of the Mental Hygiene Facilities Improvement Fund because it recognized that its approach to financing the construction of new state schools would require revenue to repay the forty-year bonds thereby mortgaging the lives of the residents with parental fees. Less apparent at the time was the fact that financing state school construction through moral obligation bonding would cost much more than through capital construction appropriations or full faith and credit bonding. At the end of the construction program, the state got less capacity at a higher cost (LCER, 1973).

Rapid Slide into Fiscal Crises

In his *Executive Budget* for 1966–1967, Governor Rockefeller claimed that, "Our executive and legislative success in achieving sound operations over the past seven years helps us meet these and other important public needs, promoting the dynamic advances in a State economy now functioning at record-breaking levels" (M.6). The governor went on to state that, "A key element in our fiscal achievements has been the financing of extraordinary capital construction programs through self-liquidating funds at no cost to the general taxpayer" (M.6). The budget proposal for 1966–67 called for an expansion in state school staffing and an 8 percent salary increase. In his 1967–68 *Executive Budget* message, Governor Rockefeller noted that the United States economy would expand in the coming fiscal year, but not as rapidly as it did in 1966. However, the governor pointed out that, "Even if the rate of growth in the national economy should slow down more than is generally expected, New York State's growth rate, based on past experience, should not decline as much as that of the national economy and a reasonably high level of revenue should still be attained" (M.16).

But by the 1968–69 fiscal year, Governor Rockefeller's *Executive Budget* message opened with "concern for economic realities" (M.5), "rising welfare costs," "escalating health care costs," and keeping recommended expenditures at "the minimum amounts required to meet essential needs" (M.13). "New York State now faces a most serious fiscal crisis" was the opening of Governor Rockefeller's *Executive Budget* message for 1969–70, but the governor placed the blame for this "austerity budget" on the "imbalance in the Federal System," and used the bulk of his message to explain how New York State was not receiving its fair share of federal funds. In 1969, Governor Rockefeller's central planning agency issued a report, *New York State: Economic Outlook for the Seventies*, in which it maintained that:

> "New York's economy in the seventies will reach record levels, spurred on by the coming of age of the postwar generation, rising incomes and the continuing emergence of new growth industries. The state's economy, undoubtedly the most advanced, complex and mature economy in the nation (and possibly the world) will continue to set the pace for the nation" (OPC 1969, 2).

A cautiously optimistic *Executive Budget* for 1970–71 was a brief respite before the 1971–72 *Executive Budget* which opened with, "We have reached a point at which the State alone can no longer meet its own needs and give adequate help to the schools and local governments" (M.5). "This is a stopgap, crisis budget," the governor stated and "Emergency financial action this year by the national government is essential to avert a major crisis" (M.5). In his *Executive Budget* for 1972–73, Governor Rockefeller began with the following statement, "Last year at this time in my Budget Message I outlined the major financial crisis that faced state and local governments in New York State and throughout the Nation. Today, I can state that my fears were well-founded" (M.5). The governor pointed out that expenditures would exceed revenues in the coming fiscal year, and temporary borrowing with tax anticipation notes would be required.

In less than five years, New York's fiscal condition had slid from "fiscally sound" to "major financial crisis." The stagflation of the national economy certainly contributed to the state's problems, but despite Governor Rockefeller's charge that New York was not receiving its fair share of federal revenues, he also conceded that his budgets had become captive to a variety of formulas for welfare and public school aid and the unstoppable momentum of the construction programs for the State University, mental hygiene institutions, and other new programs. The "major financial crisis" Rockefeller announced in 1972 was not the bottom, but it was enough to be the catalyst for the political crisis that brought the *ARC v. Rockefeller* suit at Willowbrook.

Staffing Public Institutions and New York's Political Economy

At the same time the governor was announcing yet another fiscal crisis, staffing in public institutions was rapidly increasing and changing the nature of public institutions and the economies in their locales. In the 1960s, staffing increased, became more professional, and was restructured. The state schools were transformed from administratively flat pyramids in which a handful of physician-administrators oversaw thousands of attendants, food service workers, groundskeepers, and locksmiths into complex organizations employing nurses, social workers, physical therapists, occupational therapists, and special education teachers. These increasingly complex organizations required managers who were recruited from the ranks of the therapeutic professionals and from the hospital, business, public administration specialists who were also joining the state civil service. These staffing changes within the state schools were part of a larger increase in public employment in the rapidly growing central administrations of agencies and public authorities in Albany and in the burgeoning state colleges and universities and other public programs instituted and expanded during the Rockefeller years.

The pay for those positions was increasing, making them more competitive in the overall economy. Public employment was also becoming a much more important sector in the state's economy, especially upstate, as industrial jobs declined and large numbers of baby boomers began leaving college and looking for employment. Unionization of public employees under New York's Taylor Act created a new and problematic relationship between the administration and its employees. This played out first in a strike at mental hygiene institutions in 1968, and in 1972, the dispute over staffing at Willowbrook that was the catalyst for the parents' suit.

Overcrowding and Increased Staffing and Pay

Overcrowding became the primary concern in the state schools by the 1960s, but staffing shortages were a chronic problem and threatened to delay expansion of capacity. Despite severe overcrowding and waiting lists, the opening of a new building at Craig Colony was delayed because of a lack of personnel, and the department began using a "recruitmobile" to tour communities in the western part of the state to recruit employees (DMH 1967, 6). The administration engaged a consulting firm to compare public and private pay that led to an upgraded salary plan for state employees (DMH 1965). Enhanced recruitment efforts, higher salaries, and new professional opportunities in the state's institutions soon broke the hiring logjam. From 1966 to 1968, employment in the state schools soared by 32 percent as more than 4,000 new positions were added, bringing the number of employees to 18,768 (NYS Executive Budget 1966–67, 1968–69). By the end of the decade, the Department of Mental Hygiene was aiming for a ratio of one ward service staff for every 1.5 residents of the state schools and a 1 to 1 clinical staff-to-resident ratio (DMH 1969).

Staffing increases for the overcrowded state schools were a high priority. However, the radical change in the residents to a much younger and more severely disabled population added another dimension to the problem. Additional teachers, nurses, and rehabilitation specialists were needed. In 1966, the department established 1,700 new positions in the state schools "to provide better medical and personalized care for the severely physically handicapped mentally retarded children, to staff new facilities and to employ physicians, medical consultants and specialists." The department also reported an important new source of funding for staff as it noted that more than $500,000 in federal funds were made available for hospital improvement projects in personalized care, educational programs and intensified training and rehabilitation services (DMH, 1966, 9). Nonetheless, the *Annual Report* for 1967 conceded, "Many institutions are short of essential medical, nursing, and ward service personnel" (12).

Changes in the Structure and Functions of Institutions

The recruitment of large numbers of professional staff and staffing targeted to special needs led to the reorganization of the structure of the state schools. Large wards were divided into smaller living units. A survey of the needs of children who required assistance with feeding, toileting, or ambulation resulted in more then five hundred new Attendant (primary direct care) staff being approved in the department's budget. The department instituted a system called "post staffing" in the state schools that assigned personnel on the basis of functional needs rather than overall ratios based on resident population (DMH 1962). Institution farms were closed, and staff was reassigned to new chronic intensive care units. Training and management development issues were featured in the *Annual Reports*, and "career ladders" were being built into the civil service position structure. The state schools were beginning to evolve from custodial facilities characterized by large wards staffed by attendants into more articulated organizations staffed by professionals and direct care staff organized more on the bases of resident need and functional approaches.

In 1969, the department implemented a "functional unitization" plan in which the state schools were reorganized by functional goals, and each unit was headed by a Chief of Service overseeing multidisciplinary teams (headed by Team Leaders) who were responsible for the planning, implementation, and evaluation of programs and services (DMH, 1969). These Team Leaders and Chiefs of Service became key positions in a more complex state school organizational structure. These positions provided career opportunities for clinical staff and, along with similar developments in the business offices, created a cadre of managers within the evolving state schools.

Increased Role of Government Employment in State and Local Economies

McClelland and Magdovitz (1981) tracked the changes in nonagricultural employment sectors in New York State from 1946 to 1978 from United States and New York State Departments of Labor statistics and showed the large increase and relative growth in government employment.

From 1965 to 1972, total New York State nonagricultural employment grew by 7.8 percent while total government employment grew by 29.6 percent. Moreover, the growth in government employment was greater in upstate New York where it grew by more than a third from 1965 to 1972 — from 347,000 to 463,000 (McClelland and Magdovitz 1981, 403). From 1960 to the end of the Rockefeller administration in 1972, manufacturing jobs declined from 37.9 percent of total upstate employment to 30.0 percent (McClelland and Magdovitz 1981, 400–401). Government employment, including state schools with thousands of employees in one facility, became more crucial to the local economies in which they were located.

Politics of Government Employment

The absolute and relative increases in government employment in upstate New York had important long-range political consequences. The almost exclusively Republican state legislators representing the districts in which state schools were located were conservative on social issues and continued to express traditional Republican concerns about cutting the size of government and taxes. However, the state administration could count on them for support

Table 5.1
New York State: Nonagricultural and Government Employment

	Nonagricultural (000)	Government	Govt. % of Total
1946	5,325	618	11.6
1960	6,182	838	13.6
1965	6,519	959	14.7
1972	7,028	1,243	17.7

McClelland and Magdovitz 1981, 398

for maintaining and increasing the budgets of the state and community colleges, psychiatric centers, state schools and other New York State programs in their districts along with the generous aid to school districts and local governments that provided their constituents with jobs that had become the best-paid and most secure in their localities.

Labor Turmoil: Hiring Freezes, Layoffs, and Strikes

The number of jobs in the civil service was increasing, the pay scale was increased, and more professional positions and promotional opportunities were available. Nonetheless, the late 1960s and early 1970s were marked by increasing labor problems that ultimately were the catalyst for the *ARC v. Rockefeller* suit at Willowbrook.

The public labor union turmoil began with a fourteen-day transit strike in New York City in 1966. Following this strike, the Taylor Law was passed to provide a new framework for government-public employee labor relations, substituting collective bargaining with newly certified public employee unions for the less formal salary negotiations with employee associations. This legislation passed over the strenuous objections of public employee unions about the new law's provisions for penalties for strikes. Tensions rose to the point of precipitating a ten-day strike at four state psychiatric hospitals in November 1968.

Further deterioration in the state economy and yet another fiscal crisis prompted the Rockefeller administration to impose a hiring freeze in December 1970 which resulted in the reduction, through attrition, of approximately 5,000 employees of the Department of Mental Hygiene (DMH 1971). In 1971, there were 18,553 positions authorized in the state schools, but hiring freezes had reduced the number of employees to 15,346 (*Executive Budget* 1971–72). In the opening lines of the 1971 *Annual Report*, Commissioner Miller stated, "The year 1971—hardly the best of times but surely not the worst—has seen the Department of Mental Hygiene affected by various adversities, principally in the form of public criticism and in losses of revenue with the consequent loss of valued employees." Unfortunately, the times did become worse, and in 1972, New York, for the first time since the Great Depression, laid off thousands of employees, setting off the confrontation at Willowbrook.

Chapter 6

Willowbrook and the Medicaid Intermediate Care Facilities for the Mentally Retarded Program

The wards of the State in this institution have lived and slept under conditions which members of the Commission felt could never have existed in a civilized society. There has been no adequate explanation given as to why such conditions should have been allowed to exist either by the institution or the Department of Mental Hygiene over such a period of time.

—*Moreland Act Commission Report,* 1944

Willowbrook. Willowbrook was the fulcrum of another radical departure in New York's experience with public institutions. Decades after the political and fiscal crises that brought about the parents' suit in federal court, it still deserves the attention David and Sheila Rothman gave it in their landmark book, *The Willowbrook Wars.* But Willowbrook alone did not cause the enormous changes and new directions that followed. Willowbrook was a figure in the landscape of mental retardation policy and politics during the 1970s while the Medicaid ICF/MR Program was the ground. By the time of the *ARC v. Rockefeller* suit in 1972, Medicaid had moved to the center of policy making in New York and other states. However, less-obvious features of Medicaid, especially the Intermediate Care Facilities program, coupled with Willowbrook to set the stage for the radical departure in public institutions and developmental services in New York.

Outside Forces: Pressures from the Federal Government and Other States

The appointment of a President's Panel on Mental Retardation by President John F. Kennedy was the opening of an expanded role of the federal government

129

in mental retardation issues. The panel's Proposed Program for National Action to Combat Mental Retardation gave mental retardation advocates in New York the example of a vigorous federal initiative to contrast with New York's contentious and delayed action in this area. Federal legislation provided for planning and construction funding, and, consistent with the War on Poverty metaphor of the New Frontier, guidelines for action and combat. After issuing its report in October 1962, the President's Panel was largely reconstituted as the President's Committee on Mental Retardation with a prestigious membership and professional staff. This committee provided a vehicle for advocates and analysts to promote plans that challenged prevailing concepts about the role of people with mental retardation in society and the appropriate objectives, size, and location of models of care. The President's Committee also did comparative case studies and statistical analyses of experiences in other states and countries which advocates in New York could point to as examples and guides for corrective action.

Changing Patterns in Residential Services for the Mentally Retarded (1969) contained the core reports of the panel and was most widely citied by advocates and analysts. Brent Nirje and Karl Grunewald from Sweden, N.E. Bank-Mikkelsen from Denmark, and Jack Tizard and David Norris from the United Kingdom defined the principle of normalization that would guide reformers and described community-based service systems in those countries that could act as models for what were still no more than vague plans in New York. While these might be discounted as not representative of the American situation, Robert Krugel and Wolf Wolfensberger from Nebraska, Earl C. Butterfield from Kansas, Burton Blatt from Massachusetts, and M. Michael Klaber and Robert E. Cooke from Connecticut wrote scathing critiques of large institutions in other states and described smaller facilities, community services, and new approaches that were getting underway in these other states. These were concrete examples of how other states were making progress on community services while New York was preoccupied with building institutions.

New Blood: Recruitment of Administrators from Outside New York

The impact of other states' better practices was accelerated as New York began to hire large numbers of administrators from other states. Until the 1960s, the leadership of the Department of Mental Hygiene was drawn from within the agency. Beginning in the mid-1960s, New York hired so many psychiatrist-administrators who had worked in the Saskatchewan Department of Mental Health that they became known as the "Saskatchewan mafia." Top administrators from Canada, Colorado, Texas, Connecticut, and other states were recruited to fill positions in the Mental Retardation Division of the department. The division also made key appointments of individuals who were not physicians and had been executives and managers of local mental retardation agencies in New York and other states. These administrators in an increasingly autonomous Division of Mental Retardation challenged long-standing policies and practices of the department.

The politics within the entire mental hygiene arena began to shift. New administrators from outside the state contended with more traditional directors running large institutions and the MHFIC and the governor's office implementing the construction plan. While advocates found allies in the Division of Mental Retardation, this did not eliminate the natural antipathy between the mental retardation constituency and the administration, nor satisfy concerns about a virtually nonexistent community mental retardation program. Burton Blatt and Wolf Wolfensberger moved to New York to found the Center on Human Policy at Syracuse University. Their indictments of New York's institutions and failure to provide community services, now from within the state, were especially galling to state policy makers and administrators.

Role of the Federal Courts: Wyatt v. Stickney

The outside force that would have the most dramatic impact on New York was the role federal courts were beginning to play in states' operation of large institutions. Beginning with the U.S. Supreme Court decisions in *Baxstrom v. Herold* (383 U.S. 107) in 1966, federal courts turned their attention to conditions of residents in public mental hospitals, and particularly the criminally mentally ill (Castellani 1975). The findings in *Baxstrom* were soon being applied to broader classes of persons in state facilities for people with mental disabilities, and in its 1967 ruling in *Rouse v. Cameron* (387 F.2d 241: DC Cir), the federal district court found that residents of public mental hospitals had a "right to treatment."

The role of the federal judiciary was largely limited to mental health cases through the late 1960s. In 1972, the federal courts stepped into the mental retardation arena in the *Wyatt v. Stickney* case brought against the Commissioner of Mental Health of Alabama. A class action complaint prompted by the threat of mass layoffs of institution staff and the prospect of "no treatment" was brought on behalf of the residents of Bryce State Hospital for the mentally ill. Shortly after the initial order in *Wyatt*, several national organizations, including the American Association on Mental Deficiency and the National Association for Retarded Citizens, joined the case as *amici curiae*, and the complaint was amended to include the other state institution for the mentally ill and the state institution for people with mental retardation, Partlow State School and Hospital (Castellani 1975, 1987; Yarborough 1982).

The final order in the *Wyatt v. Stickney* case was a landmark in judicial policy making in this area and established an entirely new direction for public policy. Federal District Court Judge Frank M. Johnson, Jr. found that the evidence "vividly and undisputedly" demonstrated that conditions at Partlow did not meet constitutionally minimum standards. In rejecting the argument of the Alabama Mental Health Board that the absence of adequate funding precluded appropriate staffing and facilities, Johnson stated that the implementation of constitutionally minimum standards was mandatory, and no default could be justified by the lack of operating funds. Johnson stated that if the Alabama Legislature failed to provide sufficient funds to implement these standards, the court would take affirmative steps including the appointment of a master to ensure that proper funding is realized *(Wyatt v. Stickney* 344 F. Supp. 373). The court suggested that a special session of the Alabama Legislature be held to appropriate the necessary funding, and it proffered the notion of seizing and selling state property to secure the funds if the legislature failed to act. The court also ordered the hiring of a professionally qualified and experienced administrator to oversee the reform and reorganization of Partlow. Appendix A to the Final Order and Decree in *Wyatt* was Constitutional Standards for Adequate Habilitation of the Mentally Retarded and contained forty-nine detailed standards stipulating: (1) Adequate Habilitation of Residents, (2) Individualized Habilitation Plans, (3) Humane Physical and Psychological Environments, and (4) Qualified Staff in Numbers Sufficient to Provide Adequate Habilitation (*Wyatt v. Stickney*, 344 F. Supp. 373).

The *Wyatt v. Stickney* ruling commanded the attention of administrators and advocates for people with mental retardation for several reasons. First, this was a class action suit that carried the possibility of broad application to similarly situated individuals in a state. Second, the court explicitly applied the constitutional right to treatment to individuals with mental retardation in state institutions, pre-preempting arguments that custodial care was adequate and laying the groundwork for what later became requirements for "active treatment." Third, *Wyatt* was the first case in which the court promulgated objectively measurable and judicially enforceable standards. Fourth, the court set time limits for implementation of remedial action. Fifth, although only posing the possibility, the court stated its willingness to apply sanctions as well as take implementation into its own hands by hiring a "professionally qualified and experienced administrator" to oversee reform and reorganization at Patlow (Yarborough 1982). A right to treatment, specific and measurable objectives, time limitations, sanctions, and an alternative to administrative and legislative inaction were features of *Wyatt* that advocates across the country could not ignore.

Impact of Willowbrook

In 1944, the Moreland Act Commission was expressing its shock and dismay about conditions at Craig Colony, but that observation would be readily applied to Willowbrook. The controversy following Senator Robert Kennedy's visit in 1965 and the response of the Rockefeller administration had passed, and the state as well as the mental retardation constituency were hoping that the state school construction program would relieve overcrowding and waiting lists. An evaluation team from the American Association on Mental Deficiency did a survey at Willowbrook in 1967, and while they reported a number of significant problems, their report gave the institution and the state credibility with enough equivocation about conditions and observations of "movement in the right direction" to keep Willowbrook and other large institutions out of the public eye and political agenda.

Willowbrook was not a major political priority for the ARC. The ARC was primarily concerned with access to public schools, state funding for tuition at private schools, and state funding of ARC chapters' schools, workshops, and other programs. The ARC did not openly oppose the addition of thousands of new jobs in the state schools, in Republican-represented upstate New York. However, the hostility of the heavily New York City, and Democrat leaning, leadership of the ARC to the Rockefeller administration grew as plans for state schools in New York City evaporated, and the highly touted hostel program barely inched forward.

In *The Willowbrook Wars*, the Rothmans provide a rich account of the events leading up to the Willowbrook suit. They describe the role of staff members such as William Bronston, Michael Wilkins, and Elizabeth Lee agitating for reform from inside Willowbrook and their serendipitous relationship with TV reporter Geraldo Rivera whose televised exposé in January 1972 sparked a renewed public scrutiny of conditions at Willowbrook. They highlight the role of several parents who dared to challenge the institution administration about the abuse of their children and encouraged other parents to speak out and portray institution and Department of Mental Hygiene administrators as well-intentioned, but impotent, apologists for the status quo. Staff members afraid for their jobs and forced to take on greater burdens of care as a result of hiring freezes that decreased their number by hundreds were faced with a proposed state budget that would include layoffs. In the winter of 1972, Willowbrook was in turmoil. The Rothmans point out that the Mental Health Law Project (which had brought the *Wyatt* case), along with the Legal Aid society, were preparing to bring a suit against New York similar to the *Wyatt* suit that was moving toward initial resolution in Alabama. However, they wanted the weight and legitimacy of the state's most prominent advocacy group, the ARC.

The Rothmans argue that the Mental Health Law Project had a difficult time convincing the ARC to act as the lead plaintiff in a suit at Willowbrook. They characterize the ARC as cautious (even reluctant) and point out that despite the historic antipathy between the ARC and the state administration, the ARC was an astute player in a political process that involved compromise and accommodation. By becoming the lead plaintiff in a federal suit against the state of New York, the ARC would be a party to a radically different, confrontational process in the politics of mental retardation.

The *ARC v. Rockefeller* suit focused on reforming and depopulating Willowbrook, but the case and the events surrounding it were catalysts for broader change. The 5,400 Willowbrook residents the court deemed class members "drove the agency" in the phrase that was widely used in Albany to describe their impact on managing all developmental services in the state. Policy makers also used Willowbrook as an excuse or threat to justify other changes they wished to make. In still other circumstances, Willowbrook, the ICF Plan of Compliance (which will be described in the next chapter), the exigencies of federal reimbursement, the demands of public employee unions, the opening of new institutions, electoral politics, and other events interacted in ways in which Willowbrook was the most visible, but not always the most important, factor. Nonetheless, Willowbrook had several important and long-term effects on the organization of developmental services in New York.

Willowbrook and the Role of the Courts

No matter whether the plaintiffs or the state won, lost, or tied on the seemingly endless motions and actions that marked the Willowbrook case, from March 1972 on, the federal courts became a major player in policy making and implementation. Even when the courts withdrew to the sidelines or backed away from the expansive and aggressive role on closing institutions they took in the early 1970s, their role remained a potent factor that policy makers had to take into account.

The role of courts in bringing about significant change was, nonetheless, limited. In the *Wyatt v. Stickney* case, the ultimate impact of the federal court on effecting change was stymied by the state's recalcitrance (Yarbrough 1982). Masters and review panels were powerful goads to action, but they were limited in their ability to actually bring about change, especially in the face of determined opposition by the state. From the initial order to the signing of the Consent Decree in 1975, Judge Orin Judd in the Willowbrook case expected that New York State would implement the court's orders to depopulate Willowbrook less from the ability of the court to impose and implement its will than from the state's fear that the findings of the court would demonstrate that New York was out of compliance with Medicaid regulations and would lose federal reimbursement.

Willowbrook and the Growth of Community Services

Willowbrook played a very important role in the growth of residential and day services in the community. From the inauguration of the hostel program in 1966 until the early 1970s, the growth of community residences in New York, burdened by a cumbersome process, moved at a glacial pace. The passage of the federal Supplemental Security Income Act (SSI) in 1972 allowed community agencies to use financing from the residents' federal SSI and state supplement payments to open community residences. By the time Judge Orin Judd made his initial rulings in the case, the number of hostels in New York City had grown, although they represented a minuscule resource in relation to the needs of the New York City population. The hostel program was, nonetheless, a framework that could be employed for the depopulation of Willowbrook.

In the first wave of deinstitutionalization of Willowbrook, the great majority of its residents were transferred to other existing state schools, newly opened state schools, special units on the grounds of state psychiatric centers, specialty hospitals, and nursing homes. Several hundred were "deinstitutionalized" in place as the United Cerebral Palsy Association of New York State took over the operation of a number of buildings and services at Willowbrook under the rubric of the Karl Warner Complex. Still, a large number of Willowbrook residents were eventually placed in apartments and community residences in New York City, especially following the agreement between the state and provider agencies to allow those agencies to also place individuals from their own waiting lists.

Deinstitutionalization of public psychiatric hospital residents as well as Willowbrook class members into community residences in New York City resulted in legislation that became an unexpectedly powerful tool in expanding community residences across the state. Charges of "dumping," the use of Single Room Occupancy hotels, and concentration of halfway houses and group homes in neighborhoods created a strong backlash against deinstitutionalization (Padavan, 1979). Community opposition to group homes led to the enactment, in 1978, of the "Site Selection of Community Residential Facilities Act." This statute, Section 41.34 of the state's Mental Hygiene Law, commonly referred to as the Padavan Law after its sponsor State Senator William Padavan of Queens, was intended to allow community input into the siting of group homes by establishing a notice, hearing, and appeal process for the establishment of community residential facilities. The law allowed a municipality to approve, suggest alternate sites, or object to selected sites for group homes and outlined standards for disapproval such as the concentration of similar facilities in the neighborhood (Padavan 1979). Although the law was intended to slow or even impede group home siting, it gave the commissioner of the state agency the authority to make the final decision on the site. The commissioner could unilaterally override the objection of the locality, and, in almost every instance of formal opposition to a group home since, the objection of the locality was overturned. Unexpectedly, the Padavan Law became an extraordinarily powerful tool for the expansion of group homes across the state.

Willowbrook and the Nature of Community Agencies

Willowbrook had a significant impact on the growth of the private provider agencies in the state. In *The Willowbrook Wars*, the Rothmans describe the Metropolitan Placement Unit's inability to convince most established social welfare agencies to take on the new challenge of serving severely disabled people in community settings and the successes in getting new providers (such as the Young Adult Institute, Catholic Charities, and United Cerebral Palsy of New York State) to provide residential and day services to the individuals moving out of Willowbrook and those who had been living at home.

A second feature of the growth of community provider agencies was that the state put no limit on their size or their operation of residential as well as day programs. Several other states controlled the size of provider agencies by putting a cap on the number of clients they could serve as well as the size and number of residences they could operate. There is no evidence of a formal discussion or decision on these issues in New York. The exigencies of the Willowbrook Consent Decree and the ICF Plan of Compliance made moving residents out of institutions and into community services as quickly as possible the primary consideration. If that could be achieved more quickly by having the same agency provide both the day and the residential services, then that was what was done.

Willowbrook played a crucial role in the decision to rely exclusively on nonprofit agencies for the care of people with developmental disabilities in New York. In 1973, a relatively small number of former Willowbrook residents were moved to a proprietary nursing home in New Jersey, and negotiations were underway for the transfer of additional class members to other proprietary nursing homes, including ones owned by Bernard Bergman. In the midst of the negotiations, an exposé of abysmal conditions, contributions to politicians, and Medicaid fraud in Bergman's nursing homes resulted in a Moreland Act Commission hearing. Some Department of Mental Hygiene officials who had been dealing with Bergman were reprimanded, and a stinging report was issued that insured that proprietary nursing homes or other for-profit agencies would not be allowed to provide services.

Willowbrook As a Catalyst for Changes Among Government and Constituency Groups

The Rothmans cast the adversaries in the Willowbrook Wars war as "the court and a bureaucracy dominated by a civil service that may be impervious to both the legislature and the executive," (1984, 355). They portray the bureaucrats of the Metropolitan Placement Unit as the allies of the court, and parents, various commissioners, institution directors, and other bureaucrats are cast as progressive or recalcitrant. Beyond the clash of personalities and skirmishes between the court and the bureaucracy described by the Rothmans, Willowbrook was reshaping other institutional relationships.

According to the Rothmans, in the early stages of the Willowbrook suit the Commissioner of Mental Hygiene, Alan Miller, promised that he would put up "as defenseless a defense as possible" (66). Despite Miller's intentions, the state's legal defense was in the hands of New York State Attorney General Louis Lefkowitz. Lefkowitz was not only the state's chief legal officer but also a close friend, confidante, and top political advisor to Governor Rockefeller. Although Robert Kennedy had been dead for four years, Willowbrook remained a political thorn in Rockefeller's side. Moreover, the plaintiffs' suit in federal court represented a fundamental challenge to the authority and autonomy of the state and the governor. Any awareness of Rockefeller's personal, political, and executive history would disabuse one of the notion that he would allow a "defenseless defense."

The Willowbrook case illustrated and exacerbated the administrative cleavages within the Department of Mental Hygiene. Commissioners had been chosen for their professional credentials, and Alan Miller had been elevated to the job from Assistant Commissioner of Local Services. Professional, progressive, and pursuing the same general goals of community services as the plaintiffs, Miller and his deputies had been recruited from inside and outside the state to change the institutional mind-set of the agency. They were caught between the governor and attorney general, who were not going to concede anything to the plaintiffs; the old-line institutional directors, who correctly perceived the intentions of the new leadership cadre; and new executives in the agency's Division of Mental Retardation who may have shared Miller's general goals but, nonetheless, suffered second-class status within the agency. In this latter group were psychiatrists who specialized in mental retardation, and they were also hearing the louder calls for abandonment of the psychiatric dominance of mental retardation policy and programs. The tensions within the administration during the early stages of the Willowbrook Wars presaged major administrative changes that occurred after the election of Hugh Carey: the signing of the Consent Decree, the appointment of Thomas Coughlin, a layperson, as Deputy Commissioner of Mental Hygiene, and finally the creation of a separate Office of Mental Retardation and Developmental Disabilities in 1978. These events will be examined more fully in the next chapter.

Willowbrook also involved executive-legislative relationships. The legislature had not staked out a strong adversarial position on mental retardation vis-à-vis the executive. It passed a number of bills sponsored by the ARC, but it is likely that many, such as the creation of a separate agency, were passed with the knowledge that the governor would veto them. With Executive Director Jerry Weingold as paid counsel, the ARC had a "seat" with the Joint Legislative Committee on Mental Retardation (JLC). As the parent of a child with mental retardation, Senator William Conklin, Chairman of the JLC, was sympathetic to the views of the ARC. However, Conklin was a Republican, an important player in the state party, and an ally of Governor Nelson Rockefeller. Conklin provided the ARC a platform for JLC [ARC] reports on mental retardation issues, but while sensitive to the prerogatives of the legislature, he did not provide a serious challenge to the executive's hegemony in the field. Moreover, the *ARC v. Rockefeller* suit was not only a challenge to the administration, but, as the *Wyatt* case had demonstrated, it also represented a challenge to the legislature.

Willowbrook also contributed to growing rifts within the mental retardation constituency. The ARC was the lead plaintiff in the suit, but it was a reluctant player. The ARC's main activities were advocating for and operating educational and community day services. The Rothmans suggest that not only were traditional social service agencies reluctant to get into operating community residences for Willowbrook residents, but that the ARC was also unenthusiastic about taking on this role. New and embryonic agencies, such as the Young Adult Institute, or older, non-ARC agencies, such as the Association for Children with Retarded Mental Development, greatly expanded their roles in providing residential as well as day programs. These new agencies quickly became important players, especially in New York City, offering for the first time significant alternative voices to that of the ARC.

Willowbrook was also the vehicle for a new role for agencies with the broader-than-mental retardation focus of developmental disabilities. The concept of developmental disabilities, which included a range of mental impairments other than mental retardation, had become widely accepted in the professional field. The 1970 federal Developmental Disabilities Services and Facilities Construction Act (PL 91-517) used a categorical definition of developmental disability that included mental retardation, cerebral palsy, epilepsy, and other neurological impairments occurring before the age of eighteen. The 1975 Developmental Disabilities Assistance and Bill of Rights Act (94-103) added autism to the categories. The ARC opposed the expansion of disabilities other than mental retardation in the mission of the Division of Mental Retardation, had fought for workshops exclusively for people with mental retardation, and had been unsuccessful in blocking the change of the JLC to the Joint Legislative Committee on Mental Retardation and Cerebral Palsy.

The Willowbrook suit made the United Cerebral Palsy Associations (UCP) a key partner in the state's efforts to depopulate that institution. The state maintained compliance with the court orders by turning over large portions of Willowbrook to the UCP to operate as the Karl Warner Complex. The UCP also opened a large number of apartments and community residences in New York City and, later, upstate. The UCP-Karl Warner episode was important, but there were many other instances where Willowbrook expanded the size and changed the composition of the parent-provider constituency in the state.

Willowbrook and the Nature of Public-Private Relationships

Willowbrook played an important role in shaping an exceptionally important feature of the relationship between the state and private provider agencies. That was the issue of who would control access to vacant beds. The Rothmans describe the agreement between the state and the private agencies in the depopulation of Willowbrook as involving the important incentive of allowing those agencies to fill one-half the newly created beds in community residences and apartments with individuals from their own waiting lists of people living at home. The other 50 percent of the beds were to be filled by Willowbrook residents. The Rothmans do not describe the struggle between the state and these agencies on implementation of this agreement. The most significant and long-lasting impact of the fifty-fifty agreement was the implicit assumption that the private agencies would play the primary, virtually exclusive, role in identifying which individuals from their waiting lists would occupy the new residences.

A substantial number of the community residences and apartments which were approved and funded by the state with the agreement that half of the beds would be filled by Willowbrook class members were filled exclusively or largely from the private agency's own waiting list. Not surprisingly, there are differing views and recollections of how many individuals were involved, which agencies were most egregious in reneging on promises, whether the state (MPU) misrepresented the characteristics and needs of the class members, and other aspects of these events. But the crucial issue was that private agencies, not the state, controlled access. Private agencies made the decisions about the needs of individuals for a residential placement, assessed the level and intensity of service need, and made the decisions about which individuals would be placed in which of their residences. This underlying feature of the strategic agreement between the state and private agencies is less well known but one that the private agencies fiercely defended.

Willowbrook and the Distribution of Consumers and Providers

The failure of the state to build institutions or community services in New York City and the metropolitan area was crucial to the overall lack of congruence between the location of the population and the services they required. The overwhelming bulk of public institutional services were in upstate, largely rural areas. The requirements of the Consent Decree for rapid and large-scale depopulation of Willowbrook resulted in the majority of the residents being transferred to other institutions and later, either directly or as a result of deinstitutionalization of these upstate facilities, placed into community services outside the New York City and metropolitan area. Despite the large number of community programs created in New York City and surrounding counties, the Willowbrook case contributed to an overall imbalance between population and services. Thirty years after Willowbrook, the disproportionately large numbers of consumers and community services in upstate rural counties are the long-term consequences of the depopulation of Willowbrook.

Willowbrook and the Medicalization of Developmental Services

At the same time advocates for people with mental retardation were succeeding in divorcing the administration of services from the dominance of psychiatrists and physicians, Willowbrook contributed to the medicalization of services for people with mental retardation. The constitutional bases of the rulings in the Willowbrook case and their most prominent antecedent, *Wyatt v. Stickney*, were unclear. Whether and to what extent a "right to treatment" (found, but not strictly applied, in *Rouse v. Cameron*), a "constitutional right to receive individual habilitation" *(Wyatt v. Stickney)*, or a "right to protection from harm" (which Judge Orin Judd found in his original rulings in *ARC v. Rockefeller*) was the constitutional basis for the rulings on Willowbrook, the implications for a remedy were even more unclear (Castellani 1975, 1987). Judge Frank Johnson in *Wyatt v. Stickney* reached into case law on the rights of prison inmates to fashion the remedies he ordered the State of Alabama to implement (Castellani 1975, 1987; Yarbrough 1982). It is clear that both Judges Orin Judd and John Bartels in the Willowbrook case expected (or hoped) that their rulings would prod the State of New York to meet federal ICF/MR standards of care. The Consent Decree was fashioned around the Joint Commission for the Accreditation of Hospitals *Standards for Residential Facilities for the Mentally Retarded* and the DHEW *Guidelines for Facilities for the Mentally Retarded* as their base (Rothman and Rothman 1984).

A primary objective of the plaintiffs in *ARC v. Rockefeller* was to close Willowbrook in order to allow people with mental retardation to live lives more in tune with the emerging principles of normalization in communities. Nonetheless, a major consequence of the rulings in the case was to adopt, refine, and implement higher, essentially medical, standards of institutional care. The Willowbrook case, along with the ICF Plan of Compliance, improved and strengthened institutions, at least in the short run, and contributed to the long-term medicalization of developmental services.

Willowbrook was not simply one more episode in the long political conflict between the mental retardation constituency and the state administration. It was not another chapter in the relationship between the ARC and the Rockefeller administration that had been in a rapid downward spiral since the completion of the *Comprehensive Plan* process in 1965. At its outset, it was not a new beginning. It was a final declaration by the mental retardation constituency of the collapse of their confidence that New York was willing or able to address fundamental demands it had been making on behalf of people with mental retardation. Other prosperous states would eventually be sued in federal courts, but the plaintiffs in the *ARC v. Rockefeller* suit were charging that New York shared, in Deutch's phrase, "the shame of the states," with Alabama. one of the poorest and most politically regressive states in the nation. In the distinctive, personalized terms of court cases, Governor Nelson A. Rockefeller, the progressive Republican with presidential ambitions, was charged with denying the most vulnerable citizens of the state their constitutional rights.

David and Sheila Rothman termed *The Willowbrook Wars*, "A Decade of Struggle for Social Justice." Three decades after the filing of the suit, the Willowbrook case continued to play an active role in the administration of developmental services through regular meetings of the Consumer Advisory Board, proposals and complaints by its members and their attorneys, and actions by the Office of Mental Retardation and Developmental Disabilities on behalf of the surviving Willowbrook class members. Over those thirty years, Willowbrook was never far from the center of policy making and implementation.

Medicaid and the Intermediate Care Facilities for the Mentally Retarded Program

Willowbrook and the Medicaid Intermediate Care Facilities for the Mentally Retarded (ICF/MR), working in tandem, had enormous significance for public institutions and the shape and direction of developmental services in New York. There were key features of New York's Medicaid program and its initial implementation that were especially significant.

Medicaid: Four Key Features of New York's Program

The fiscal implications of Medicaid were unknown at the time of its passage by Congress and adoption by New York. Earlier in the book, the immediate realization of the magnitude of the costs of Medicaid to New York State and the federal government was described and cutbacks in eligibility and benefit levels were discussed. The lack of awareness of the potential fiscal *benefits* of Medicaid is illustrated by the following passage from the *Executive Budget, 1966–67*:

> "In 1966–67 it is estimated that the State will receive approximately $6.0 million from these sources [Medicare and Medicaid]. The total amount of Federal funds which will eventually become available to the State from these sources is estimated at $25.0 million" (487).

These benefits of Medicaid began to emerge from the confusing mélange of eligibility requirements, exclusions, cost-sharing arrangements, applications, and administrative mechanisms that Medicaid entailed. Four sets of factors had significant long-term consequences for the financing and organization of developmental services in New York: the waiver of parental liability, local government share in the state's costs, the application of Medicaid in public institutions, and administrative requirements and mechanisms.

Waiver of Parental Liability

New York's Medicaid statute waived familial responsibility for the costs of Medicaid. Children's assets would not be taken into account in establishing the eligibility of a medically indigent parent for Medicaid, nor would their income or assets be tapped to offset any of the costs of Medicaid-funded services once the parents had "spent down" to Medicaid eligibility. The less immediately apparent, but crucial, impact for parents of children with mental retardation was that they would no longer be responsible for a portion of the costs of care for Medicaid-eligible children. The full implications of this watershed change fully blossomed in the 1970s. With the waiver of parental, filial, and spousal fiscal responsibility, Medicaid, enacted as a program for the aged and medically indigent, became a middle-class entitlement.

Local Share

A 25 percent local government share of the costs was another feature of New York's Medicaid program that shaped the organization of developmental services in the state. A local share of costs was an anomaly in comparison to the typical state government-federal government share of costs in almost every other state. In New York State, the 50 percent of the costs not paid by the federal government were split between the state (25 percent) and local governments (25 percent). This local share was a major source of opposition to the program as state legislators protested the impact of the program on local taxes. As the state's experience with Medicaid grew, several reforms aimed at alleviating the full impact of the local share were enacted (e.g., Chapters 620 and 621) which largely exempted local governments from their Medicaid share of former long-term residents of state institutions. Nonetheless, the local share provision remained a part of New York's Medicaid program, and the design, development, and implementation of many Medicaid-funded community services had to be done with an eye to their impact on the local share.

Federal Reimbursement for Institutional Services

From the enactment of the Social Security Act in 1935, federal financial participation (FFP) in the costs of public assistance was prohibited for otherwise eligible persons who were "inmates" of any public or private institution other than a medical institution or were patients or residents of a public or private institution for mental diseases. The Social Security Act did not prohibit federal reimbursement for public assistance paid for persons disabled by mental disorders who were cared for in either general hospitals (including their psychiatric wards) or in private nonspecialized, nonmedical facilities such as boarding homes or child care facilities, or in public or private nursing homes (Boggs 1981).

Medicaid permitted federal financial participation for the costs of care of mentally disabled persons over age 65 in "institutions for mental diseases." However, the definition of "institutions for mental diseases," which had up to that point been broad and inclusive of facilities for the mentally retarded, was narrowed by regulation to public or private mental hospitals offering active treatment (Boggs 1981). The Medicaid statute also permitted inpatient Medicaid coverage of persons otherwise eligible for categorical public assistance who entered skilled nursing facilities meeting federal standards.

The effect of the statute was to provide Medicaid coverage for low-income elderly persons disabled by mental illness as inpatients in public or private specialized psychiatric or general medical facilities. Facilities for the mentally retarded were no longer included as institutions for mental diseases and were considered nonmedical unless they met the standards either for specialized hospitals or skilled nursing homes. Persons in private nonmedical institutions for the mentally retarded could qualify for public assistance and for outpatient medical assistance. However, the same persons in public institutions were not eligible for income maintenance and inpatient coverage under Medicaid. States could recover FFP for indigent elderly and disabled persons who required personal care and were in private congregate facilities and were eligible for Aid to the Permanently and Totally Disabled (APTD), but at much lower rates than patients in Skilled Nursing Facilities (SNFs).

The fiscal incentives and disincentives of where patients were served were immediately apparent to states, and they began to move (or plan to move) large numbers of categorically eligible elderly and disabled adults from facilities not certified by Medicaid into facilities certified as SNFs. Illinois, for example, planned mass transfers of residents of public institutions for the mentally retarded to private nursing homes in order to secure federal reimbursement for their costs of care (Boggs, Lakin, and Clauser 1985). Other states began to convert their institutions for the mentally retarded into SNFs, and many states began moving residents of public institutions into private boarding facilities where their costs of care would be federally reimbursed under APTD and Old Age Assistance (OAA).

New York, along with several other states, did not plan mass transfers but, instead, applied broad eligibility criteria to whom among the residents of their state institutions would be eligible for federal financial participation. In federal fiscal year 1969, New York claimed reimbursement for 12,828 eligible patients in state institutions for the mentally retarded, by far the largest number among the states and almost three times more than those claimed by California (Boggs, Lakin, and Clauser 1985, 1–10). A subsequent review by the federal Government Accounting Office (GAO) found that a large number of the claims states had made were based on deficient applications of eligibility criteria. The GAO also found that states were using broad interpretations of the "maintenance of effort" requirement in order to use federal funds to replace rather than augment state funding for the cost of care in institutions.

It was apparent at the outset that the states' applications of the fiscal incentives in Medicaid were creating unintended consequences. In 1967, Congress authorized payments to states (at Medicaid percentages) for the assistance costs under ATPD and OAA for adults who needed care beyond room and board, but not at Skilled Nursing Facility levels, at an *intermediate* level of care. The adoption and implementation of the Intermediate Care Facilities legislation and regulations will be discussed in more detail later. There were other problematic features of Medicaid statute and regulation that were less apparent than the SNF incentive but which had unintended consequences.

Administrative Responsibility and Mechanisms

New York's appreciation of the fiscal incentives surrounding the application of Medicaid in public and private facilities was bolstered by administrative structures and mechanisms that allowed the state to take advantage of those incentives. In New York's enabling statute, the state Department of Social Services was designated the "single state agency" administering Medicaid as required by the federal regulations. However, New York also devolved significant administrative responsibility over key aspects of the program to the Department of Health and to the Department of Mental Hygiene. This had a significant impact on the direction Medicaid took in New York and on the organization of developmental services in the state (Sparer 1996).

An essential feature of Medicaid is federal reimbursement of the costs of actual services provided by states. While this may seem self-evident, one of the hallmarks of New York's approach to Medicaid was an early recognition of the importance of establishing a large and aggressive cost-finding system. The *Executive Budget* for 1966–67 pointed out that, "The staff of this [Reimbursement] section has been unable to keep abreast of the increased workload caused by increasing admissions and the availability of new sources of revenue such as insurance and pension rights and social security entitlements" (492).

The estimate that Medicaid would eventually produce $25 million a year for New York was belied within months of its implementation. Once the unanticipated magnitude of federal reimbursement for Medicaid services in Department of Mental Hygiene facilities became apparent, this agency moved quickly to set up the machinery to maximize federal financial participation. The *Annual*

Report for 1968 pointed out that, "The department has begun work on a cost reporting-cost distribution system, to be operational September 1, 1970. The system will be designed to collect data on the actual treatment costs for services to individual patients and categories of patients. The purpose of the system is twofold: (1) to provide the accurate cost data demanded by Medicare, Medicaid, and insurance companies in billing for services rendered to individual patients, and (2) to provide the department administration with valuable management reports to assist in making program decisions" (24). The *Annual Report* for 1968 went on to explain that, "As of December 30, 1968, the department had 38,931 patients enrolled in the Title XIX Medicaid program. For the first time, about 12,000 mentally retarded were included under the Federal Government's Aid to the Totally and Permanently Disabled Program. In addition, 1968 was the first year that substantial Medicaid claims for dentures, eyeglasses, and other prosthetic devices were submitted and approved by the Federal government" (24). In 1970, the department reported:

"Another program of central management moved a step forward in 1970, when a schedule of rates for patient services was established. This increased the income to the department from Medicare and Medicaid and was the result of establishing a cost distribution system set up the previous year to produce these rates" (18).

Throughout the successive fiscal crises that marked virtually every New York budget from the late 1960s through the late 1970s, additional positions for the department's Reimbursement Section were added even though hiring freezes and layoffs were ordered for other state employees. In the "austerity budget" of 1969–70, for example, the governor recommended the abolition of 450 positions in the Department of Mental Hygiene but added positions in the agency's Reimbursement Section, noting that "each new reimbursement agent will produce approximately $250,000 in added revenue" (407). As the following table from the *Executive Budget* for 1969–70 shows, the exponential increases in Medicaid as a source of revenue shifted the focus of the Department of Mental Hygiene's Reimbursement Section from extracting fees from the parents of state school and psychiatric hospital residents to maximizing FFP. This became a first principle of operation in the Department of Mental Hygiene that has endured.

There was considerable confusion and uncertainty about how states could employ Medicaid in public institutions. A critical feature of New York's approach to Medicaid was the early development and continued strengthening of a management capacity to maximize federal reimbursement. Whenever and whatever opportunities emerged from the sometimes confusing and overlapping elements of Medicaid, the ICF/MR program, and other new sources of funding, New York State was in a position to take advantage of them. The following table illustrates the early results of this approach.

Table 6.1
Sources of Revenue of the Mental Hygiene Services Fund

	1966–67	*1967–68*	*1968–69*
Direct Fees	41.1	41.5	43.0 (millions)
Medicare	.9	5.2	7.0
Medicaid	33.5	105.3	166.5

Executive Budget, 1969–79, 507

The ICF and ICF/MR Program:
Perverse Incentives with Unintended Consequences

Not only was the Medicaid program rife with unanticipated consequences, but the measures taken to remedy some of its anomalies created additional problems and more unexpected outcomes. The 1967 authorization of an intermediate level of care was a response to the large and increasing number of elderly people admitted to Skilled Nursing Facilities (SNFs) who did not need the medical and nursing services required in this setting. The Congressional Conference report on the 1967 amendments that created the ICF level of care concluded:

> "This amendment could result in a reduction in the costs of Title XIX by enabling States to use lower cost facilities more appropriate to the needs of thousands of persons, thus avoiding the higher charges for skilled nursing homes when care of that kind is not needed." (Boggs, Lakin, and Clauser 1985, 1–14)

Intermediate Care was also viewed as a way to provide services in smaller facilities, which although technically classified as nursing homes, could not meet Title XIX standards for Skilled Nursing Facilities. (Later, the significant unintended consequences of this notion that smaller facilities would be more appropriate will be described.) ICFs were expected to save money by delivering less-costly support in place of expensive medical services in smaller, less capital intensive settings. While the intent seemed clear, advocates and analysts debated its consequences. They had already seen states' plans for transferring large numbers of individuals to proprietary nursing homes to make their costs of care eligible for federal financial participation. They were concerned that states were maximizing Medicaid reimbursement for elderly patients in public and private psychiatric hospitals by diverting funding from institutions for people with mental retardation. But at the same time, advocates were worried that increased federal funding would underwrite the long-term survival of large public institutions. According to several individuals who participated in the debates within the National Association for Retarded Children (NARC), new federal funding was regarded as a potential Faustian bargain.

In 1967, NARC issued a white paper calling on the federal Department of Health, Education, and Welfare (DHEW) to write implementing regulations for the ICF amendment to encourage the development and improvement of public and private ICFs for people with mental retardation and to encourage existing public institutions to provide ICF services (Boggs, Lakin, Clauser 1985). This prompted a series of letters and exchanges between the NARC and DHEW in which DHEW argued that Section 1121 (which authorized ICFs) did not modify prior exclusions of "payments to or care on behalf of any individual who is an inmate of a public institution (except as a patient in a medical institution)" (Boggs, Lakin, and Clauser 1985, 1–19).

Despite the apparent setback dealt by DHEW and Congress to broad interpretations of the applicability of ICF funding in public institutions, advocates continued to press the case under the umbrella of the general welfare reform efforts underway at the time. According to Boggs, Lakin, and Clauser (1985), in meetings with Secretary Wilbur Cohen and his staff at DHEW, a working group from NARC (which included Elizabeth Boggs) argued that states paying for SNF level nursing care in public institutions were displacing funds needed for less costly rehabilitation under a "developmental model" of care.

There was nothing in the track record of private proprietary nursing homes that indicated they were superior to publicly administered care. The states' expenditures to upgrade mental hospitals to meet standards required for federal Medicaid reimbursement for eligible over-65 populations was diverting funds from needed improvements in public institutions for the mentally retarded. Advocates saw the 1967 ICF legislation as a potential model for flexible nonmedical residential services, which if made available in public as well as private institutions which met appropriate federal standards, would result in substantial improvements in the quality of care for residents.

In 1970, in the context of Congress' consideration of President Nixon's sweeping welfare reform proposal, the Senate added a new Section 269(b) to the statute which added intermediate care to the list of services fundable at state option under Medicaid and authorizing inclusion of public institutions for the retarded as ICFs as long as recipients were receiving "active treatment" and the non-federal expenditures for these eligible recipients was not reduced because of federal reimbursement.

There was no agreement between the House and Senate on the welfare reform legislation that included the new Section 269(B) in1970, but in December 1971, Congress passed PL 92-223 that, effective January 1, 1972, added a new optional service to Medicaid by transferring "intermediate care facility services for the mentally retarded and persons with related conditions" to the Title XIX program.

Implementing Regulations

The federal Social and Rehabilitation Service announced the availability of intermediate care services under Medicaid in early 1972, covering those services under preexisting regulations. However, it would January 1974 before DHEW would issue final ICF/MR regulations as the federal government, state governments, and advocates debated various low, moderate, and stringent standards for ICF/MR participation. The regulations that were issued in January 1974 contained over one hundred specific standards of compliance and established what most participants agreed was a moderate level of standards for participation (Boggs, Lakin, and Clauser 1985).

Once again, this new element of the Medicaid program had many anomalies and uncertainties that resulted in unintended consequences that had strategic importance for the direction and shape of developmental services in New York and other states. By adopting more than minimum standards for participation, DHEW assumed that most participating states would have to make substantial improvements in the physical plants of public institutions in order to comply. The most problematic regulations for states were those permitting no more than four beds to a room and a minimum of 60 square feet per occupant. Recognizing that this would require some time, DHEW issued an interim set of regulations in 1974 that would require the states to meet the minimum acceptable standards of participation by March 1977 (Boggs, Lakin, and Clauser 1985). The interim standards also covered administrative policies and procedures, resident living standards, and professional services requirements. Congress and NARC advocates expected that the statutory requirement for "active treatment" would replace custodial care with training and habilitation and establish standards for quality of care in public institutions that had come under increasing negative scrutiny. Advocates had managed to build at least the skeleton of the developmental model into the Congressional record which referenced such key elements as individual participation, medical, social, and psychological evaluations, written plans of care with specific goals and objectives, annual reviews, and post-institutional plans.

Boggs, Lakin, and Clauser (1985) argue that "this amendment [PL 92-223] was a relatively little noted addendum to the section transferring authority for federal financial participation in the cost of vendor payments for certain aged and disabled recipients of public welfare from Title XI of the Social Security Act to Title XIX," and was "not much heralded at the time" (1985, 1-1). However, like its umbrella Medicaid, the ICF/MR program would have an unforeseen and large fiscal impact on the federal government and would be a primary force shaping the organization of developmental services in

New York. That was a result of the cumulative impact of at least ten anomalous, but crucial, factors built into it that created large unintended consequences in New York's and many other states' ICF/MR programs.

Ten Congenital Anomalies

First, one of the most important features of the ICF/MR program was that states that were receiving the federal reimbursement for the operation of public institutions as ICFs/MR, were also charged with the initial certification of these facilities as meeting the federal standards.

Second, the states receiving the federal reimbursement were also required to undertake the quality assurance monitoring of their own operations to maintain certification and federal reimbursement. While "look behind" audits by federal surveyors eventually provided some occasional outside oversight, they could not compensate for the initial certification of the facilities and the structural incentives of states monitoring their own activities.

Third, the ICF/MR program carried forward the Medicaid principle of "reasonable cost-related reimbursement" for federal financial participation. However, there was little or no reliable data on the costs of providing care for individuals in the institutions and facilities that were now becoming ICFs/MR since state budgets and appropriations were not accurate measures of actual costs. Clauser, Rotegard, and White (1985) examined various approaches to cost finding taken by states in their ICF/MR rate methodologies and found wide variations in the ways states established cost centers and assigned and allocated costs. The absence of clear and uniform guidelines left great discretion to states, like New York, who took aggressive and broad approaches to "reasonable costs" to be reimbursed by the federal government.

Fourth, the ICF/MR program was new and evolving, requiring upgraded physical plants and new types, levels, and intensity of professional and ancillary services. For much of the early implementation of the ICF/MR program, states designed their own programs under interim regulations. Final regulations adopted years following the initiation of the ICF/MR program had to be applied in the context of large state programs already underway.

Fifth, many states used private, for-profit providers to deliver ICF/MR services, and a strong underlying assumption in the design of the program was that states would proceed to contain the costs generated by their rate-setting methodologies. However, the cost-saving incentive largely evaporated when states operated their own ICFs/MR.

Sixth, the states could choose from a variety of rate-setting methodologies that had different consequences for the costs generated and reimbursed by the federal government. New York adopted a prospective reimbursement methodology, which, at the time, was generally assumed to have more cost-containment incentives than a retrospective cost methodology. In fact, Clauser, Rotegard, and White (1985) cited New York's rate-setting and reimbursement system as "an attempt to slow system growth and contain program costs" (8–7). However, prospective systems with generous inflation adjustments and high percentile ceilings can have an opposite effect, and the history of what actually occurred in New York demonstrated the unanticipated impact of New York's choice.

Seventh, Congress and NARC advocates expected the requirement for "active treatment" to replace custodial care with training and habilitation and establish standards for quality of care for institutions. The legislation creating the ICF/MR program authorized federal funding for the purpose of providing health *or* rehabilitative services, but the ICF/MR, a subset of Medicaid, quickly became a medical model of services.

Eighth, advocates argued that the legislative history of the ICF/MR program showed that the federal government never intended the program to provide comprehensive funding for an entire residential service system, both institution *and* community. However, the original regulations implementing the 1971 amendments provided not only for large institutional settings but also for facilities of "four or more" individuals. Moreover, the 1974 regulations established ICF/MR categories of those housing sixteen or more or those housing fifteen or less residents and included more flexible regulatory stipulations for the fifteen or less category. Congress and advocates expected that the ICF/MR program would remove incentives for placement of residents of public institutions into private ICFs solely to claim federal reimbursement. However, it is unlikely anyone anticipated New York's wholesale conversion of its public and private community programs to the "small" ICF/MR program.

Ninth, it is clear that Congress intended the ICF/MR program to act as an incentive for states to upgrade both the physical plants of public institutions as well as provide enhanced care and habilitative services under the rubric of "active treatment." The ICF/MR program would provide the funds for states to upgrade care in public institutions for people with mental retardation by offsetting part of the costs of institutional care, but federal funds were intended to augment, not supplant, state funds (Boggs, Lakin, and Clauser 1985). With the overall costs of institutional care growing at double-digit rates at the time, no one was able to reliably calculate (or challenge) whether and to what extent states were using federal ICF/MR funds as a substitute for state tax dollars.

Tenth, and finally, the ICF/MR program was originally created as a cost-saving measure for individuals who did not need the skilled nursing level of care. The legislative and regulatory history surrounding the creation, implementation, and early development of the program did not contain any recognition of the possibility that a state would find that *spending* rather than saving money would have important political and economic benefits. The opportunity to *find* costs that could then be shared with the federal government would be the most rational operational, political, and economic approach to the understanding that "Every dollar of expenditure is someone's dollar of income" (Castellani 1987, 50).

Each of these anomalies had significant and long-term consequences. The fundamental fiscal dynamics that support the organization of developmental services in New York (including the persistence of large and small, public and private institutions) were established in the confusing context of statute, regulation, and implementation that marked the establishment of the basic structure of federal and state fiscal relations in this area. The history of statute, regulation, and oversight by the federal government for the next twenty-five years were, in many respects, attempts to remedy the congenital errors committed during the early period. New York's relationship with the federal government from the 1970s was, in many respects, an effort to preserve and enhance the advantages in the flawed design the state perceived and built into its financing and organization of public institutions and developmental services.

Part 3

The Big Bang

Chapter 7

Creating a New Universe of Developmental Services in New York State

And you didn't even ask me what OPM stands for: Other People's Money.

—Garfinkle, *Other People's Money*

The forces that created the institutional crises that erupted at Willowbrook and New York's fiscal collapse finally broke apart the century-old foundations of services for people with developmental disabilities. But rather than spinning away from each other into separate institutional and community systems (as happened in many other states) the major elements in New York coalesced in a series of revolutionary changes between the early and late 1970s.

Adversaries became allies. Advocates became providers. Public institution employees delivered community services. Entirely new administrative arrangements at the state and local level were put into place. Significant policy and operational responsibilities were devolved to private entities. Costs became sources of reimbursement and engines of local economic development. The entire system of public and private, institutional and community services was refinanced with federal funds. A new universe of developmental services was created.

The critical events of the 1970s occurred with such speed that key actors were often surprised by how quickly large-scale change took place. Many of the most significant effects of policy decisions were unintended and unanticipated. Statutes designed to address the needs of the poor became middle-class entitlements. Reimbursement mechanisms intended to save money created incentives for states to spend money. Regulations intended to create nonmedical habilitative alternatives to institutions reinforced clinical and medical models of services.

Radical changes in this field were obscured by the economic and political turmoil in the state and nation. The country was wracked by the Watergate

155

scandal, and the resignation of President Richard Nixon in 1972 had an enormous impact on New York when President Gerald Ford selected Governor Nelson Rockefeller to be his vice president. The political turmoil continued as it became evident that Lieutenant Governor Malcolm Wilson's ascension to the governor's office would be as short-lived as Rockefeller's tenure as vice president. The state's chronic deficits of the early 1970s would pale in comparison to the fiscal crises that gripped New York City and New York State in 1975.

Federal financing of developmental services was crucial to the changes that took place. However, Medicaid, Supplemental Security Income, and the Intermediate Care Facilities and Intermediate Care Facilities for the Mentally Retarded programs had unclear and overlapping boundaries and perverse applications with respect to which individuals were eligible for what services in what settings. New federal funding had important, but often uncertain, consequences for state funding of institution and community programs, parental fees, and state and local shares of the costs of services. New types of funding for private agencies had complex linkages to other federal and state financing and important implications for key features of rapidly expanding community services.

The significant changes that took place during this critical period were often on parallel, but linked, tracks, and the linkages were not always apparent. The Willowbrook Consent Decree and the ICF/MR Plan of Compliance were the twin engines of deinstitutionalization and the creation of new community services, and these were mirrored by agreements among the state and its public employee unions, the state and local governments, and the state and existing private provider agencies. The creation of a new universe overlapped and was entwined with the collapse of the old system. As the Willowbrook Wars were being fought, the adversaries were moving toward a historic compromise that would dramatically alter the political foundation of developmental services for the remainder of the twentieth century. However, as adversaries battled, formed new alliances, and planned a new political order, they had to identify and make decisions about what remnants of the old could be discarded, what could be refashioned, and what could be melded with new components. New and complex systems of budgeting, rate-setting, and capital financing of public and private, institution and community services were put into place. Various financial instruments and mechanisms operated in a new environment of overlapping intergovernmental and interorganizational environments.

Each of these forces and factors created uncertainty, conflict, and opportunity. The importance of New York's experience was that state and local government policy makers and the developmental disabilities constituency groups fashioned a strategy. The approach was strategic because, by pulling together existing instruments, developing new organizational frameworks, and designing new fiscal techniques and mechanisms, New York aimed at rearranging the fundamental ways of financing and organizing developmental services. The four main objectives of this strategy were established early. They were to: (1) shift the costs of developmental services to the federal government, (2) create and finance a strong network of private community agencies, (3) minimize the financial impact on local governments, and (4) use federally financed state and private agency employment to maintain and enhance local economies. These goals would be achieved by *spending*, not saving, other people's money.

Deinstitutionalization was the framework within which most of these changes occurred. This large-scale movement of the residents of public institutions to group homes and day services in communities will be described in the next chapter. This chapter will describe the fiscal, administrative, and organizational foundations on which deinstitutionalization rested and explain how why the decisions and actions taken had long-term consequences.

The Five-Year ICF Plan of Compliance and the Creation of Statewide Community Services

The Willlowbrook suit led to a substantial increase in community services in New York City and the metropolitan area, but the growth of these services was neither sufficient nor appropriate to the needs of all class members, especially as private agencies filled many of the new community residences with individuals who had been living at home. While Willowbrook was the focus of public attention and court action, the other nineteen state schools remained severely overcrowded and unable to meet the demands of the waiting list. The conversion of the state schools to ICFs/MR also aggravated the capacity problem since they were not in compliance with the federal regulations under which they were operating. These problems were systemic and statewide, and despite the importance of the Willowbrook suit, it would be the ICF Plan of Compliance, along with the mechanisms crucial to its implementation, that would result in the rapid deinstitutionalization of the state schools and creation of community services across the entire state.

The features of New York's ICF Plan of Compliance and the decisions that worked with the Willowbrook Consent Decree included the bold approach the plan took, new leadership in the Division of Mental Retardation (and later the Office of Mental Retardation and Developmental Disabilities), and key changes in administrative approaches and mechanisms for certifying and managing developmental services statewide and at the local level.

New York's Broad and Bold Approach to an ICF Plan of Compliance

Between the issuance of the interim ICF/MR regulations in 1972 to the adoption of final ICF/MR regulations in 1974, New York converted its state schools to ICFs/MR and billed the federal government for the "reasonable allowable costs" of operating this new program. DHEW had acknowledged the difficulties states would have in converting their public institutions to the new physical plant configurations required by the regulations. New York made little progress on meeting the requirements of the interim regulations, especially the requirements of no more than four beds to a room and a minimum of 60 square feet per occupant. In fact, most states made little progress toward compliance (Boggs, Lakin, and Clauser 1985).

From 1972 to the adoption of the final regulations in 1974, the census in New York's state schools (now ICFs/MR) dropped from 25,866 to 21,460 (DMH 1972, 1975). In 1974, following the requirements of the final regulations, New York filed its Five Year Plan of Compliance with DHEW, expecting to join the overwhelming majority of the other states in negotiating extensions of the deadlines for compliance. New York's position was especially precarious because its budget deficits were again approaching crisis proportions, and the state was not spending the funds necessary to bring the institutions into compliance even though federal reimbursements for these ICFs/MR had increased to over $125 million a year (*Executive Budget* 1975).

New York faced the threat of losing the $125 million in federal reimbursement now generated by the state schools, but it could not afford the cost of bringing 20,000 beds into compliance with ICF/MR standards. Meeting the minimum ICF/MR occupancy space requirements would also mean that over 2,000 beds would have to be phased out. Moreover, overcrowding in the facilities virtually erased the state's ability to reconstruct the facilities to meet the standards because there was not sufficient space to do the required renovations with the residents still in the buildings—a lack of "turn around space" as it came to be called.

With these circumstances as the background, New York turned from a reactive to a proactive posture. The New York State ICF/MR Plan of Compliance committed the state to renovating only those state school buildings with long-term residential value. This would require moving 8,800 residents from the state schools to community residential programs within five years— community residential programs that did not exist. This broad and bold approach rested on several factors: a new governor and administration, new leadership in the Division of Mental Retardation, the large fiscal liability noncompliance presented, and the requirements of the Willowbrook Consent Decree. This contained high risks, but gave the state more latitude in implementation than the more cautious and reactive strategies pursued by most states. It was an approach that would be repeated thirteen years later in the decision to close several developmental centers.

New Leadership

Congressman Hugh Carey was elected Governor of New York in November 1974, defeating Malcolm Wilson who had succeeded Nelson Rockefeller. During the campaign Carey had formed an alliance with key mental retardation constituents, especially those involved in the Willowbrook Case, and his election signaled a resolution of the suit favorable to the plaintiffs. Indeed, shortly after taking office in January 1975, Carey directed the state's attorneys to negotiate a Consent Decree which established the framework for the depopulation of Willowbrook. The new leadership in the Department of Mental Hygiene's Division of Mental Retardation decided to apply the basic guidelines of the Consent Decree statewide. This universality was an important feature in the overall organization of community developmental services because, in contrast to early deinstitutionalization in many other states, it required that day as well as residential services be established for each individual moving from the institutions to community programs.

Governor Carey also changed the administration in the Department of Mental Hygiene (DMH), naming Dr. Lawrence Kolb Commissioner to replace Dr. Alan Miller. In September 1975, Thomas Coughlin was appointed as Deputy Commissioner for Mental Retardation in the department. Coughlin's appointment was made directly by Carey, not Kolb. It was made with the understanding that Coughlin—a former State Trooper, parent of a daughter with mental retardation, leader in the ARC, and an active participant in Carey's campaign—was to run the Division of Mental Retardation as a largely autonomous entity within DMH until the promised legislation creating a separate mental retardation agency could be passed.

With a strong personality and the backing of the governor's office, Coughlin quickly linked with the new cadre of mental retardation professionals who had joined the department from outside and had been chafing under the mental hygiene yoke. Coughlin also brought into the division several individuals who had been managers of community agencies in New York and other states.

Administrative and Operational Factors

Several administrative and operational factors were also important in the implementation of the Five Year Plan of Compliance: control over the budget, rate setting, certification, and quality assurance monitoring; a local management structure and approach; and enhanced management capacity.

The Division of Mental Retardation had been gaining autonomy within the department for several years before Coughlin's appointment, but in many critical areas the division remained subordinate in the mental health orientation of the department. Control over its budget was the most problematic. During the Rockefeller administration, the governor's *Executive Budget* moved away from a detailed line item format (listing each position and specific category of expenditure) to more general areas of expenditure. The appropriations bills passed by the legislative followed this flexible and ostensibly progressive budgetary approach. The effect was to give the executive greater latitude to move funds among expenditure categories. Through the fiscal crises of the late 1960s and early 1970s, millions of dollars budgeted and appropriated in mental retardation accounts were underspent and, towards the end of the fiscal year, transferred to mental health areas of the budget or outside the department altogether. Coughlin had the mental retardation section of the department's budget office report directly to him, and the transfer of funds out of mental retardation accounts ceased. This budget control would become crucial when the DMR, and later OMRDD, began using Purchase of Services contracts to expand community services.

Another significant administrative change Coughlin instituted was the creation of District Developmental Services Offices (DDSO). The DDSOs were intended to bypass county governments, which had been given primary local funding and operational roles by the state's 1954 Community Mental Health Act, and which, twenty years later, were doling out a meager 13 percent of total state aid to local mental retardation programs (LCER, 1973b). Coughlin and the new leadership wanted nothing to do with counties. The DDSO Director was the Director of the Developmental Center (former state school), the Director of State-Operated Community Services, and responsible for management and oversight of the privately operated services in that district. Centered on each of the developmental centers, the scope of the directors' responsibility was focused on one institution and state and privately operated community services in geographic areas substantially smaller than the huge areas covered by DMH's one New York City and three upstate regional offices.

The DDSO directors had the primary management responsibility for services in their locales, but they were well-staffed with managers from their inception, which typically included Deputy Directors for Administration, Quality Assurance, Community Services, and Institutional Services. The availability of a substantial number of well-paid senior management positions in twenty DDSOs was a major attraction to recruitment and quickly provided the local management capacity to implement deinstitutionalization and development of state and private agency community programs required by the Plan of Compliance.

Control of Certification, Rate-Setting and Quality Assurance

In contrast to most other states in which certification, rate-setting, and quality assurance were separated from the operational agencies, New York effectively centralized those functions in the Department of Mental Hygiene, effectively the DMR (Sparer 1996). Although it was the agency New York formally designated as its single state Medicaid agency, the Department of Social Services allowed the DMR to do its own surveys for certification of the ICFs/MR. In the state's original structuring of its Medicaid program, the Department of Health was given (to its surprise) a role in quality assurance monitoring (Benjamin and Hurd 1984). However, DMH (later OMRDD) quality assurance teams monitored the private agency programs. Rate setting was exclusively in the Department of Mental Hygiene, and Coughlin quickly moved to separate and bolster that already significant capacity in the Division of Mental Retardation. The combination and concentration of program certification, quality assurance, and rate setting within the Division of Mental Retardation was crucial to the division's ability to rapidly implement community programs needed to meet the Plan of Compliance.

The Division of Mental Retardation also hired the person in the federal Health Care Financing Administration (HCFA) who had played the lead role in writing the ICF/MR regulations. This helped ensure that New York State would develop the ICF/MR programs consistent with HCFA regulations and would also enhance its position on differences of opinion between the state and federal government on the meaning or intent of those regulations. The Division of Mental Retardation also retained a leading Washington law firm to represent its interests with the federal government and contracted with a major accounting firm to assist in calculating rates and undertaking supporting fiscal analyses.

Financing the Rapid Expansion of Community Service

The Willowbrook Consent Decree and the ICF Plan of Compliance committed the State of New York to the creation of a very large number of new community residential and day programs within a very short time. The targets were relatively clear, but, in 1974 and 1975, there was still limited experience in establishing these programs, and the fiscal and organizational frameworks that would be required to meet those targets were embryonic at best.

Almost twenty years after the passage of the Community Mental Health Services Act in 1954, community programs for people with mental retardation, other than public schools, were almost exclusively workshops and related day services operated by ARC chapters. The framework for the acquisition and construction of hostels by the Department of Mental Hygiene was established in 1966. The first hostel opened in 1968, but by 1972 there were only twelve hostels operating in the state. Although $1.5 million was appropriated in the 1971–72 state budget for fifteen additional hostels, a decrease in the Local Assistance portion of the budget and the state's fiscal crisis did not hold promise for a rapid increase in state financing for community residential development (DMH 1973; LCER 1975; ARC 1989).

Supplemental Security Income (SSI)

The federal Supplemental Security Income (SSI) program became an important source of funding for community residential programs, especially at a time when New York State's fiscal crisis severely constrained the amount of state funds that could be channeled into new services (Berkowitz 1987). Under SSI, monthly payments provided a personal allowance of $25 per month to eligible persons living in state institutions (Boggs 1985). However, substantially higher congregate care payments were allowed for room and board for persons living in state or private community residences. States were allowed to add supplements to the basic federal rate, and New York did provide a supplement to the federal payment. Another especially important feature of SSI was that instead of reimbursing states for a percentage of their expenditures, which was the case in the various aid to the aged, blind, and disabled prior to SSI, the SSI benefit was paid directly to the eligible recipient (or his/her designee). SSI payments made directly to the residents of group homes provided sufficient funding to allow private agencies to begin to expand at a more rapid pace than they had under the state's hostel program.

State Aid to Community Residences and Community Residence Contracts

Community Residences, which supplanted "hostel" in the terminology, became the primary community residential program until the creation of small ICFs/MR in the late 1970s. Under the regular state aid formula that had been in effect since the 1954 Community Mental Health Services Act, the local governments were reimbursed for 50 percent of the net operating costs of each program. Local governments, however, had provided paltry funding for mental retardation programs even after the state paid them in advance rather than reimbursing them for funds already spent (OMRDD 1979).

The 1972 legislation that created Section 41.33 of the New York State Mental Hygiene Law provided for state aid grants for up to a maximum of 50 percent of the operating expenses of Community Residences. The state provided one-half the operating budget of the Community Residence, and the resident's SSI provided the other 50 percent. Overall funding for the program depended on yearly appropriations, and funding for specific Community Residences was executed through annual contracts between the Department of Mental Hygiene and the operating private agency.

Chapters 620 and 621

Based on New York's per capita income at the time of the creation of Medicaid, the federal share of New York's overall expenditures in the program was set at 50 percent. However, New York was one of only twelve states that required its local governments to share in the costs of Medicaid, requiring local governments to contribute 25 percent of the total cost. This cost-sharing element of New York's Medicaid program had an impact on the design and implementation of Medicaid services since their inception in 1966.

Recognizing that local governments would resist the implementation of programs that had a local fiscal impact, in 1974 the legislature passed one of the first statutes that exempted a local government share to facilitate the development and expansion of Community Residences. Since a substantial number of the individuals living in Community Residences had been in state schools and were Medicaid-eligible, Chapters 620 and 621 provided for state assumption of all county Medicaid costs for residents who had resided in a state institution for five or more years, approximately 95 percent of developmental center residents (OMRDD 1979). This legislation removed an important fiscal impediment to the expansion of Community Residences.

New Funding and Mechanisms for Spending for Developmental Services

SSI was an important new source of federal funding, but it alone had not fueled the amount of new programs necessary to meet the targets of the Consent Decree or the Plan of Compliance. State Aid to Community Residences had been negligible, and Chapters 620 and 621 were not themselves a source of funding but rather mechanisms to exempt localities from sharing in the costs of Medicaid-financed programs. Despite the extreme fiscal crisis the state faced, funding for developmental services did rise substantially from the mid-1970s (Martiniano 1984; McClelland and Magdovitz 1981; *Executive Budgets* 1970–1980; LCER 1980; 1986). However, the Consent Decree and the Plan of Compliance had diffuse statewide effects on where appropriated funds were spent. Coughlin's commitment to extend most of the Consent Decree stipulations statewide also made it virtually impossible to tie specific increases to the Decree, the Plan, or an enhanced commitment to fund services for people with mental retardation. New funds could be appropriated, but meeting the specific targets of the Decree and the Plan required that they be expended quickly.

Purchase of Services Contracts

Purchase of Services (POS) contracts between the state and private agencies were arguably the most important mechanism in the rapid expansion of community programs during the mid- to late 1970s. The head of the Metropolitan Placement Unit, Barbara Blum, had used foundation grants to fund Purchase of Services contracts during her tenure with the New York City Department of Special Services for Children as a vehicle for providing start-up funds for small agencies to open group homes for homeless children (Rothman and Rothman 1984). The Carey administration continued the use of broad "Maintenance Undistributed" (MU) budgets that provided latitude and flexibility within broad categories of funding, and it saw Purchase of Services (POS) contracts fitting nicely into this approach. In the 1976–1977 fiscal year, New York began to appropriate funds for "purchase of services" (*Executive Budget* 1976–77).

As an OMRDD report explained, "Purchase of service is designed as a temporary funding mechanism to foster the development of new community services and provide full funding for clients placed into those programs until they can be assimilated under a standard funding formula" (OMRDD 1979, 23–24). These POS contracts were in addition to the regular 41.13 contracts that funded Community Residences.

OMRDD had almost unprecedented latitude in how much could be paid in the POS contract and for what purposes. Each budget-based contract was negotiated separately and was based primarily on the staffing needs of the individuals being served, but could vary widely depending on start-up costs, capital costs, and other projected expenditures. Very quickly, POS contracts became the vehicle for funneling large amounts of funds to private agencies. By the late 1970s, POS contacts had become critical to underwriting many private agencies on-going as well as start-up costs. This reliance on POS contracts that resulted in a major restructuring of the financing of community programs will be discussed later in this chapter. However, between 1976 and 1980, POS contracts were the primary fiscal mechanism for funding a rapid expansion of community programs.

Purchase-Lease/Loan of Community Facilities

Purchase of Services contracts were not the only fiscal mechanisms Coughlin and his executive team used to finance the rapid expansion of community programs. Private agency operating costs could be reimbursed through contracts, but the costs of property acquisition could not be included. The statutory and fiscal frameworks for reimbursing private agencies for the acquisition of property were virtually nonexistent. Many of the early community residences operated by the private agencies were in properties purchased by the

State of New York and loaned to the agency for its use without cost. Many "community" agencies operated (rent and maintenance free) out of state developmental centers.

Rapid expansion of community programs, however, would require that private agencies acquire their own property as private entities rather than waiting for the state to go through the lengthy and cumbersome process involved in acquisition of property by the state. However, these small parent-run agencies usually did not have funds available for the purchase of property. To circumvent this problem, private agencies were encouraged to set up subsidiary corporations solely for the purpose of purchasing property to lease to the parent agency, which could then include the cost of the lease as a reimbursable operating expense in POS or 41.13 contracts. The difference between the costs of acquisition and what agencies included in their contracts as lease expenditures paid to their subsidiaries proved to be such a lucrative source of income for agencies that within a few years, more than 50 percent of all agencies funded by OMRDD were using related property companies. A subsequent audit by the Office of State Comptroller charged that many not-for-profit agencies were earning substantial profits by leasing space at excessive rental rates (OSC 1990). However, in the late 1970s, this fiscal mechanism not only facilitated the acquisition of property for the rapid expansion of community programs but was also a new source of funding for private agencies.

Technical Assistance and Shared Staffing

The state provided extensive technical assistance to private agencies that was critical to their creation, early survival, and eventual expansion. "Shared staffing" was the euphemism used to describe the large numbers of state employees (direct care workers, clinicians, program administrators, and support staff) who were simply assigned to work in the private agencies' residential and day programs. Many of these state employees worked in private agencies for years, supplementing and substituting for private agency staff. Extraordinary amounts of "technical assistance" were also crucial to the creation and early survival of private agencies as OMRDD attorneys drew up incorporation papers and handled the bulk of legal work associated with getting new agencies underway. OMRDD fiscal and budget staff worked with the agencies to set up payroll, accounting, billing, and other financial management mechanisms, often operating these systems for extended periods of time. In addition to the staffing and technical assistance, many of private agencies used state staff and resources in the developmental centers as integral components of their programs. Medical, dental, and auxiliary health services based in the developmental centers were routinely provided to the clients of private agencies. "Shared staffing" was also an early mechanism for using federal Medicaid funding in community programs. The state staff that was being "shared" with private agency (as well as state community) programs was institution staff financed increasingly through Medicaid reimbursement.

Creating the Private and Public Community Organizational Infrastructure

The notion of an "incubator" was not abroad during the 1970s, but the blurred distinctions between the state and many fledgling private agencies often fit this pattern. The state needed a rapid and large-scale expansion of residential and day programs in the community in order to meet the targets of the Consent Decree and the Plan of Compliance, but expansion required an organizational infrastructure within which they could be created and grow. Two organizational changes that had enormous impact on the growth of services were the expansion of parent-run and other community groups into a statewide provider network of agencies and the use of state-operated community programs.

Expansion of Existing vis-à-vis the Creation of New Private Agencies

In 1974, in addition to state institutions and community programs, there were 101 private agencies providing residential and day services (Castellani et al. 1995). Twenty years later in 1994, even with a large increase in total number of private agencies, the 101 "original" private agencies accounted for 75.8 percent of the total residential, day, and waiver enrollments in the state (Castellani et al. 1995). In implementing the Willowbrook Consent Decree and ICF Plan of Compliance, New York chose to increase its residential and day community services capacity largely by expanding the agencies that were in existence at the time the period of rapid growth began. This contrasted with policies in many other states that limited the size of agencies and expanded community services by adding new agencies (Castellani 2000). Moreover, New York differed from most other states in the mid-1970s in that its private agencies (primarily the ARCs) had chosen to operate services in addition to acting as advocacy and parent support organizations.

New York also did not restrict agencies to the operation of one type of service (again in contrast to many other states). Private agencies in New York began providing day programs (typically workshops and educational programs), expanded into residential programs, and later added family support, transportation, and a variety of other services as they grew. The exigencies of the Willowbrook Consent Decree and the ICF Plan of Compliance made moving residents out of institutions and into community services as quickly

Made in the USA
Las Vegas, NV
24 February 2022

44452303R10115

as possible the primary consideration. If that could be achieved more quickly and efficiently by having the same agency provide both the day and the residential services, then that was what was done. As difficulties of placing Willowbrook class members in New York City and metropolitan area agencies were encountered, the state directed and coordinated the movement of large numbers of class members to existing small private agencies upstate. These individuals became the base on which very large complexes of residential and day services were built in rural areas. In this "big bang" approach to creating the universe of providers, rapid expansion was achieved by expanding those agencies present at the beginning.

State Operated Community Programs: The Morgado Memorandum

Besides the expansion of existing private agencies New York also created a large number of state-operated community residential and day programs. This decision to create a dual, public and private, system of community services was not the outcome of careful planning but the result of a combination of situational and political considerations that demanded a quick resolution. Nonetheless, as the pieces were being put in place, the strategic consequences of the decision were widely understood and agreed upon.

Two factors have already been discussed. The first was that community residential and day programs were not being created in numbers large enough or quickly enough to meet the deadlines of the Willowbrook Consent Decree and the ICF Plan of Compliance. The pace of development in the private agencies was still too slow—and made slower once the option of using proprietary nursing homes was removed by the Bergman-Willowbrook scandal. The second related factor was that public employees were already working in increasing numbers and roles in community programs—in "shared staffing," technical assistance, clinical, and various other roles, especially in agencies upstate. In New York City, it was becoming apparent to public employees and their unions that the downsizing of Willowbrook would ultimately mean the loss of jobs at that institution. These factors were the proximate causes of the decision to formally create state-operated and staffed community programs.

Willowbrook was again the catalyst. The spark that set off the firestorm that would result in the strategic decision was Gouverneur. Gouverneur was a dilapidated hospital in Manhattan into which 160 very disabled children from Willowbrook had been moved. The abysmal conditions and threat of condemnation by the fire department forced a search for an alternate site. The Gouverneur Parents Association had become a very vocal and politically active organization. They blocked the parceling out of the residents to various other centers and were successful in getting the Consent Decree Review Panel and the state to look for another a site for the entire group.

At this time, the Roman Catholic Archdiocese of New York was seeking to operate a medical school. The diocese proposed taking over New York Medical College (a private institution in serious financial difficulty) and merging it with the diocese's Flower and Fifth Avenue Hospital to create the medical school. This was facilitated by the fact that Westchester County, where the medical college's Mental Retardation Institute (MRI) clinic was located on the grounds of the county medical complex at Valhalla, and the New York State Facilities Development Corporation, the successor of the Health and Mental Hygiene Facilities Improvement Corporation, were among those to whom the medical college owed large amounts of money.

The governor's office brokered a complex plan which brought the several parties together and revolved around the proposal to have MRI operate "showcase" clinical services for the Gouverneur residents at Flower Fifth Avenue Hospital in which the key component was to allow New York Medical College and MRI to operate the program at $250 a day per individual—double the current reimbursement rate—on the basis of the extraordinary needs of these individuals. The income generated by that high reimbursement rate would allow the archdiocese to purchase New York Medical College and the hospital. The Gouverneur parents would have their children moved to Flower Fifth Avenue Hospital, the archdiocese would have its medical school, New York Medical College and MRI would be bailed out, and the FDC and Westchester County would be repaid.

The impending deal infuriated the public employee unions who had already mounted a loud and public campaign against the state's policy of deinstitutionalization. Although virtually all individuals moving out of developmental centers were placed in highly structured day and residential programs, early signs of homelessness and people with mental illness on the streets and in Single Room Occupancy hotels were painted with the broad brush of "dumping." Public employees saw their jobs threatened while mental patients were being "dumped" on the streets and private institutions were being "bailed out."

Other problems with rapid deinstitutionalization contributed to the use of state-operated community residences. A substantial proportion of the residents of Willowbrook were minorities as well as being profoundly and severely disabled. The core of many of the community agencies consisted of white parents who had kept their relatively less-disabled children at home. While many community agencies welcomed clients regardless of racial and ethnic background, some agencies were reluctant to serve individuals with different backgrounds. OMRDD had limited success in encouraging the creation of new minority-operated agencies in New York City. The problems of start-up were especially difficult, and this was compounded by the lack of experience these new as well as established community agencies had in dealing with profoundly and severely disabled individuals now coming to them.

Other kinds of problems arose. For example, in some upstate areas the leadership of ARC chapters was made up of older, working-class parents who were reluctant to become involved in rapid expansion to serve individuals coming out of the developmental centers. In some of these areas, the state reached out to newer United Cerebral Palsy Association chapters where the membership and leadership had more professional-business middle-class background. Several of these agencies proved to be much more entrepreneurial in expanding their programs by serving not only their children who had been at home but individuals coming out of local developmental centers, and later, individuals moving from the New York metropolitan area. None of these issues stopped the rapid growth of community services, but institution-at home, racial, ethnic, class, and age factors were important in setting the stage for the use of state-operated Community Residences and the movement upstate of individuals from the New York metropolitan area.

Under increasing pressure on all these problems during the 1978 reelection campaign, Governor Carey's chief political and administrative aide, Robert Morgado, issued a memorandum to the Department of Mental Hygiene which outlined an agreement with the unions calling for a rough parity between community programs operated and staffed by state employees and those operated by private agencies (Morgado 1978). The core of the agreement was the state's promise to open fifty state-operated community residences to absorb Willowbrook employees that might otherwise be laid off in the downsizing. Few government memorandums achieved legendary—almost mythical—status as quickly as the Morgado Memorandum. Despite the fact that it focused on state-operated group homes in New York City, it was soon interpreted by the unions to be a commitment by the state for overall parity in state-operated and private agency operated community programs. The Morgado Memorandum joined the Willowbrook Consent Decree and the ICF Plan of Compliance as the founding documents of the contemporary organization of developmental services in New York. Fifty-Fifty became a central tenet in the doctrine of deinstitutionalization.

Conversion of Community Residences to ICFs: Rebuilding the Foundation

By the late 1970s, the Office of Mental Retardation and Developmental Disabilities was riding a fiscal tiger. Rapid expansion of community residential and day programs was occurring, but problems financing the expansion and operation of community programs were emerging.

The notion that community services cost less than institutional services had already become axiomatic in the developmental disabilities field. Regardless of the validity of this comparison, by the late 1970s, it was becoming apparent that the basic fiscal framework for paying the costs of day and residential services was out of balance. The combination of clients' SSI (including the state supplement), private agencies 41.33 State Aid contracts, property cost pass-throughs, shared staffing, and Purchase of Services contracts was proving insufficient for the creation, expansion, and operation of community programs, especially in New York City where the costs of acquiring real estate and paying utility costs were especially high. Deinstitutionalization began at the depths of the city's financial crisis, but as its economy began to improve, housing costs rose. Opposition to siting of community residences continued to impede expansion regardless of the ultimate override of the Padavan Law. The availability of housing that would accommodate four or more clients, many with severe mobility problems, was extremely limited. In addition, the "house mother/father" model of the first hostels was no longer a viable staffing option; not only because of the absence of real estate that would accommodate several disabled persons and live-in staff, but also because there were not anywhere near the numbers of individuals who wanted to adopt this kind of life to staff the hundreds of community residences required. While staff in private agency community residences had never been well-paid, those agencies still had to pay salaries that were somewhat in line with similar jobs in nursing homes and a growing home-care industry—jobs which often did not bring the level of challenge involved with caring for people with severe disabilities (O'Neill et al. 1985).

The initial concern was with meeting the demands of the Consent Decree and the Plan of Compliance, but cost problems began to loom. OMRDD estimated that the average cost per resident in community residences in New York City was double that in the rest of the state (CQC 1980, 2). By the late 1970s, Purchase of Services contracts, which had been introduced to pay start-up and extraordinary costs had become vital to private agencies' ongoing budgets, still not sufficient to resolve what had become "an immediate fiscal dilemma" facing private agencies operating community residences (CQC 1980). Federal funding, largely residents' SSI payments, accounted for less than 15 percent of the total costs of the community residences.

Small ICF/MR Program to the Rescue

Federal financial participation was the solution to the fiscal dilemma OMRDD faced. Federal financial participation in the costs of the state's large institutions, now converted to large ICFs/MR, had become an increasingly important component in financing all New York's developmental services. Those involved in the creation of the ICF/MR program believed that the federal government never intended the program to fund both institutional and community services (Boggs et al. 1985). The "four of more" clause in the regulations implementing the 1971 amendments was included in the context of large institutions and apparently not intended to define small facilities. Nonetheless, Minnesota, which had a reputation for progressive and innovative developmental service programs, interpreted the ICF/MR regulations to encompass small community residences and succeeded in getting federal financial participation in their costs. New York State officials looked to the federal regulations and Minnesota's experience in obtaining Medicaid funding for its community programs.

Once it became clear that Minnesota's initiative was not going to be overturned by federal Medicaid officials, OMRDD sold the scheme to the Division of the Budget (which applauded the very positive fiscal impact of federal financial participation in a heretofore state-funded program), and argued to other state oversight agencies that "the immediacy and seriousness of the fiscal situation confronting the more costly community residences" warranted immediate action despite concerns about the appropriateness of this institutional model of care and the many regulatory, fiscal, and operational implications (CQC 1980). These concerns would be resolved with relative ease, and, more importantly, problems became opportunities.

Costs and Benefits of ICFs

Initial estimates of the costs of converting Community Residences to small ICFs was that they would cost 45 to 70 percent more than the average rate for a Community Residence in New York City (CQC 1980). Of course, with the Medicaid match, anything under 100 percent of the cost of a Community Residence would be a net gain for the state. But that still did not take into account the other half the equation—and a central argument of this book— that the preoccupation with the costs ignores the benefits.

The Commission on Quality of Care report on conversion of Community Residences pointed out that the ICFs higher administrative costs, increased direct care staffing requirements, clinical services, and recreation, transportation, and other auxiliary services "lessen considerably the attractiveness of their increased federal reimbursement" (CQC 1980, 11). But it was these *costs* that were additional *benefits* of the ICF conversion. In the late 1970s, New York was still in a recession that would prove to be deeper and longer than the national recession. Tens of thousands of baby boomers were graduating from the state's enormously expanded university system. The state was losing thousands of industrial jobs to the south and to foreign competition. The additional administrative, direct care, clinical, and auxiliary service costs of ICFs were not fees paid to some outside entity but *jobs*—well-paying, professional, *federally funded* jobs.

This point cannot be overemphasized because it has been largely ignored and misunderstood in this policy area. The conversion of state-funded Community R esidences to federally funded ICFs had two significant benefits, the net reduction of expenditures as a result of federal financial participation *and* the additional employment of thousands of administrative, professional, clinical, and direct care staff. Later chapters will explain how New York's aggressive approach would eventually maximize federal reimbursement to the point where it produced a *surplus* over the direct total costs of operating ICFs. Two critical problems had to be resolved before the conversion to ICFs could be implemented.

Medicaid Eligibility: The Dogs That Didn't Bark and District 98

The first was whether the soon-to-be residents of Intermediate Care Facilities (ICFs) were eligible for this Medicaid-funded program. It was virtually certain that the overwhelming majority of the individuals who had been in developmental centers prior to moving to Community Residences met Medicaid eligibility standards. However, increasingly large numbers of people in Community Residences had moved to these residences from home. Were these individuals Medicaid eligible? There are undocumented accounts of junior OMRDD staff being stared down by agency executives when they had the temerity to raise this issue, and it became prudent to not ask the question. The question of Medicaid eligibility also appears to have been set aside in the other agencies with key roles: the Department of Health, and Department of Social Services.

There were concerns that the Commission on Quality of Care (CQC), a semi-independent oversight agency whose commissioners were appointed by the governor, might raise objections. After the mass conversion of Community Residences to ICFs, the CQC issued a report on the process, *Converting Community Residences into Intermediate Care Facilities for the Mentally Retarded: Some Cautionary Notes* (CQC 1980), which indicated the position it took as the conversion was being planned and implemented. It dealt with the issue of initial Medicaid eligibility of the individuals in Community Residences by asserting that, "a review of the federal ICF-MR regulations indicates that a significant proportion of the clients in converting community residences are eligible for ICF-MR care" (CQC 1980, 23). Other than this single assertion based on review of the regulations rather than the clients in the residences, the commission did not delve into what proportion of residents might not be eligible but raised concerns for eventual disallowances and the need for "a careful assessment of the needs of developmentally disabled persons for this level of care" (CQC 1980). The bulk of the report focused on cautions about cost containment and the need to maintain Community Residences as an option in the continuum of care. The message embedded in the oblique language of regulators was that there would be no *prior* challenge to the initial mass determinations of Medicaid eligibility and need for ICF level of care, rather *post hoc* reviews. Indeed, for a period of time in the 1980s, OMRDD and private agencies did have to contend with a series of adverse level of care determinations. These were addressed without major disruption to Medicaid funding and eventually faded from regulators' attention. Key agencies with regulatory and oversight responsibilities for Medicaid and programs for people with disabilities were like Sherlock Holmes' dog that didn't bark. There would be no regulatory roadblocks from state-level agencies on the critical question of Medicaid eligibility.

State oversight and regulatory bodies appeared willing to give OMRDD and the private agencies a "bye" on the initial determinations of Medicaid eligibility involved in the conversion of Community Residences to ICFs. However, county Social Service Commissioners immediately perceived that a program that was funded entirely from state funds would be converted to one which New York's Medicaid statute would require a 25 percent local share. County Social Services Commissioners played a formal role in "signing off" on Medicaid eligibility determinations that could block the mass conversion of Community Residences to ICFs. In an arrangement similar to Chapters 620 and 621 that exempted localities from the local Medicaid share of former residents of state institutions, OMRDD and the state negotiated an arrangement with county Social Services Commissioners that would exempt localities from their share of the costs of ICFs. The mechanism was the creation of District 98, an artificial statewide location for the assignment of residents of ICFs and other Medicaid-funded programs that allowed the state to assume both its and the counties' share of the Medicaid costs.

The counties' agreement to effectively take themselves out of initial determinations of eligibility and level of care removed another impediment to the devolution of power to OMRDD and private agencies. Moreover, the District 98 device laid another piece of the foundation that remained largely in place for the next twenty years. Local governments would be largely held harmless from the Medicaid-funded initiatives of OMRDD and its private agency partners. While controversies about local costs continued in the mental health area, large-scale OMRDD and private agency initiatives in Medicaid-funded programs were uncontroversial and barely noted in the broader political arena.

Other Critical Elements: Determining Eligibility and Level of Need

Embedded in the eligibility determination issue was the tacit agreement between the state and its private agencies that the *provider* would make the initial assessment of Medicaid eligibility and determination of level of care. In contrast to the practice in many other states which exercise rigorous *prior* gate-keeping on these decisions, this initial, critical element of control would be devolved to the private providers in New York—a prerogative they have since vigorously defended.

The mass conversion of Community Residences to Intermediate Care Facilities involved two basic features of organization of developmental services in New York. The first was the shift from financing the cost of community programs from largely state funding to federal funding. Despite the assertions that the ICF program was never intended to finance a state's entire developmental services system (Boggs et al. 1985), the conversion of Community Residences to ICFs accelerated the aggressive approach New York had already begun with its initial ICF financing of large institutions and its ICF Plan of Compliance. From this point on, maximization of federal financial participation of every possible element in New York's public and private, institutional and community, services would be fundamental strategy.

The second basic feature of the organization of developmental services in New York was also formed in the process of converting Community Residences to ICFs—the partnership between the state and its private agencies. The hostility that marked the relationship between private agencies and the state was not simply lessened; rather, a grand alliance was forged. The conversion of Community Residences can be seen as a treaty between the state and the private provider sector. These private agencies would set aside concerns about the appropriateness of ICFs as community residences, allowing the state to shift the financing of all developmental services to the federal government. The state would devolve essential elements of control and financing to the private agencies. Private agencies, not the state, would maintain control over their waiting lists and access into their day and residential programs. The private agencies, not the state, would make the critical initial assessments of Medicaid eligibility and level of care determination.

New Universe of Developmental Services

The changes that took place during the 1970s radically reordered developmental services in New York. At the outset of the 1970s, the financing of developmental services was largely the state's responsibility. New York's aggressive approach to pursuing Medicaid reimbursement for the residents of its institutions and its subsequent conversion of those institutions to large Intermediate Care Facilities for the Mentally Retarded (ICFs/MR) set New York on the path to federal financing of the bulk of its developmental services. The federal Supplemental Security Income (SSI) program provided substantial federal funding for the Community Residences, and their conversion to small ICFs/MR secured federal Medicaid funding for New York's public and private, institutional and community services.

The focus on the ICF Plan of Compliance, like the Willowbrook Consent Decree, is usually on the large-scale deinstitutionalization that ensued. By the end of the 1970s, developmental services in New York shifted to a large and growing, public-private partnership. The number of residents in the state's twenty developmental centers dropped from more than 25,000 at the beginning of the decade to less than 15,000 by its end, and the number of individuals living in group homes grew exponentially (OMRDD 1984).

While the ICF Plan of Compliance resulted in a census in the state's institutions that was smaller, the plan made those institutions *stronger*. New institutions were occupied, older institutions were completely refurbished, living quarters were reconstructed from huge dormitories into semiprivate rooms, and other major improvements were made in the physical plants of the twenty large facilities. Most importantly, the active treatment requirements of ICFs resulted in a radical shift in the staffing of these institutions. The young professionals recruited to implement the active treatment requirements replaced the ranks of ward attendants and changed the operational and administrative structure of the institutions. The ICF Plan of Compliance resulted in smaller, less crowded institutions vital to the financing of the entire system of public and private developmental services.

The conversion of Community Residences to ICFs/MR meant that there would no longer be a clear distinction between institution and community. There would be large and small ICFs/MR, almost identical clinically and fiscally, and, in the case of small ICFs/MR, operated by both the state and private sector. Residents of large institutions could be moved out to virtually the same program—and moved *back* to the same type of program. Institution vis-à-vis community, public vis-à-vis private would no longer be zero-sum games in New York State. The ICF/MR program integrated the organization of developmental services in New York and solidified the role of institutions.

At the beginning of the 1970s, a number of private agencies operated day programs. These were largely ARC sheltered workshops. A handful of agencies opened hostels. By the end of the 1970s, the parent organizations that had reluctantly started and operated sheltered workshops were being transformed into complex service providers for thousands of individuals moving out of large institutions as well as people who had been living at home. Large numbers of United Cerebral Palsy Association chapters and independent provider agencies had joined the Association for Retarded Citizens in what had heretofore been that organization's predominant, almost exclusive, role as provider and advocate. Relatively small parent organizations were being now operating large numbers of day and residential programs. Hostels and Community Residences were being converted to the ICF medical model with its physical plant, clinical staffing, programming, and other regulatory requirements.

The rate-based structure of ICF funding meant that private agencies would no longer be dependent on annual contract renewals. Instead, once their rates were established, they were virtually guaranteed permanent funding. This was crucial to creating the fiscal foundation of steady, predictable income that would bring long-term stability and growth.

In 1972, the long-standing hostility between advocates for people with mental retardation and the state resulted in the *ARC v. Rockefeller* suit in federal court. By the end of the 1970s, the major parent organizations had forged an alliance with the state government. By the end of the 1970s, state employee unions that had launched campaigns against deinstitutionalization were guaranteed jobs in state-operated community programs. Local governments which had resisted expansion of community programs were effectively neutralized by statutes (Chapters 620 and 621; Padavan Site Selection) and administrative mechanisms (District 98) that held them fiscally harmless and politically impotent as well more economically dependent on jobs created by publicly funded community services.

In 1978, a new state agency for the administration of developmental services was created—the Office of Mental Retardation and Developmental Disabilities. This formalized what had already become an assumption of management control by nonmedical professionals with extensive experience in and ties to private community agencies. The creation of twenty well-staffed District Developmental Services Offices with direct responsibility for institutional *and* public and private community services established a strong local management capacity. More staffing, ongoing consultant assistance in rate-setting and powerful law firms enhanced the state's already potent capacity to maximize federal financial participation.

At the beginning of the 1970s, developmental services were still largely a matter of state and local public policy in New York. By the end of the 1970s, the role of local governments had been severely limited, and the organization, operation, and financing of developmental services in New York State rested on the relationship between the state and the federal Medicaid agency.

The impact of all these changes was the *integration* of large public institutions in the context of a public *and* private, institution *and* community system of services. From the late 1970s on, no one component of public or private, institutional or community developmental services in New York could be divorced from the role it played in an integrated fiscal, operational, political, and economic context.

Of course, tensions existed and differences between the key players had to be continually negotiated, but the fundamental nature of the relationships changed. From the late 1970s forward, New York State and the private agency sector forged an operational, fiscal, and political partnership. The financial stability and growth of the private agencies was ensured. Growth would be largely within existing nonprofit agencies that could operate residential as well as day programs. Private agencies would be given substantial autonomy in such key areas as controlling access to (and within) their own programs, determining eligibility and level of care, and the assessment of the client characteristics that determined rates.

Strategic decisions and actions were taken even though the long-term implications of some of them were not clear to all the parties, nor their consequences fully realized. In the near-term, the partnership allowed New York State to meet the requirements of the Willowbrook Consent Decree and the ICF Plan of Compliance. In the long-term, this partnership allowed the state to create thousands of new, well-paying, federally funded jobs; to maintain the employment of unionized state employees by providing jobs in community programs as well as in institutions; to replace a dwindling upstate industrial economy with a human services industry while holding local governments financially harmless; and to do all this by spending *other people's money.*

Chapter 8

Deinstitutionalization:
Reorganizing and Refinancing Institutions and Community Services

If it moves, Medicaid it; if it doesn't depreciate it.

—Anonymous

Deinstitutionalization is usually portrayed as the breakup of the old system of services, downsizing institutions and creating community programs. In New York, a more complex reality lay beneath the simplistic implications of the term. Downsizing began before the Willowbrook Consent Decree and the ICF Plan of Compliance that marked the formal start of deinstitutionalization in 1975—a point at which the number of people in New York's developmental centers had dropped to 20,062 from the peak census of 27,544 in 1967 (DMH 1968,1976). Nonetheless, the almost fantastical placement goals in the ICF Plan of Compliance, the looming presence of the federal court at Willowbrook, and the increasing dependence on funding from a federal government bent on Medicaid reform and closing large institutions were among the factors threatened to destabilize a newly created and complex constellation of public and fiscally fragile private services.

Like riding a bicycle, staying upright is easier when one goes faster rather than slower, and during most of the 1980s, New York raced ahead with large-scale depopulation of its institutions. From 1975 to the 1987 announcement of the intent to close several developmental centers, the population in New York's twenty developmental centers dropped to 9,742—by far the largest and most rapid deinstitutionalization in any state (Braddock et al. 1995). But these statistics deflect attention from the other aspects of deinstitutionalization that stabilized and solidified public institutions in a reorganized system of developmental services.

179

As the ICF Plan of Compliance was the critical *döppleganger* of Willowbrook, the success of deinstitutionalization depended on the large-scale expansion of a private provider network and an orderly transition of state employees from institutional to community services. This depended on stable funding for the private sector through the new ICF rate-setting structure and turning the developmental centers into cash cows that would finance institutions and virtually all state and most private agency operations. Creating a community-based system of services depended to a great extent on moving people out of their communities to upstate rural enclaves of developmental services. Deinstitutionalization relied on a "continuum of services" in which developmental centers and specialized state-operated behavior, geriatric, and forensic programs provided backup for individuals who were either "not appropriate for" or had "failed" in private community agencies.

A Medicaid-financed rate system for private residential and day programs inextricably linked, rather than separated, the public and private sectors. A variety of fiscal mechanisms were used to *medicaid* residential and day service programs and finance property acquisition and create highly structured organizational formats, approaches to service delivery, and program designs. Innovative financing formed the basis of a highly concentrated, vertically and horizontally integrated industry. Family support service contracts and federal funding intended for independent planning were employed to integrate smaller providers and advocacy organizations into a cohesive fiscal and political framework. Developmental centers became cash cows as New York used aggressive cost finding, a large fixed cost base, and a base-year trended rate system in which institutions financed themselves and large portions of the public and private system of community services.

Broad Factors Driving Deinstitutionalization

The Willowbrook Consent Decree and the ICF Plan of Compliance were critical for initiating a broad policy of deinstitutionalization and shaping its direction, but New York's experience was also shaped by other factors as it proceeded to reorganize its services.

Role of Federal Courts

The Willowbrook case remained at the center of deinstitutionalization in New York. From the filing of the *ARC v. Rockefeller* suit in 1972, to the Willowbrook Consent Decree of 1975, and in all the subsequent skirmishes between the state, the plaintiffs, and various oversight panels that continued for years, the state and the various parties, along with the federal court itself, had to keep developments in the federal courts in mind as deinstitutionalization unfolded. Despite a pullback from an era of judicial activism by federal courts in the early 1980s, New York and other states were pursuing deinstitutionalization under the penumbra of various federal court decisions: from improving the institutions in *Wyatt v. Stickney*, to improving and offering alternatives in *ARC v. Rockefeller*, to closing the institutions in *Halderman v. Pennhurst* (446 F. Supp. 1295, 1978). For most of the 1980s, "Willowbrook drove the agency" in many operational respects, but the potential for the federal courts to significantly reshape policy was never far from policy makers' considerations.

Normalization and Least Restrictive Alternative: A New Political Ideology

The President's Panel on Mental Retardation in the early 1960s and subsequent papers developed through the President's Committee on Mental Retardation provided a framework and vehicle for advocates and analysts to promote plans that challenged prevailing concepts about the role of people with mental retardation in society and the appropriate objectives, size, and location of models of care. The principle of "normalization," originally articulated by Nirje (1969) and Bank-Mikkelson (1969) and modified by Wolfensberger (1972) was at the core. The essential features were best expressed by Lakin and Bruininks, "This standard (normalization) dictates that the residential, educational, employment, and social and recreational conditions of the individual must be close to the cultural norm for a person of that age as the extent of the individual's disability reasonably allows" (1985, 11).

Normalization gained added potency as it was paired with the principle of least restrictive alternative (originally articulated in the 1969 United States Supreme Court decision in *Covington v. Harris*) that a disabled person's needs be provided, to the maximum extent possible, in the types of community settings that are used by nonhandicapped persons. The concepts of normalization and least restrictive alternative formed a framework and political ideology within which deinstitutionalization took place. They were principles easily and widely understood, and not able to be met in institutions.

Federal and State Legislation

Deinstitutionalization evolved within a context of new federal and state statutes that provided a variety of legal mandates and supports for community services. The Developmental Disabilities Services and Facilities Construction Act of 1970 provided federal funding for community services. Section 504 of the 1973 Rehabilitation Act revised and expanded vocational rehabilitation programs and, very importantly, prohibited exclusion from participation by an otherwise qualified handicapped person in any program receiving federal funds.

The 1975 Developmental Disabilities Assistance and Bill of Rights Act required states to spend at least 30 percent of their formula grants on deinstitutionalization and to include deinstitutionalization in the state plans required by the statute. The 1978 Rehabilitation, Comprehensive Services and Developmental Disabilities Amendments added functional definitions of developmental disabilities, authorized protection and advocacy systems in states, and called for a shift in "priority services" that would support community living (Braddock 1987; Castellani 1987).

In 1975, Congress passed PL 94-142, the Education for All Handicapped Children Act, which greatly expanded funding for special education but also mandated a "free and appropriate public education for all handicapped children between the ages of three and eighteen" (Laski 1985). In New York, the Padavan Site Selection Law became a critical instrument in deinstitutionalization by giving the Commissioner of Mental Hygiene (later OMRDD) unilateral power to override local government objections to placement of group homes.

Medicaid Reform

There probably has been no major federal or state program in which reform began as quickly after initiation as in Medicaid. New York's deinstitutionalization, relying heavily on the creation and expansion of ICFs/MR, Day Treatment, and other Medicaid-financed programs, took place in the shadow of three major elements of federal Medicaid reform.

The first was Medicaid waivers. The Home and Community Care Waiver was passed as a part of the Omnibus Budget Reconciliation Act of 1981, and it permitted states to develop a variety of community-based alternatives to ICFs/MR (Gardner 1986). New York, which was perfecting the maximization of federal reimbursement, resisted federal pressure to employ Medicaid waivers (with a few targeted exceptions) until the early 1990s.

The second strand of Medicaid reform affecting deinstitutionalization was federal legislation proposed by Senator John Chafee, the Community and Family Living Amendments of 1985. The Chafee Bill was intended to permanently restructure Medicaid services for people with developmental disabilities, largely by establishing strong fiscal disincentives for federal reimbursement of services in large institutions (more than fifteen-bed ICFs/MR). The Chafee Bill never passed, but through the 1980s, it served as a focal point for opponents of large institutions, for advocates for community services less medicalized than small ICFs/MR, and for federal policy makers hoping to cut their reimbursements to states operating increasingly costly ICFs/MR. In the hearings on this bill, New York was typically cited as the prime example of the need for reform. While New York policy makers did not expect the bill to ever pass (largely because many other states also depended on federal reimbursement of their institutional and small ICF/MR costs), the Chafee Bill did bring unwanted attention to New York's maximization of Medicaid strategy.

The third strand of Medicaid reform was heightened oversight of New York's Medicaid programs by the federal Health Care Financing Administration (HCFA). This was the primary area of concern for New York as Medicaid-financed deinstitutionalization proceeded. New York's 1969 reimbursement claim for 12,828 eligible patients in state institutions for the mentally retarded, by far the largest number among the states and almost three times more than those claimed by California (and later found by the GAO to be based on deficient applications of eligibility criteria and broad interpretations of maintenance of effort requirements), put HCFA on early alert to scrutinize New York's Medicaid program (Boggs, Lakin, and Clauser 1985). New York's massive conversion of Community Residences to ICFs/MR in the late 1970s was another goad to federal oversight. Virtually from the beginning of deinstitutionalization, and carrying through the 1980s, fending off and dealing with federal "look behind" surveys, special audits, disallowances, alternate care determinations, and threats of decertifications in developmental centers became a central element in the overall strategy of OMRDD, assisted by outside law firms, financial consulting firms, and the state's representatives in Congress. HCFA oversight was not as visible in Medicaid reform as waivers or the Chafee Bill, but it was the most important to OMRDD because of its potential for substantial fiscal impact.

Important Features of Deinstitutionalization in New York State

The role of federal courts, the political ideology of normalization, a broadening statutory base undergirding community programs, and Medicaid reform were largely exogenous factors shaping the direction and pace of deinstitutionalization in New York. There were other features of New York's deinstitutionalization that had significant long-term effects on the organization of developmental services and on the persistence of institutions.

Rapid Rate and Large Scale of Deinstitutionalization

The most outstanding feature of New York's deinstitutionalization was its rapid rate and large scale. The following table illustrates its dramatic pace.

Table 8.1
Census of Residential Alternatives: 1975 to 1986

	Developmental Centers	Community Residences	ICFs/MR	Family Care
1975	20,062	850	55	3,651
1976	19,160	1,225	55	3,831
1977	18,438	1,760	212	3,940
1978	16,441	2,420	868	4,052
1979	15,636	3,270	848	3,860
1980	15,066	3,620	1,376	3,947
1981	13,771	3,919	2,576	3,905
1982	12,826	4,334	3,209	3,846
1983	12,123	4,558	4,303	3,747
1984	11,624	4,856	5,368	3,846
1985	11,162	4,900	5,934	3,700
1986	10,522	5,200	6,500	3,600

OMRDD, 5.07 Plans, 1980, 1984, 1987

From 1975 to 1986, the number of residents in the state's developmental centers and special units was halved. The number of community ICF/MR beds had reached 6,500 by 1986, an increase of over 350 percent since 1980, and Community Residences had increased by 47 percent by 1980 to 5,200 beds. Family care decreased by 13 percent from 1980 to 1986 to about 3,500 beds, fewer than the 3,600 family care beds at the beginning of deinstitutionalization in 1975 (OMRDD 1987, 66).

Linking a day service to a residential placement for every individual coming out of a developmental center, whether or not that person was a member of the Willowbrook class, was one of the key strategic decisions OMRDD made as it began deinstitutionalization. That meant that a new day service "slot," as they were termed, had to be created for every new residential "bed." The following table shows the dramatic changes in day services.

Table 8.2
Census of Day Service Alternatives: 1978 to 1986

	Day Treatment	Day Training	Sheltered Workshops	Total
1978	3,394	7,349	11,612	22,355
1982	8,041	2,118	16,696	26,855
1986	11,346	3,950	19,592	34,888

OMRDD, 5.07 Plans, 1984, 1987

While the overall growth in residential capacity was modest during these years, the overall capacity in day services increased substantially. State-funded Day Training programs were converted to Medicaid-funded Day Treatment programs and grew significantly, while capacity in sheltered workshops almost doubled. Unlike residential services that were reorganized and only grew modestly in capacity, day services grew by more than 56 percent from 1978 to 1986.

Recreating Institutional Models of Service in Group Homes

With Willowbrook as the national symbol of institutional abuse and neglect, New York policy makers and administrators proudly pointed to the fact that the state was undertaking the largest and most rapid deinstitutionalization in the country. New York's system of community residential and day services were shaped by the need for rapid progress. Many important elements of the community programs were largely recreations of institutions in other places. New services thought to embody principles of normalization and least restrictive setting locked in mid-1980s models.

The oft-repeated observation in the field in the late 1970s and early 1980s was that deinstitutionalization would have stalled if not for the rectories and convents being vacated by priests and nuns leaving the church or taking up vocations in various kinds of community rather than parish service. Indeed, large numbers of ex-priests and nuns and clergy took up service and administrative roles in OMRDD and the private agencies. The supply of rectories and convents, however, dried up quickly, and housing suitable for individuals with severe disabilities, often in wheelchairs, became more scarce and costly. OMRDD found that, "Often, the only limitation to community living for thousands of people has been the scarcity of housing stock which is appropriate for the special needs of these people" (OMRDD 1986, ii). New construction, using predetermined formats, would be needed to solve this problem.

Five residential "models" were developed to represent state-of-the-art architectural and engineering concepts and yield significant savings in time and construction costs by allowing earlier decision-making, more certain time and cost schedules, and fewer architectural review requirements. The model plans even included suggestions for coordination of interior materials and colors, "a unique and personalized environment tailored to the individual needs and characteristics of those who will eventually call this their home" (OMRDD 1986). Home, however, was a twelve-bed ICF/MR since OMRDD's fiscal experts calculated that twelve beds would provide the optimum reimbursement. The waggish tale that twelve beds filled two vans is certainly apocryphal.

The five core models were not ready when they were announced, and the speed of approvals for projects using the models did not measurably increase. Some DDSOs lost considerable time waiting for these ostensibly "off-the-shelf" designs to actually become available. One DDSO director who selected only one model for all its homes since they were very similar to what had worked well in the past said, "God help us if we picked the wrong one!" The five models were large, congregate care facilities that required extensive land for employee and van parking, and did not look anything like "home."

Another important issue was whether community residences would be built to institutional specifications. Chapter 21 of the state's Life Safety Code, focusing on the time required for a resident to evacuate a board and care home in an emergency, required sprinklers, fire-rated materials, and other physical plant modifications. Chapter 12 of the Health Care Occupancy Code known as the "institutional code," assumed the need for preservation in place and, consequently, required institutional sprinkler systems with a separate water supply, wide corridors, exit signs, and a variety of enhanced structural features in the facility.

As deinstitutionalization progressed at a rapid pace, community residences housed thousands of individuals who were aging and becoming medically frail. In early construction, houses were built to Chapter 21 specifications. Later, areas were modified for occupancy by individuals whose inability to evacuate required Chapter 12 specifications. Planners in OMRDD argued that the community residences would have to accommodate more individuals with medical and related needs in the future as well as those who would develop more severe disabilities as they aged. A decision was made to build all new group homes to Chapter 12 institutional code, and the twelve-bed ICFs/MR became mini-institutions inside as well as outside.

In many cases deinstitutionalization went only to the perimeter or immediate vicinity of the developmental center. The costs of rehabilitating buildings dating from the late nineteenth and early twentieth century to meet ICF/MR standards had been a significant problem from the inception of the ICF Plan of Compliance. Even with extensive reconstruction to meet life safety codes, the centers were still left with buildings that were too large and ill-suited to contemporary notions about appropriate programming. At the same time, these centers often had hundreds of acres of unused space. In the mid-1980s, the notion of Small Residential Units (SRUs) percolated up from the field, and at Newark Developmental Center, eight twelve-bed ICFs/MR were built on the perimeter of the campus in what was known as Cobblestone Terrace. They were similar to other community residences, but these were grouped in a cul-de-sac and used shared staffing arrangements, and day programming and other services at the center rather than operating independently. The Medicaid reimbursement rate for SRUs was also higher than for comparable ICFs/MR in the community.

OMRDD's plan to use more SRUs in deinstitutionalization came under attack by advocates who argued that SRUs would perpetuate institutions by their location on the center campuses and by their reliance on developmental center day programming and other supports. Other advocates, particularly those that were also provider agencies, saw the use of state employees in SRUs as a potential reneging on commitments to deinstitutionalization, with large parts of developmental centers merely being reconstituted as SRUs. Nonetheless, OMRDD issued a policy paper to support its position, Small Residential Units: A Residential Alternative (OMRDD 1985), and proceeded to develop SRUs.

Bonding and Mortgaging

New construction of community residences needed to be financed. The Carey and Cuomo administrations adopted the creative approaches of the Rockefeller administration and expanded the use of public authority bonding to finance construction of community services. Private agencies financed new construction largely through bank mortgages with substantial assistance from the state in a variety of "prior property approval" guarantees, advances, and reimbursement mechanisms such as funded depreciation. Nonetheless, the underlying premise was the same as that which financed the large institutions. The bonds would be repaid by the Medicaid fees generated by the residents of these new facilities over the next forty years for twelve-bed ICFs, built to nursing home standards, and unlikely to ever be used for anything other than a mini-institution. The twelve-bed ICF/MR was the predominant residential model. However, OMRDD allowed several private agencies to open ICFs/MR housing more than 60 individuals (a few housed more than 100 residents), and they looked like, and were operated as, institutions.

Strengthening the Continuum: Specialization and Integration of Programs by Sector

The notion of creating a continuum of services went back at least to the ten models of Community Residences and ICFs/MR in the late 1970s. OMRDD's 1987–1990 5.07 plan was titled, Strengthening the Continuum, and the thrust of the plan was to describe how the agency was putting into place an integrated range of more to less intensive services that individuals could move along (OMRDD 1987). Continuum also carried with it the notion of "backup." Individuals placed in what was thought to be an appropriate residential settings on the continuum (usually an ICF/MR) rarely moved to less intensive settings. However, individuals with special medical needs or behavior problems might "retreat" to a more restrictive residential setting. These backups were typically the state institution or specialized, often remote, state-operated community programs (Castellani, Epple, and Sirmans 1985). Continuum also effectively meant that private and public community programs would use medical and ancillary health services located in the developmental centers, especially in upstate areas. Continuum meant that deinstitutionalization in New York was not simply an emptying of all the residents and all the programs and services in large institutions in favor of concomitant community services. In addition to built-in "backups," specialized programs for specific types of individuals were created in state and private agencies.

No Single Point of Access

From the historic agreement at Willowbrook with the parent-run agencies that they would serve people coming out of institutions in return for what they took to be a sacred commitment to serving their own waiting lists, private agencies expanded this agreement into an understanding with the state that they would be the primary, virtually exclusive, arbiters of who entered their residential and day services. Any attempt to mitigate that control through a "single point of access" was vehemently opposed. In contrast to state and/or local government control, or cooperative involvement with provider agencies in other states, this became a core feature of deinstitutionalization.

A Cooperative Regulatory Approach

Another feature of New York's deinstitutionalization was the state's approach to the regulation of the private agencies. It was designed on the assumption that these parent-run agencies were providing services to the sons and daughters of members of the boards of directors, executives, and many employees of these organizations and would be largely self-regulating. It is also important to remember that in the initial design of New York's Medicaid program, rate-setting, program certification, and important features of quality assurance were decentralized to the operating agency—the Department of Mental Hygiene and its successor, OMRDD. During deinstitutionalization, OMRDD's focus was on rapidly expanding services in private agencies, not on enforcing stringent regulatory standards. Even within this initial lenient context, deregulation and "regulatory reform" became OMRDD initiatives (OMRDD 1987). Reduction of paperwork requirements and various self-assessment approaches were featured in this "reform" agenda, but the reductions in oversight staff in OMRDD was undoubtedly effective in leaving all but the most egregious private agencies in a comparatively benign regulatory environment. In fact, through the 1980s, most of the regulatory problems faced by OMRDD were from New York State Department of Health reviews and federal look behind surveys focused on developmental centers and state-operated community programs.

Opening Institutions

Deinstitutionalization was complicated by the opening of several long-delayed new institutions under construction since the Rockefeller era. In contrast to the existing centers that typically housed several thousand individuals, these new centers for several hundred residents were regarded as substantial improvements. They were intended to house individuals closer to home rather than in the distant larger institutions, and the opening of these new architecturally innovative centers was favorably anticipated by parents and professionals. Some advocates and professionals felt that the centers were still too large and services could best be provided outside an institutional setting. The opening of new developmental centers in the Bronx and in the Albany area illustrated how opening the new centers complicated deinstitutionalization and ultimately played a role in the 1987 decision to close several developmental centers.

Bronx and O.D. Heck Developmental Centers

The new Bronx Developmental Center became the most prominent symbol for the growing disenchantment with new buildings that were architecturally interesting but functionally at odds with a community approach to services. The opening of the facility, in the midst of the negotiations around the Willowbrook Consent Decree, created hostile relations among key actors and organizations in the borough and demonstrated the powerful fiscal, political, and functional impact of an institution, no matter how new or small.

Dr. Herbert J. Cohen was the first director of the Bronx Developmental Services Office, and prior to the opening of the developmental center, he established a "community services team" approach to providing services that depended on services throughout the borough linked to various diagnostic, training, research, and medical resources (Cohen 1975). In describing his plans for the role of the new developmental center in the community services approach, Cohen said he hoped to alter the original character and purposes of the building to have apartment-style living quarters, intensive habilitation for both children and adults, day programs, workshops, inpatient physical rehabilitation services, crisis and respite care, plus innovative educational programs (Cohen 1975, 401).

The original plan for a 1,500-bed facility had already been scaled back to a little under 400, and Cohen and advocates involved in the Willowbrook case wanted the facility to house no more than about 150 residents (Rothman and Rothman 1984). During the trial that considered the placement of Willowbrook class members in the new Bronx center, Cohen testified that he thought the building was too large and not compatible with his community services approach. OMRDD Commissioner Coughlin testified that had the center not already been built, "I would not build it" (Rothman and Rothman 1984, 147). However, the exigencies of the Willowbrook Consent Decree and the "fiscal and political pressures" created by the completion of a $26 million dollar facility (Cohen 1975, 418) ultimately resulted in the opening of the center for several hundred residents.

A similar story unfolded at the Oswald D. Heck Center, named after the long-time Republican Speaker of the State Assembly from New York's Capital District, which was also under construction in the midst of deinstitutionalization. Hugh LaFave, one of the several physicians who had come to the Department of Mental Hygiene from Saskatchewan was named director of the district office. The dichotomy between LaFave's expectations for community services in the locale and his orientation toward the facility under construction was signaled by the name he chose for the overall district office: the Eleanor Roosevelt Developmental Services Office. As the center neared completion, LaFave was necessarily drawn into planning the layout and other features of the buildings, while simultaneously arguing, first, that he did not want a developmental center in the district, and, if one was obviously going to be opened, that it be much, much smaller than what was close to completion. With the backing of a group of parents, advocates and like-minded professionals, LaFave attempted to continue to operate a network of community services without opening the now-completed facility. However, three sets of factors ultimately led to the occupation of the center by long-term residents.

Ironically, the first was the deinstitutionalization of Willowbrook. As the state began to depopulate Willowbrook in order to meet court mandates, residents were moved to other, newer facilities such as O.D. Heck that were just beginning to open. Second, while some parents and professionals felt that individuals could be better served outside a developmental center, this was not a widely held position in the early-to mid-1970s, and many people with a family member at a distant developmental centers wanted the new centers to open to allow their family member to live closer to home. Finally, there was a very important fiscal imperative. The construction of the new centers was financed by bonds whose amortization depended on the revenues generated through Medicaid reimbursement, and there was no way that the state was not going to open them.

The opening of the Bronx and O.D. Heck Developmental Centers showed that deinstitutionalization was haunted by decisions made twenty years earlier as institutions were being planned. Although they were much smaller than the original plans, by the time they opened they were considered relics of an earlier era by progressive elements within OMRDD who were building twelve-bed ICFs/MR in the community. These were institutions, albeit smaller, and their opening cemented institutional patterns of service delivery.

Creation of New Mini-Institutions: DRUs, RBTUs, and MDUs

While deinstitutionalization was underway, the state also moved residents from overcrowded facilities into empty space at the state's psychiatric centers that had experienced a large drop in their censuses. These Discrete Mental Retardation Units (DRUs) each housed hundreds of individuals. A number of Regional Behavior Treatment Units (RBTUs) and Multiply Disabled Units (MDUs) were also established around the state as separate units on the grounds of one of developmental centers or psychiatric centers to provide special programming and segregation for individuals with severe behavior problems.

Rapid Deinstitutionalization and
Skewing the Distribution of Clients and Types of Services

There were a variety of geographic and situational factors in deinstitutionalization that had important consequences for the perseverance of institutions and the long-term organization of services.

Movement of Willowbrook and Former NYC Residents Upstate

In spite of the rapid drop in institution census, community residential and day programs were not being created in numbers large enough or quickly enough to meet the deadlines of the Willowbrook Consent Decree and the ICF Plan of Compliance, especially in New York City. OMRDD's 1988 *Report on Community Development* was a recap of the problem that was apparent at the beginning of deinstitutionalization. In a report, *The Crisis in New York City Community Residential Bed Development*, OMRDD conceded "despite a massive capital development and client placement effort, only 700 new beds have been added to the New York City residential capacity in over a decade" (21). With more than forty percent of the state's population, New York City had slightly more than twenty percent of the noninstitutional beds in the state (OMRDD 1988). The report cited rising real estate costs; zoning, administrative and approval procedures that were too slow; inadequate housing stock appropriate to the needs of severely disabled, nonambulatory persons; limited vacant land for new construction; and a booming real estate industry reluctant to become involved in cumbersome administrative and payment mechanisms (OMRDD 1988, 19). OMRDD policy makers realized that in order to meet the goals of both the Consent Decree and the ICF Plan, the expansion of community programs would have to take place upstate. They employed two new variations of the overall deinstitutionalization strategy in expanding existing and creating of new types of private agencies and using large-scale state-operated community programs.

The expansion of existing private agencies upstate had to overcome a number of problems. The first was, like their New York City counterparts, the core of many of these agencies were parents who had kept their relatively less-disabled children at home, enrolling them in sheltered workshops and other day programs. They had little experience with entirely new intensive services such as ICFs and Day Treatment programs required by the severely disabled residents in developmental centers. Many of these agencies operated on a fiscal shoestring, and, as one regional manager pointed out, the working-class backgrounds of many of the parents made them extremely cautious about taking on new, large, and financially complex programs to serve individuals coming out of developmental centers in addition to their own family members.

OMRDD undertook a massive effort to expand private agencies upstate. Some expansion took place in the existing agencies that overcame their reluctance and started new group homes and day services for the former residents of institutions in their area. If the local ARC chapter was reluctant to expand rapidly, OMRDD would focus on other agencies. In one area, a small United Cerebral Palsy chapter with an entrepreneurial executive director and a board willing to take up OMRDD's offer of substantial assistance became a major provider of programs for individuals coming out of the local developmental center as well as many from downstate. Willowbrook class members presented the biggest problem for OMRDD. Where expansion in existing private agencies was not proceeding fast enough, OMRDD identified what became known as "Willowbrook agencies." These agencies, often in very rural upstate counties, received extraordinary assistance from OMRDD to start-up and expand ICF and Day Treatment services for large numbers of Willowbrook residents. All these private agencies grew exponentially with expansion into every program offered through OMRDD. Some were so successful that other state and local government agencies asked them to take on heath, education, foster care, and other social services. These agencies invested heavily in construction of buildings in which to provide these services so that after several years the agency campuses were virtually indistinguishable from small institutions. This pattern of concentration of a comprehensive array of developmental services on one campus was repeated in a number of upstate areas.

Concentration of State-Operated Programs Upstate

While the initial focus of the Morgado Memorandum was in New York City, its most significant and long-term impact was upstate. The staff in upstate institutions was more experienced in caring for the typically more disabled residents than the staff in the private agencies. So, as the residents moved out of upstate developmental centers, it was efficient and politically prudent in the context of the Morgado memorandum to create and expand state-operated residences and day programs. Not only did Willowbrook residents move to upstate community residences but, in many instances, state employees moved upstate with them.

The result of these approaches and tactics used to achieve deinstitutionalization and creation of community programs was a long-term skewing of individuals and services in the state. The concepts of normalization, least restrictive alternative, and other tenets in the philosophy underpinning deinstitutionalization anticipated disabled individuals living in their *own* communities. One of the most important and lasting outcomes of New York's rapid deinstitutionalization was the movement of more New York City residents to upstate enclaves of services to join other former New York City residents who either remained in or were being moved out into the immediate vicinity. Another lasting outcome was the transformation of many small private agencies into large, complex organizations serving hundreds of individuals (wildly out of proportion to the numbers in those rural areas) often on campuses indistinguishable from modern public institutions. Deinstitutionalization resulted in concentrations of former institution residents in certain localities rather than the diffusion in communities anticipated by its political ideology.

Outcomes of Deinstitutionalization

The Emergence and Solidification of Patterns of Service Delivery

The strategic choices made by OMRDD and provider agencies along with a variety of situational factors established a relatively stable pattern of provider agencies across the state. By the mid to late-1980s, in each locale there was typically one large state agency (DDSO), a small number of large, multi program private agencies, a few single program agencies, and a number of family support agencies. The DDSO and one or two large private agencies typically accounted for at least 50 percent of the enrollments in routine residential and day services (Castellani et al. 1995). Some private agencies became virtually the only provider of services in rural counties while other agencies tended to specialize in certain types of clientele. Even in urban areas there were tacit allocations of clients and services along geographic, historical, ethnic, and other dimensions. Despite the fact that there were a number of large provider agencies in each DDSO, as one upstate DDSO executive put it, "We have unbundled the programs, but virtually everybody gets their services from the same agency." This executive estimated that 95 percent of individuals in his district were getting all their services from the same agency.

The very rapid pace of deinstitutionalization demanded approaches that could be readily implemented. Moving residents in blocks of twelve into ICFs/MR models built to institutional standards, often in clusters on the perimeter of developmental centers facilitated the deinstitutionalization. Expanding existing provider agencies rather than creating new agencies was much more efficient in rapidly increasing capacity. Encouraging private agencies to develop comprehensive arrays of residential, day, and ancillary services allowed deinstitutionalization to proceed rapidly. Moving residents of developmental centers upstate rather than waiting for difficult-to-develop residences in New York City was efficient. Creating state-operated residential and day programs was politically expedient and established specialized services and "backups" in the community as well as in the institutions.

By 1987, on the threshold of the decision to close several institutions, developmental services in New York State appeared to have changed since 1975, and indeed they had. However, the rapid depopulation of the institutions was achieved at the price of establishing community residential and day programs much in the image of institutions. Institutional models were disaggregated and moved off campus or to the perimeter of the campus. Many private agencies expanded into supermarkets of comprehensive programs often providing services on campuses as large as contemporary institutions. New institutions were opened, mini-institutions were created for special populations, and the creation of specialized services in a continuum established a more highly integrated system of public and private institutional and community services than existed in 1975.

Finally, one of the most important features of deinstitutionalization in New York was that overall residential capacity was largely reconfigured, but not greatly expanded. Despite the large-scale and rapid pace of New York's deinstitutionalization and creation of community residential beds in ICFs/MR and Community Residences, from 1980 to 1986, total residential capacity only increased by 8 percent. In fact, when measured from 1967, the peak year of developmental center census, there was an overall decline in residential capacity. The issue of waiting lists reemerged, and various surveys and estimates found that between 8,000 and 12,000 individuals had been waiting for a residential placement at least a decade after the official initiation of deinstitutionalization (OMRDD 1987). Deinstitutionalization was important for the restructuring of developmental services in New York and the expansion of the private sector, but it did not significantly expand the amount of core residential programs in the state. And undergirding the reorganization of services was a refinancing of those services.

Private Agency Funding: Stabilizing the Fiscal Foundations for Long-Term Growth

Launching deinstitutionalization by converting private agency-operated Community Residences to small ICFs/MR for funding the rapidly expanding community services was a bold strategy. It shifted the burden of financing from the state to the federal government while holding the localities harmless for their share of Medicaid. It was designed to solve the structural imbalance between the costs of providing these services and what the state could pay through regular 41.33 contracts and the "start-up" Purchase of Services contracts. This strategy also rested on implementing ICF/MR rate methodologies to replace the Community Residence contracts. Moreover, a set of related complex fiscal mechanisms supplemented these methodologies. Base year trended, subsidiary property corporations, funded depreciation, and a variety of instruments did not have the *cachet* of "plastics" in this decade. In fact, they were usually ignored or dismissed (to the delight of those who designed and implemented them) as "technical." But, these were the mechanisms that generated the income—and surpluses—that were crucial to building, cementing, and transforming a fragile array of parent-run agencies into an "industry."

Small ICFs and Rate-Setting Systems

The conversion of private agency Community Residences to ICFs/MR required that OMRDD move from an annual contract to a fee-based model of reimbursement. Initially, these fees were based on six models of ICFs/MR (A through F) that were classified by the level of disability of each of the residents and adjusted for the size of the residence. The assumption was that ICFs/MR housing more disabled residents would require more staffing and would be more costly. However, the six-model system added complexity to an already unclear linkage among the factors accounting for staffing and the costs of providing services, and neither the state nor the federal government had an independent basis for predicting those relationships (CQC 1980; Clauser, Rotegard, and White 1985).

What was clear was that the conversion to the ICF/MR model not only shifted the costs to the federal government but also increased these costs. Higher administrative costs, increased staffing in what was essentially a variation of a nursing home, and ancillary costs in ICF/MR rates not included in Community Residence budgets were elements in the new methodology that produced *initial* rates 45 to 70 percent higher than the average Community Residence in New York City (CQC 1980, 11). While New York's Commission on Quality of Care and federal Medicaid funders saw these features as problems, astute financial managers in OMRDD and private agencies began to see that these features also created opportunities.

Budget-Based Model

In 1984, OMRDD scrapped the six-model rate method and shifted to a budget-based rate approach for financing the entire ICF/MR site. The case-mix methodology at the core of this new rate system was based on a composite "score" for each ICF/MR. The variables included the characteristics and needs of the residents, the size of the facility, whether it had shift or live-in staffing, and geographic location (as a proxy for labor cost variation). Direct care and clinical staffing "screens" were derived using an algorithm based largely on the specific needs of each resident of the ICF/MR, and a *per diem* rate for the ICF/MR site was established—essentially the budget-based cost of the site divided by the number of residents divided by 365 (OMRDD 1987). A key problem was how to measure the characteristics of the residents in a way that would translate into levels of need for type and intensity of clinical and direct care staffing (FTEs). Clauser, Rotegard, and White's review of the wide variety of ICF/MR rate systems adopted by the states found that "little is known about the influence of facility, geographic, and level of care variables on cost differences within and across state ICF-MR systems (1985, 8–17). They also pointed out that, "There is precious little research analyzing facility costs by differences in client characteristics" (8–17).

The relationship between resident characteristics, staffing, and costs may have been unclear, but New York had to create an instrument for measuring these characteristics that were central to its rate-setting algorithms. To accomplish this, OMRDD designed the Developmental Disabilities Information System (DDIS) in 1978 and began implementing it in 1979 (OMRDD 1978). The DDIS measured categories of need (none, mild, moderate, and severe) in several "domains" such as behavior, medical, and intellectual functioning. The DDIS was experimental, and it had substantial problems in validity and reliability. However, it was probably as good or better than the instruments used in other states, and the federal government had no standards against which it could be evaluated.

There was another feature of the role of the DDIS in the initial rate-setting system that had long-term implications. The DDIS, and the Developmental Disabilities Profile (DDP) that replaced it, was completed by the provider agency. The provider of service, without close oversight or monitoring by OMRDD, made the assessment of the characteristics of the individuals they would serve that would be a central element in the rates they would receive. This was critical to rate setting and a fundamental feature in the relationship between OMRDD and the private provider agencies. It was not until the mid-1990s that OMRDD began a limited number of *post hoc* reviews of day programs where "DDP creep" appeared to be driving excessive rates. Well before these reviews, however, a mini-industry of DDIS and DDP consultants emerged to assist provider agencies in administering the assessment instruments.

A Cost-Based Methodology and Base-Year Trended

In 1985, OMRDD began its initial comprehensive cost finding for private agency operated ICFs/MR in order to move to a cost-based rate methodology.

OMRDD gathered cost reports from the agencies and determined, subject to some negotiation with the agency, the costs of operating each ICF/MR (OMRDD 1987). These initial costs established 1986 as the base year for the cost-based rate system that was implemented in 1988. However, staffing, the largest cost, was variable, with direct care, supervisory, support, and clinical positions shared among several sites and among other programs. Other nonpersonal service costs were also difficult to assign to specific sites. While OMRDD had developed cost-finding techniques to maximize federal financial participation, it did not have extensive experience in determining private agency costs. Moreover, while the industry as a whole may have been in its adolescence, some agencies were more advanced than others in their financial sophistication. A substantial number apparently understood the long-term consequences of OMRDD's initial cost-finding and deferred expenditures and "found" extraordinary amounts of ICF/MR costs that could be included in the 1986 *base year* for the new methodology (CQC 1995a).

The importance of establishing as large a base year as possible was that a central feature of the new methodology was *base year trended*. Each year, the state Department of Health calculated a trend factor based on the rise in the Consumer Price Index along with some factors specific to health care costs, and OMRDD used this trend factor for a yearly increase in the base year rate for each ICF/MR. From the 1986 base year to 1994, when a new base year was established, this trend factor cumulatively increased private agency operated ICF/MR rates by over 67 percent. Moreover, once the initial rate for the specific ICF/MR was established, there was no statutory or regulatory obligation for the agency to actually expend the resources that drove the costs that were included in the base year. The only regulatory obligation of the agency was to maintain a level and quality of services sufficient to meet ICF/MR certification standards, measured by periodic quality assurance surveys. Once the initial case-mix rate was set for each ICF/MR, the provider agency continued to receive that rate for that ICF/MR, regardless of whether client characteristics changed or less disabled residents replaced more disabled residents. The replacement of more disabled for less disabled residents invariably led to a rate appeal. Very quickly, a large number of agencies began to spend less than base year costs and generated substantial *surpluses* from those programs.

Rate Appeals

In addition to a basic rate-setting process that provided generous funding to the rapidly expanding private provider sector, rate appeals played a big role. Rate appeals were not rare occurrences, and, once granted, they had significant, long-term consequences for agencies' funding. A study of rate appeals by the Commission on the Quality of Care for the Mentally Disabled found that over

30 percent of the private agencies that operated ICFs/MR and Community Residences had their rates increased through appeals, and over 50 percent of all ICF/MR sites had rates that included "rolled over" appeals into future years (CQC 1995a). This study found a number of problems in the appeals process: poor documentation on the part of the provider agency, systemic flaws in OMRDD's review process, improper calculations of the occupancy levels, double reimbursement of property costs, and reimbursement of nonallowable costs (CQC 1995a).

Day Treatment: Variable Fees and Day Lite

Day Treatment was a Medicaid State Plan service New York established in the late 1970s as the day program corollary to the ICF/MR. Individuals who were Medicaid-eligible for the ICF/MR residential program would now attend a Medicaid-funded day program. As in the case of ICFs/MR, the initial costs were higher than in non-Medicaid programs such as sheltered workshops, and they provided state and private agencies additional opportunities to maximize federal reimbursement for fiscal growth and stability.

Day Treatment programs were initially funded through a flat fee reimbursement mechanism. During the 1980s, additional tactics were employed to "medicaid" previously non-Medicaid reimbursable services and make this an even more fiscally lucrative program. One very successful innovation was the creation of "Day Lite." In the original flat fee reimbursement for Day Treatment, there was a provision for half-day services, but that required three to five hours of participation in the program. Under "Day Lite," agencies could bill one-third the Day Treatment per diem rate for individuals in (non-Medicaid) sheltered workshops who occasionally needed some additional services or attention, for example behavior modification, and that service could be for as little as one hour per day. In the 1980s, OMRDD also switched from the flat fee reimbursement for Day Treatment to a variable rate methodology based in large part on variation in consumer characteristics (measured by the DDIS), but also including add-ons for staff training, variations in regional costs, and utility and property costs (OMRDD 1987). The new variable Day Treatment rate provided an enhanced rate for all consumers as well as add-ons for difficult-to-care-for consumers, measured by the DDP that replaced the DDIS. The DDP was a more valid and reliable instrument. However, like its predecessor, it was independently administered by private agency staff. The new rate methodology produced more income, and the virtually inevitable "DDP-creep" contributed to increased reimbursement. Day Treatment became the private agencies' fiscal engine in day services, generating operating surpluses along with ICFs.

Clinics and Early Intervention Programs

As deinstitutionalization progressed, the expectation was that people with developmental disabilities would get services from a greater number of sources, particularly health and medical services from so-called generic agencies. However, in New York a number of private developmental services agencies established Medicaid-funded clinics under Article 28 (NYS Department of Health regulations) or Article 16 (OMRDD regulations). This allowed them to provide a variety of medical and health-related services to their own clients rather than sending them to generic health providers. The substantial fiscal benefits accruing to these agencies and the problems of rapidly escalating costs with limited means of oversight led to OMRDD establishing a moratorium on new Article 16 clinics. However, those agencies that managed to get clinics established before the moratorium found them to be important sources of income as well as another component in their increasingly comprehensive service organization.

During the 1980s, the costs of early intervention programs for children with developmental disabilities under the age of five skyrocketed. Funding for these programs was largely under the aegis of local Family Courts which approved packages of early intervention services, including transportation, that were presented to them by parents and state-funded local advocacy agencies (Early Childhood Direction Centers) often working in close collaboration with the agency which was going to provide the services. Many private agencies began or increased delivering early intervention services and used the largely unregulated reimbursement as an additional source for expansion and fiscal stability (LCER 1984; Bird, Castellani, and Nemeth 1990).

Reimbursing Administrative Costs

New York's success in early maximization of Medicaid was dependent on quickly developing the management capacity to take advantage of the opportunities of Medicaid funding. The management capacity of parent-run agencies had to be quickly enhanced if they were going to operate within these increasingly complicated fiscal schemes. Generous allowances for administrative costs were included in the rates in the first instance. However, the rates for ICFs/MR and Day Treatment also allowed for what was called a "direct charge method" in which an agency could allocate administrative costs among programs and sites. The problem for OMRDD and the opportunity for provider agencies was that the private agencies were operating numerous day and residential programs for OMRDD, rehabilitation programs for the Office of Vocational Rehabilitation and the Office of Mental Health, early intervention programs through Family Courts, school programs through the State

Education Department, and various other services funded by federal, state, and local government, insurers, and private payers. Provider agencies could shift administrative costs among programs and among payers. For example, if an agency actually spent less than the amount for administration allowed in the ICF/MR rate methodology, it could shift administrative costs in from programs that did not have generous administration allowances or from a program where an agency may have overspent on administration. Neither OMRDD nor the other public agencies had a clear idea of what the provider agencies were doing. It was becoming clear that agencies that developed good fiscal management capacity and had the ability to hire accounting firms and consultants were able to grow and become financially stable. Few in the public sector wanted to stifle what was viewed as an overall positive development despite grumbling about the large increases in some private agency executive salaries.

Ultimately, New York instituted a Consolidated Fiscal Report that was intended to provide one overview of public funding, but it proved difficult to administer and monitor. A "ratio value method" was later adopted to diminish the ability to arbitrarily assign administrative costs, and the allowances for administration in the rates were substantially reduced. Nonetheless, the mechanisms used during most of the 1980s were important in allowing the private agencies to enhance their management capacity.

Paying for Property: Capital Financing of Community Programs

In the mid-1970s, OMRDD and private agencies circumvented the ban on including the cost of purchasing property in 41.33 and Purchase of Services contracts by encouraging and assisting those agencies to set up subsidiary corporations to purchase property and pass through the costs as leases in the contracts with the state. By the mid-1980s, an audit by the Office of State Comptroller found that at least 50 percent of the private agencies that operated ICFs/MR had established related property companies (OSC, 1990). This audit also found that, "many not-for-profit private agencies have been able to earn substantial profits by leasing space for services to the developmentally disabled from related property companies at excessive rental rates" (OSC 1990, MS1). The OSC audit found that, "OMRDD, either through inaction or by the constraints of its regulations, has permitted the property companies to charge excessive rents" (OSC 1990, MS2). The OSC report provided a variety of examples of how related property companies loaned the excess profits back to the parent agency and subsequently forgave those loans. Reminiscent of Inspector Renault's "shocking" discovery of illegal gambling at Rick's Café in the movie *Casablanca*, OMRDD called the use of the word *profits* in the audit, "inflammatory," "misleading," and inappropriately implying that "something illegal had taken place" (OSC 1990, A2).

Funded depreciation was another mechanism created to provide additional funding to private agencies. In OMRDD's rate methodologies, a private agency could receive depreciation reimbursement for capital costs. The purchase of buildings, costs of construction and rehabilitation, renovations, and fixed equipment in excess of the principal portion of payments made on indebtedness incurred for these items could be included in an agency's rates if the agency "funded" this excess by depositing it to a separate interest-bearing checking account or other OMRDD-approved investment (OMRDD 1987, 83). With this device, OMRDD effectively granted the private provider agency, up front, the dollar amount of capital expenditures, which was then supposed to go into a "locked box" for the purpose of replacing this equipment at the end of its useful life. At the same time, OMRDD allowed the agency to depreciate the cost of that equipment or capital expense in its rate, thus effectively paying twice for the private agency's costs.

Other key elements in private agency capital financing were Prior Property Approvals and State Aid Grants. Since banks were reluctant to lend to private agencies, OMRDD issued a Prior Property Approval that gave the banks an iron clad commitment that everything in the purchase was in order for the agency to get reimbursement of capital costs through the rates. The State Aid Grant solved the problem of banks not lending 100 percent of the costs of a project by making up the difference between the costs of the project and what the banks would lend.

The cumulative impact of all of these new and restructured funding sources and mechanisms was to stabilize and solidify the fiscal foundations of private agencies and link, not separate, public and private, institution and community services.

Family Support Services and Other Funding Sources for Private Agencies

New York also used a number of mechanisms to integrate private providers of support and ancillary services as well as "independent" planning and advocacy organizations within the overall strategic framework of developmental services.

Developmental Disabilities Planning Council Contracts

In 1970, the federal Developmental Disabilities Services and Facilities Construction Act authorized and funded state Developmental Disabilities Planning Councils (DDPC) which were expected to plan, monitor, evaluate, and advocate on behalf of developmentally disabled people in conjunction with the state agency. The DDPC was to be comprised of interested citizens, along with nongovernmental agencies, and representatives of public agencies who would advocate for services, identify issues to be addressed by state policy makers, and develop long range plans *independent* of the state's developmental disabilities agency. While these bodies operated more or less independently in many states, New York's DDPC operated *within* OMRDD until 1982 where funding was used for a variety of planning, research, and demonstration projects under the complete control of OMRDD executives. After 1982, New York's DDPC was officially located outside OMRDD, and the governor's office appointed council members and executive directors. However, executive staff had very close ties to the legislature, the governor's office and OMRDD. The "citizen" representatives were largely parents drawn from major provider agencies. OMRDD staff drafted the DDPC Plan, and DDPC funds financed a variety of demonstration projects in OMRDD as well as in the agencies represented on the DDPC.

The DDPC brought advocacy groups who were not major providers of services into the network by making grants to them for various information and public education programs. The amount of DDPC funding was minuscule compared to OMRDD's budget, but careful investment of that funding paid large dividends in cementing the relationships among the private provider agencies, advocacy groups, and OMRDD.

Family Support Services

By the early to mid-1980s, the full range of core residential and day services was being implemented in the state and private sectors. Private agencies, however, claimed that they were providing "soft" services to families who kept their children at home. These included respite, recreation, family counseling, information and referral, and parent training, and these were not part of regular programs and their funding was limited and uncertain (Castellani et al. 1986). OMRDD, using DDPC funding, launched an initiative that renamed these "Family Support Services." Dovetailing with the strengthening families theme in Governor Mario Cuomo's first term, they became a new category of state funding.

Family support services were implemented through annual contracts and never cost more than a small fraction of total OMRDD and private agency expenditures. Nonetheless, providing occasional weekend respite to allow a family to deal with an emergency or to take a vacation and supporting recreation programs and transportation to them proved to be enormously popular. The families receiving these services became a bulwark of political support for OMRDD and were carefully nurtured in regional and statewide Family Support Councils. Family support contracts were used by the larger private agencies to cover the costs of previously underfunded services. Larger agencies also used family support services for vertical integration. With these "feeder programs," as one private agency executive called them, providers of adult services could deliver after-school recreation, respite, and other programs for parents of younger children with disabilities who would be likely to enroll their children in these agencies when they needed adult services.

By the end of the 1980s, virtually all of the private agencies that delivered core residential and day services were operating one or more of the 950 separate family support programs around the state (Castellani et al. 1995). By the late 1980s, more than 250 additional private agencies had contracts to deliver only family support services (Castellani et al. 1995). Many of these were religious organizations, neighborhood groups, and community agencies whose political importance far outweighed the cost to OMRDD and the state.

Cementing the Linkages: Provider Councils, Statewide Associations, and Planning

From the creation of the Association for Retarded Children in 1948, to the filing of the *ARC v. Rockefeller* suit in 1972, and at least until the signing of the Willowbrook Consent Decree in 1975, the relations between the state and the main advocacy organizations were hostile. The election of Hugh Carey as governor in 1974, the signing of the Willowbrook Consent Decree, and the creation of a separate Office of Mental Retardation and Developmental Disabilities were turning points in the relationship. However, it was not until the operational and fiscal partnership between the state and the ARC and UCP chapters that emerged from the ICF Plan of Compliance was a new political relationship with the private sector defined and cemented.

Provider Councils were semiformal bodies that emerged to broker relationships between OMRDD and its private provider partners. The Day Services Provider Council and the Residential Services Provider Council were the most important. These councils consisted of the executives of the major provider agencies and OMRDD top fiscal executives. Meetings were wide-ranging discussions on the implications of new rate-setting mechanisms, rate appeals, budgets, and whatever other fiscal issues needed to be addressed. Since most of the large agencies were providing both residential and day services, the overlap resulted in frequent and highly integrated attention to these issues.

Provider agency associations also became critical players. The Inter-Agency Council (IAC) was formed as a consortium of the private agencies in New York City and had a permanent professional staff that coordinated the activities of the member agencies and lobbied on issues for its membership. OMRDD executives routinely attended IAC meetings and hashed out a range of operational and fiscal issues, especially with the largest agencies known as "the big six." Of course, IAC agencies were also on the provider councils.

The New York State Association for Rehabilitation Facilities (NYSARF) was formed to represent workshop and other day service agencies, and a New York State Association of Community Residence Agencies (NYSACRA) was created to represent operators of residential services. Once again, the fact that most large agencies operated both residential and day services resulted in a high degree of overlap among the associations and the provider councils.

The unique organizational structure of the largest provider agencies was another important element in cementing linkages. In New York, the sixty-two chapters of the Association for Retarded Citizens are subsidiaries of one statewide private corporation with a large central professional staff. While the chapters operate semiautonomously, this single corporate structure provided a vehicle for an unusually high degree of coordination in articulating positions on a variety of issues with OMRDD. The United Cerebral Palsy Association has a similar statewide structure for many of its constituent agencies. Despite the fact that there are hundreds of private agencies providing developmental services in New York State, the high degree of overlap among the major providers as well as the statewide associations and structure of the ARC and UCP meant that OMRDD could address and resolve problems with a relatively small and cohesive number of providers.

The Rockefeller administration was an era of planning. However, as described earlier, the elaborate, and overlapping, planning processes exacerbated the hostile relations between the state and the mental retardation constituency. The new direction New York and the parent agencies took in the mid-1970s was without an explicit plan. Plans, however, became an important component in defining and cementing the new relationship between OMRDD and its private agency partners and other constituents.

An amendment to the Mental Hygiene Law in 1977 created Section 5.07(b) that required the constituent agencies of the Department of Mental Hygiene, which included OMRDD, to submit five-year comprehensive local and statewide plans for services. The requirement for "5.07 Plans," as they were known, became an important vehicle for the newly created OMRDD to develop and articulate policy goals and objectives. OMRDD's 5.07 Plans were comprehensive documents that described the various facets of the developmental services system and laid out plans for policy and practice in the area. By the mid-1980s, the plans included extensive "policy papers" on priority goals such as prevention, early intervention, managing the system, and serving older individuals. As well as touting accomplishments, these plans were used to articulate and test major new policy directions, for example, "Continue Developmental Center Closures and Deinstitutionalization" (OMRDD 1987).

The development of the plans was carefully controlled by OMRDD and overseen by the governor's staff and other control agencies. Nonetheless, OMRDD invited a variety of outside experts to participate, created a number of plan advisory committees, and, very importantly, conducted extensive hearings on the draft plan in various locations around the state. Elements of the 5.07 Plans were designed to deal with emerging problems and new constituencies and included sections on serving minority populations and people with low-incidence and other developmental disabilities not represented by the major providers. Throughout the 1980s, OMRDD's 5.07 Plans became a vehicle for constituency input, articulation of goals and objectives, and cementing politically important linkages among disability groups, geographic regions, racial and ethnic minorities, and other constituencies.

The Local Government Plan (LGP) was a subset of the 5.07 Plan and was organized around counties. Counties, the long-despised bastion of psychiatrist dominated Community Mental Health Boards, had been largely cut out of developmental services by Coughlin in the creation of DDSOs. The LGP process was a prickly affair, and OMRDD managed to keep counties in the process, albeit at the margins.

The federally funded Developmental Disabilities Planning Council (DDPC) was required to produce its own five-year plan. OMRDD planning staff played a central role in producing the DDPC Five-Year Plan. While the main objectives of the DDPC plan were dictated by the federal government, OMRDD used the DDPC plan process as an adjunct of the 5.07 Plan, ensuring that all players were singing from the same song book.

An Integrated Political Constituency

There was competition between agencies. There were regional tensions. County governments were surly participants on the margins. Advocates for racial and ethnic minorities expressed dismay at the lack of agencies and services in their locales. Parents of children with low-incidence disabilities felt their concerns were neglected. Nonetheless, the crucial element in the success of OMRDD's strategy was to turn the relationship between itself and its constituents from an adversarial to a political partnership and to use a wide variety of mechanisms and processes to resolve conflict *within* the partnership. Using its own frameworks, and those it controlled, OMRDD dealt with disagreements in semiprivate venues. The 5.07 and DDPC Plans provided continuing articulation and negotiation around major policy objectives.

The creation of a large and increasingly integrated network of providers rested on generous funding (and long-range, built-in funding mechanisms) that allowed private agencies to expand horizontally and vertically. While the various rate schemes and mechanisms stabilized and enhanced private agency fiscal well-being, they depended on an increasingly large fiscal management capacity—one that could administer many complex rate and contract systems for private agencies *and* integrate them with the similarly complex rate and reimbursement systems on the state side. Large numbers of existing and some new agencies were brought into the network of providers with family support services and DDPC contracts where relatively small amounts of state funding provided an exponential political impact. By the 1980s, when the key actors "went downtown," as the presentations to the legislature and the governor's office were characterized, they went as partners and ensured that OMRDD and its private agencies got their "fairer share."

A decade after the Willowbrook Consent Decree and the ICF Plan of Compliance, the relatively simple fiscal world of annual 41.33 and Purchase of Service contracts had been transformed into the complex business of case-mix methodologies, variable rates, screens, algorithms, and trend factors. The private sector in New York had grown exponentially, had become fiscally stable, and was well on its way to becoming "the industry." In contrast to the experience in many other states, public institutions and private community agencies were not locked into a zero-sum game. The well-being of this private sector was crucial to the vitality of public institutions.

Developmental Centers: The Cash Cows

Virtually every study of large public institutions focuses on their costs. Trent (1994) explained "the abandonment of the institution after 1970," by arguing, "the federal policy of deinstitutionalization resulted from an ironic convergence of developments: a combination of civil-libertarian and advocacy groups joined with state officials hoping to trim the ever-rising costs of state institutions" (4–5). It became axiomatic among advocates that institutions should be closed because they cost more than superior community services. But, public institutions persist in New York because of the integral role they play in a developmental services system *and* because their fiscal benefits outweigh their costs.

Growing Role of Federal Reimbursement

In New York fiscal year 1975, with Medicaid reimbursement limited almost exclusively to state institutions, the federal government provided approximately 35 percent of total state-federal expenditures for developmental services (*Executive Budget* 1976–77). New York took an aggressive stance toward maximizing this federal reimbursement. A massive conversion of Community Residences to ICFs/MR, the conversion of state-funded Day Training to

Medicaid-funded Day Treatment, and the use of Medicaid-funded Personal Care in Family Care were other elements in what would become a permanent strategy of "medicaiding."

Cost Finding

New York's strategy was to find costs in those Medicaid programs that could be billed to the federal government. While the census in developmental centers was dropping, their costs, and the amounts billed to the federal government, rose substantially. Three major factors accounted for this dramatic increase in the institutional reimbursement rates: cost finding, fixed costs, and base-year trended.

Developmental center rates were derived from a "universal" survey of costs that included both fixed and variable costs, and the net was cast as broadly as possible. Developmental center costs included not only the salaries of the employees of these facilities but also salaries of OMRDD central office staff whose efforts could be legitimately charged to aspects of developmental center operations as well as the salaries and related costs of employees in other agencies who performed fiscal, personnel, auditing, quality assurance, and other functions related to developmental center operations. The large increase in institutional rates was a result of OMRDD's successful effort in finding institution costs reimbursable by the federal government.

Fixed costs were the other central element in calculating institutional rates. As the census in the developmental centers declined, variable costs such as food went down. However, a large proportion of the fixed costs of developmental centers, primarily those related to maintaining the capital plant, remained. These fixed costs were spread over a smaller number of residents as deinstitutionalization progressed causing the *per diem* rate to increase. As long as OMRDD operated all twenty developmental centers for a decreasing number of residents, the fixed cost portion of the institutional rate played an important role.

Developmental centers are large ICFs/MR, and, in the same fashion as the small ICFs/MR, their rates were also increased by a trend factor calculated by the Department of Health based on the rise in the Consumer Price Index along with other costs specific to health care. These latter costs increased substantially from the mid-1970s through the 1980s and played an important role in trend factors that had a cumulative impact on developmental center rates. Aggressive cost finding, spreading fixed costs among fewer residents, and trended rates resulted in the large growth of developmental center *per diem* rates from the outset of deinstitutionalization to the decision to close several facilities in 1987 as shown in the following table.

Table 8.3
Developmental Center Per Diem Reimbursement Rates: 1975 to 1987

Fiscal Year	Per Diem Rate
1975	38.90
1976	48.00
1977	57.10
1978	71.80
1979	89.10
1980	97.50
1981	120.00
1982	145.80
1983	155.68
1984	162.72
1985	194.87
1986	201.71
1987	218.85

OMRDD, 2000

By the mid to late-1980s, cost finding and base-year trended transformed New York's public institutions into Medicaid-fed cash cows and became more, not less, important in the fiscal foundations of developmental services in the state.

Part 4

Closing and Not Closing Institutions

Chapter 9

Closing Institutions:
The Right Thing to Do

Closure is the right thing to do.

—Arthur Y. Webb, Commissioner of OMRDD

Deinstitutionalization radically reduced the number of residents in New York's developmental centers, but the state was still operating twenty public institutions when, in 1985, Governor Cuomo announced that Willowbrook would be closed. In 1986, OMRDD said it would close Westchester Developmental Center, and, in 1987, it announced that Bronx, Craig, Manhattan, Newark, and Rome Developmental Centers would close by 1991. These decisions to close seven developmental centers in a short period of time were sweeping changes in public policy, especially when other states were moving more slowly and reluctantly to close public institutions one at a time.

Closure Policy: Precursors and Contributing Factors

By 1986, a number of factors pointed toward institution closure. The federal courts had given some strong messages directed toward closure. There was an anti-institution stance at the federal Health Care Financing Administration, and the position that all institutions should be closed gained momentum in several policy communities. However, New York's twenty developmental centers played important operational and financial roles in the overall service system. Closure was not inevitable. Moreover, how closure got on the policy agenda, the timing of the decision, its scope, how political support was gained, and how the policy was implemented were all critical to the success of closure—and what happened later.

211

Governor Cuomo Announces the Intent to Close Willowbrook

In 1982, Mario Cuomo was elected governor and inherited Willowbrook. Cuomo and his new administration at OMRDD were determined to end that legacy. OMRDD fiscal staffs had already done analyses of the large operational costs of the Willowbrook case rulings as well as of the growing problem of the capital construction costs of operating large institutions for smaller numbers of residents. Soon after Arthur Y. Webb was appointed Commissioner of OMRDD, he directed his staff to analyze the fiscal and operational ramifications of closing Willowbrook. The fiscal analyses showed that closing Willowbrook would be cost neutral. The governor's staff was assured that state employees would be protected and that there would be no negative political consequences of a closure decision. After several weeks of closely held discussions, it was decided to take the initiative to close Willowbrook and seek a final settlement to the suit (Webb 1988).

In his *State of the State* message in January 1984, Governor Cuomo announced that Willowbrook (renamed the Staten Island Developmental Center) would be closed. Although Willowbrook had been dealt with as a very special case since the Consent Decree in 1975, the decision to close Willowbrook established essential guidelines and decision-making frameworks that would show how closing other institutions could be fiscally, politically, and operationally feasible. This was especially important because other experiences around actual closures had left disturbing memories for agency policy makers and managers.

Closing Small Facilities: Earlier Closure Failures

The Morgado Memorandum which endorsed the state-operated and staffed community programs was, as the Rothmans put it, "political horse-trading" (Rothman and Rothman 1984, 300). The Gouverneur experience served as a lesson that making significant changes in the system of services, moving large numbers of individuals, appropriating and spending large amounts of money, and affecting the interests of powerful organizations and constituencies were unalterably political issues.

New York had closed other facilities for people with mental retardation before the 1987 closure policy initiative. Even though they involved hundreds of residents, these institutions were so much smaller than the other developmental centers that their closing was hardly noted outside the agency and did not create political problems. Discrete Mental Retardation Units (DRUs) at state psychiatric centers closed by transferring residents to developmental centers. Their closing did, however, require surprisingly large amounts of staff time at the sending and receiving facilities as well as in central office in negotiating the placement of the residents, notifying and getting the approval of family members, and dealing with the court if Willowbrook class clients were involved. These small closures made it evident to frontline managers that movement of any significant number of residents would require more time and effort than most had anticipated and provided valuable experience for the managers about the problems involved with closure.

Closing other "small" facilities proved to be more than managerial challenges. For example, when, in 1972, the state decided to close the Sampson Division (for Mental Retardation) of Willard State Psychiatric Hospital by transferring the 200 residents to newer and unquestionably better facilities, the move provoked a substantial and unexpected controversy. Parents, employees, and the management at Sampson joined the local community in protests. Formation of "Save Sampson" committees, visits to state and local political figures, and other similar tactics were used to convince the state to keep the facility open. Ultimately, the residents were bused through picket lines, with television and print media from across the state recording protesters being dragged from the road in front of the buses. The Sampson experience had a lasting effect as a signal to policy makers that even what seemed to be an unreservedly positive move for residents could provoke major employee, parent, community, and general public relations problems.

J. N. Adam, originally a tuberculosis sanitarium, operated as an annex of the Gowanda State Psychiatric Hospital, and was considered for closure in the late 1970s. Notions about closing the aging facility had routinely circulated within OMRDD, and an informal "plan" for closing was discussed and shared with the staff of the facility. Word of this plan quickly reached the state legislators from the area. They were so successful in raising objections to the "plan" for closing the facility that a new, heretofore unrequested building for the center was included in that year's budget at the behest of the legislative leadership—a clear demonstration of the consequences of not having local political leaders on board for any decision to close a facility.

Craig Developmental Center had also previously been proposed for closure. By the early 1980s, the crisis in prison space was beginning to become acute, especially after the defeat of a prison construction bond issue. Through deinstitutionalization, Craig had reduced its census to around 325 residents. The new Commissioner of Corrections, Thomas Coughlin (who had been the first Commissioner of OMRDD) was aware that the Craig campus was large, and the facility had a power plant with increasing overcapacity. In January 1983, the governor's proposed budget called for the closure of Craig by April 1984 and the use of the campus as a prison. The strong negative reaction on the part of parents, local legislators, unions, and other constituency groups resulted in a compromise solution which would retain the developmental center with approximately 120 residents with a portion of the property to be used as a prison. Craig remained open, but not only did resentment on the part of parents and employees remain, but the prison co-location issue became embedded in closure politics.

Factors Favoring Keeping Public Institutions Open

Deinstitutionalization pushed New York State to the threshold of closure. There were, however, a number of powerful factors favoring their continuation.

Institutional Roles of Developmental Centers

Developmental centers typically housed people with the most severe disabilities, usually those with severe medical or behavioral problems (OMRDD 1989). Many of these individuals had moved out of the centers but continued to return as they encountered problems adjusting to community life. As long as the center remained, it often functioned as the "backup" to community services.

Many of the specialized services in a local service system, particularly medical, dental, and ancillary health services, remained in the large institutions. Access to medical and dental care for people with developmental disabilities was often difficult in the community because of antipathy, ignorance, lack of community health services, and low Medicaid reimbursement rates for office visits. Developmental center medical, dental, and health service staff often provided care for individuals living in state and private agency community residences and for people living at home with no access to generic providers. Most administrative and support services in the area also remained at the developmental center, which functioned as the operational hub of services in the district.

Institutions as Employers

Deinstitutionalization resulted in census declines, but the centers still had the largest number of employees in the district. Local government officials were concerned about the dispersal of employment and its economic impact on the immediate community. From the late 1970s, New York used a combination of state and private agency-operated day and residential community programs to serve both those individuals who had never lived in an institution and former residents of the developmental centers. However, there was an important differential impact on employees. Day programs for developmental center residents were provided on-site by professional employees represented by the Public Employees Federation (PEF). In the community, day programs were largely operated by private agencies, while community residential services were provided through state-operated as well as private agencies. With closure, those day program positions would have to be transferred to the private sector, obviously jeopardizing the state work force.

By creating state-operated community residential programs, the jobs of direct care workers, who were represented by the Civil Service Employees Association (CSEA), would remain in the public sector. In fact, the numbers would likely increase with the richer staffing patterns in community residential programs. However, CSEA also represented the bulk of employees in support staff positions at the developmental centers. Groundskeepers, power plant operators, locksmiths, and similar positions would be lost with closure. Safety officers were members of another union, Council 82, and dealing with multiple public employee unions was a challenge in formulating a closure policy. While employees in the institution could take examinations for community program positions, it usually meant a radical change in one's occupation. The transfer of seniority for job location, shift, and pass day preferences was an issue that did not usually occupy policy makers, but its implications for the reorganization of institution and community staffing created unexpected problems.

The major public employee unions had substantial political power in the legislature and had been strong supporters of Mario Cuomo in his 1982 and 1986 gubernatorial races. These unions had also taken strong positions on deinstitutionalization, particularly with charges that the state was "dumping" individuals with mental illness onto ill-prepared community resources and contributing to homelessness and poor care for this vulnerable group. In the Gouverneur-Flower Fifth Avenue Hospital episode, the administration made important concessions to the unions. Public employees expected that the assurances in the Morgado Memorandum would apply to the new closure policy.

Caution of Parents

The parents of people in the institutions were generally older than those who were putting their children directly into community programs, and they were skeptical about closure. They advocated for better conditions in the developmental centers, but they saw the institutions as places where their children would be safe and cared for, especially after their death. Many still viewed community programs as ephemeral and less likely to provide that assurance of life-long care. They were also keenly aware of the difficulties of getting access to medical care in the community.

Concerns of Private Provider and Advocacy Organizations

Despite their long-standing advocacy for people with mental retardation, none of the major provider organizations took strong positions in favor of the closure of developmental centers prior to the 1987 announcement. The ARC, the lead plaintiff in the *ARC v. Rockefeller* suit at Willowbrook, became the largest statewide network of private provider organizations. With assurances that private agencies would continue to be able to serve people directly from their large waiting lists, the individuals they served were more likely to come from those living at home than from the individuals with more severe disabilities who were living in the developmental centers. Some providers saw the severely disabled people in the centers as potential competitors for resources.

Role of Institutions in the Fiscal Structure

The costs associated with operating the large institutions were important components in the overall federal reimbursement. By the late 1980s, the statewide rate for developmental centers was about $300 per day per resident, and accounted for a substantial amount of the total annual federal Medicaid reimbursement—approximately $370 million of the total $500 million. The impact of closing centers with varying costs and numbers of residents was complex. The fixed costs of operating developmental centers would remain as populations declined, and it was likely that transition costs in closure would differ from those experienced in deinstitutionalization. While many advocates argued that the costs of community programs would be less than those of the institutions, this had never been clearly demonstrated. Moreover, budget officials were very cautious about the complex and uncertain implications of closure for Medicaid reimbursement.

Factors Favoring the Closure of Public Institutions

The role of federal courts, the political ideology of normalization, a broadening statutory base undergirding community programs, and Medicaid reform had varying effects on New York's experience. Beyond the specific demands of the Willowbrook case, the possibility that federal courts would play a larger role loomed, then receded, but never disappeared. Federal legislation, especially PL94-142, had important long-term effects in solidifying parental expectations and experience in legally mandated services from an early age. With rapid deinstitutionalization, the state and private provider agencies could claim adherence to the principles of normalization and least restrictive alternative. With large-scale downsizing of developmental centers, the state was addressing at least one aspect of Medicaid reform by lessening its vulnerability in the largest and most easily targeted Medicaid-funded programs. These factors, combined with Willowbrook and the ICF Plan of Compliance, pushed New York to pursue deinstitutionalization as quickly as possible.

Diseconomies of Scale and OMRDD's Capital Plan

OMRDD had a five-year capital budget planning cycle that included both developmental center and community programs. The plans for construction and renovation were based on reviews of the conditions of the physical plants at the centers and in the community in conjunction with the agency's analyses of such factors as the movement of residents among centers, new admissions, and numbers of people to be moved from the centers to community programs. While this capital planning process was important, it was not usually central to creating overall agency policy. Therefore, it was noteworthy that in October 1985, the OMRDD *Program-Capital Plan: 1986–91* contained the following statement: "Westchester Developmental Center, on the Harlem Valley Psychiatric Center campus, will be closing (including the MDU and RBTU) within the next few years" (OMRDD 1985, 91). The capital plan indicated that individuals would move to other upstate facilities and community residences. It was important that such factors as the cost of rehabilitating buildings on a psychiatric center campus led capital planners to project, and "announce," the closing of a facility well before a closure policy statement by senior agency management. Westchester was not a typical developmental center, but the capital plan was an important early signal of one basis of a statewide policy.

The 1986–91 *Capital Plan* for Rome Developmental Center showed how capital costs played an important role in the decision to close several developmental centers. Rome was one of the oldest centers in the state and, at its peak census of 5,166 in 1960, one of the largest. On March 31, 1985, the census at Rome Developmental Center was 706 (OMRDD 1985). The *Capital Plan* outlined a "dramatic reconfiguration" of the Rome campus. With the assistance of a construction consulting firm, the plan consisted of major renovations of several residential and program buildings, abandonment of many of the scores of other buildings on the campus, consolidation on one end of the campus, and construction of 144 replacement beds in Small Residential Units (SRUs) at the perimeter of the campus. The plan called for a census reduction to 270 individuals over the next five years that would leave 144 people living in twelve SRUs, and 126 individuals in renovated buildings on the old campus. No sooner had the *Capital Plan* been completed than the planning and budget staffs began to discuss the self-evident diseconomies of a major renovation of the campus for 126 people. This alone did not "drive" policy, but the inherent inefficiencies of renovating and operating old and large institutions, which had housed thousands at their peak, for a few hundred residents moved capital cost issues toward the top of the agency's policy agenda. Moreover, the employment of a fixed number of "institutional" staff such as groundskeepers, safety officers, and power plant operators became less cost effective as the census dropped, and these issues also appeared more prominently in the analyses that budget and fiscal staff presented to senior executive staff.

Role of Developmental Center Staffing in the OMRDD Budget Structure

In addition to the diseconomies it created in "institutional" staff, deinstitutionalization also created imbalances in direct care and clinical staff levels between the developmental center and community programs. Community day services were most often provided by private agencies in sheltered workshops and day treatment programs. This created a surplus of clinical staff positions at the developmental centers. Much of the discussion around this problem was subsumed under the technical budget term, the "third header issue." This involved accounting for staff justified in the budget for institution functions but actually working in community programs which local managers felt were inadequately staffed, especially in support services areas. Moreover, the district offices argued that they often provided clinical supports to private agency programs that were not taken into account in staffing allocations. As deinstitutionalization increasingly shifted the individuals to community programs, these issues became more prominent in the discussions between the central and district offices in OMRDD and between OMRDD and the Division of the Budget. While the particulars in each district varied, the overall problem loomed large at the beginning of 1986 and became a catalyst for the crafting of a closure policy.

Commissioner Webb as the Policy Entrepreneur

Personalities played a role in the decision to close several institutions, and the Commissioner of OMRDD at this time, Arthur Y. Webb, was instrumental in moving OMRDD from deinstitutionalization to closure. In many respects, Webb fit the model of "policy entrepreneur" (Kingdon 1984). A focus on innovation and other hallmarks of policy entrepreneurship became central themes of his administration. Webb had served in the Division of Budget and in senior level positions in a number of state agencies before being named Commissioner of OMRDD in 1983. His appointment coincided with a severe fiscal crisis in the state that resulted in a large number of layoffs in the district offices and in the central office. This provided one rationale for change. Webb began a strategic planning initiative with Kepner-Tregoe Associates, reorganized central office staff, decentralized more authority to district office directors, and began a series of task forces, directors' retreats, policy papers, statewide meetings, and hearings around the state on "the community challenge." Webb also backed a proposal to significantly restructure the fiscal relationship with the federal government through the 1115 Waiver proposal. It was apparent that Webb had laid the basis for and was personally predisposed to take any opportunity to make significant policy departures.

Management Capacity and Experience in OMRDD

Another factor favoring a policy to close institutions was the OMRDD's managerial capacity and experience. OMRDD now operated a very large number of the community residential and day programs as well as the developmental centers, and much of the large-scale deinstitutionalization had been done directly by OMRDD in conjunction with private agencies. In the central office most of the senior staff in the Program Operations Division, who had served in district offices, shared a strong progressive position that institutions should be closed. OMRDD not only had the managerial capacity to undertake closure, but deinstitutionalization provided the extensive experience in most of the key activities that would be required to close several institutions (Gargan 1981). In the three years prior to the closure decision, over 4,100 new community residential places had been developed. In the five years prior to the closure decision, over 700 people each year had been moved out of the centers. By January 1987, OMRDD and private agencies were establishing community programs at a rate of over 1,500 residential beds and about 3,000 day program places per year.

Deinstitutionalization involved setting up organizations, processes, and staffs to undertake that level of program development. Additionally, the complex web of relationships with the large number of other state governmental agencies, federal agencies such as HUD, banks, and others involved in this extensive an undertaking were established. Formal and informal decision rules, routines, coordinative mechanisms, and crisis management techniques had been tested. OMRDD was able to take the initiative in making a policy decision to close several centers in large measure because it believed that it already had the managerial capacity and experience in the areas that would be required to implement such a decision.

Support for Closure in the Field

The attitudes of the district office directors and their senior managers would be very important to the closure decision, and Webb was confident that he could count on support for closure in OMRDD field offices. OMRDD had decentralized considerable authority to the districts by using the notion of "commissioners-in-the-field" to signify the enhanced role expected of DDSO directors. This decentralized authority was to be applied particularly in streamlining development of community day and residential services. Their success was measured not only with respect to maintaining institutional standards for certification but also on the pace of their deinstitutionalization.

It was apparent that virtually all district directors and their senior staffs would support closure. As a group, these individuals were relatively young, and had joined the system in the mid- to late-1970s. Unlike many of their counterparts in the mental hospitals, they were not physicians (most had clinical/habilitative backgrounds or were professional administrators), and they had transferred among the facilities and through the central office regularly. There were no long-standing institutional identifications, either by length of service or clinical orientation. Some directors had already expressed opinions in favor of closure, and a few had even informally told their senior staffs that they expected to close their developmental centers. It was important that, for DDSO administrative staff, closure would not be an occupational threat. Unlike psychiatric center directors and their senior staff, the OMRDD district office directors were responsible for the network of state and private agency operated programs in their districts, and this would continue after closure. Indeed, a disproportionate share of the problems that district office executive staff faced were associated with maintaining ICF/MR certification in developmental centers. The closure policy rested heavily on OMRDD executive staff assumptions that the district offices had the experience and capacity to implement it.

Field Testing Closure Policy and Closure Implementation

OMRDD was able to satisfy the governor's office that it could manage a broad-based closure policy by field-testing it in two cases.

Westchester as a Test Case for Closure Policy Making

In virtually all other DDSOs, the developmental center had been the historical core and focus of services, predating by many years the establishment of any community-based services. In Westchester, the developmental center had been a recently added component of the service system, had always been geographically removed, and had the peculiar status of being on the grounds of another institution and transferred from another DDSO. The co-location with the psychiatric center as well as a secure Division for Youth facility at Harlem Valley were concerns of the staff and constituency groups. The Office of Mental Health periodically expressed interest in reoccupying the buildings being used as the developmental center. These factors and the inordinate costs of renovating the facility led to the "announcement" of the plan to close Westchester in the *1986–91 Capital Plan*.

The background to that announcement was critical to crafting a closure policy. A planning group including representatives of Westchester County and OMRDD central office and district staff held extensive discussions with community groups, parents, providers, employee representatives, and local government leaders. The matter-of-fact reaction in Westchester and throughout the state to the December 1986 announcement that Westchester would close showed leaders in the executive and legislature, unions, private agencies, parents, and advocates that OMRDD could craft a closure policy with a high likelihood of success and limited negative political impact. The fact Westchester was in the district of the (Republican) Chairman of the Senate Committee on Mental Hygiene and no opposition was heard from that quarter also gave a clear signal that a decision to close the center would not create a political problem for the Cuomo administration.

Willowbrook as a Test Case For Closure Implementation

Westchester was a test of closure policy making. Willowbrook was a test of closure implementation. Closing Willowbrook posed an enormous problem for OMRDD, especially since it remained under the oversight of the court. The closing of Willowbrook provided an opportunity for OMRDD to test elements of its plan to close other developmental centers. Successful resolution of work force issues, community relations, and alternate use of the facility would be crucial in getting the governor's support for a broader closure policy.

There was a long history of difficult labor-management relations at Willowbrook, and the decision to close the developmental center uncovered a number of new problems concerning job security and the difficulties of making the transition to positions in community programs. Willowbrook was located on Staten Island, closer to New Jersey than the other five boroughs of New York City, and many of the direct care workers lived in New Jersey. The prospect for employees of transferring to positions in other boroughs was daunting. To deal with this and other work force issues, an Employee Services Office (ESO) was established as part of a joint labor-management agreement. The first director of the ESO had headed a similar effort in the closing of Ford's Mahwah, New Jersey plant. This individual established the reputation of the ESO as an "honest broker" in the transition and closure process, organized job fairs, trips to other facilities in New York City, the metropolitan region, and even to the Sunmount District Office in the Adirondack Mountains, where a surprising number of long-time Willowbrook employees ultimately took positions. The Willowbrook experience demonstrated that an Employee Services Office would be key to a successful closure.

Another important element of the work force strategy was the use of state-operated community programs (as sanctioned by the Morgado Memorandum). In New York City, state-operated programs absorbed many state employees who might otherwise have been laid off with the closure of Willowbrook. Overall, only 271 of the 1,700 employees at the institution who left the payroll were laid off, and less than twenty of those had not been offered other positions. This served to significantly lessen the opposition of the unions and the consequent concern of the legislature and the governor's office (Webb 1988). The Employee Services Office proved so successful that it was adopted in other closure facilities and eventually extended statewide to all agency offices.

Relations with the Community and Alternate Use

In many locales the developmental center formed a part of the community's physical and mental landscape. In the Willowbrook closure that landscape created substantial problems in community relations. To build houses on the perimeter of the old campus, it was necessary to fell several trees in Corson Brook Woods. The community's response was intense and negative. Neighborhood protests, negative television and press coverage, and a lawsuit seeking to stop the site preparation created a period of extremely tense and adversarial relations with the community. The negative publicity surrounding the Corson Brook Woods issue severely tested the governor's office confidence in OMRDD's management of implementation. After a visit to Willowbrook by Governor Cuomo, another site on the campus perimeter was chosen for the small residences.

Alternate use of the campus was another community relations issue. At the time, New York City was in the midst of a real estate boom. The prospect of a several hundred-acre developmental center campus becoming available drew extensive interest in the real estate community. Following a number of proposals for various private and public development projects, the issue was resolved in favor of consolidation of the College of Staten Island on the campus. OMRDD and the governor's office drew praise from community groups for their efforts in bringing this about. Successfully dealing with these problems in that highly charged environment was a major factor in allowing OMRDD to go ahead with a broader closure policy.

Importance of Maintaining Control

The twenty-five year history of dealing with federal courts on Willowbrook made it painfully evident that the extension of judicial oversight to the closing of other developmental centers would effectively give the courts control of virtually all OMRDD operations. Several other states were involved in court-ordered and court-monitored closings. It was becoming apparent that closures would eventually occur as a result of a variety of factors, and the longer New York waited, the greater was the likelihood that one or more court-ordered closures would eventually occur. If Willowbrook "drove the agency," then two or more court-ordered closures would place implementation of closure and virtually all operations in the agency under the aegis of courts for years. On the other hand, if the state took a broad initiative to close several centers, it was likely that court-ordered and court-monitored closings would be forestalled. The state administration, not the courts, would exercise control.

By 1986 the logic of closure was becoming compelling. Litigation could have a broad impact on OMRDD for years. Deinstitutionalization made the diseconomies of scale self-evident in the operation of several developmental centers. The *Capital Plan* made the long-term physical plant problems apparent. Although developmental centers continued to play a central role in the overall structure of federal reimbursement, the increasing difficulties of meeting ICF standards presented the possibility of large fiscal liabilities and the reality of more and more staff time and energy devoted to maintaining certification. The imbalances in the structure of the budgets of the centers created by large expansions in community programs were becoming increasingly difficult to cover. While "Closure was the right thing to do," (Webb 1988), it was not inevitable.

There were still many powerful factors to support keeping large institutions open. The uncertain fiscal ramifications, the likely disruption of a large number of employees, the concern for stability on the part of parents, the wariness of private providers about the impact, and the centrality of the institution to the traditional organization of services in a locale were among those important factors. In addition to these specific factors supporting the continuation of the centers, there was an overarching issue that forestalled a closure policy. The closure issue was systemic. New York's twenty developmental centers were, by far, the largest institutional system in the country. New York's deinstitutionalization and community development programs were also the most extensive and the largest in the country. Moreover, this depopulation of the centers and creation of new community services had occurred almost simultaneously across each of the districts in the state. The result was that the institutional issues were more or less the same across twenty developmental centers. In those states that had pursued closure, the process had almost always been one facility at a time taking several years to accomplish. This often resulted in wide variations across the state in the mix of institutional and community services. The continuing operational and fiscal dynamics of deinstitutionalization in New York would not allow for closure of one or two facilities over many years, with sixteen or eighteen others open with few residents and extraordinary costs. Closure still presented daunting policy and implementation problems.

The Closure Decision

The closure decision was embodied in a series of policy processes that stretched from the budget and policy planning within OMRDD through the Summer of 1986, tightly held negotiations with the governor's office during the fall of that year, the formal announcement by Governor Cuomo in January 1987 of the decision to close several developmental centers, and the Closure Bill passed by the legislature in the spring of 1987. As in the precursors of the closure decision described earlier, elements of each of these had an impact on the eventual shape of the policy, its implementation, and the subsequent decisions to close all centers—and later to suspend the closure of all centers.

Policy Entrepreneurship: Linking Problems, Solutions, and Politics

In Kingdon's model of policy making, separate "streams" of problems, solutions, participants, and choice opportunities run through organizations. Kingdon argues, "the organization is a collection of choices looking for problems, issues and feelings looking for decision situations in which they might be aired, solutions looking for issues to which they might be the answer, and decision makers looking for work" (Kingdon 1984, 91).

Support for closing large institutions was abroad among the various interests and constituencies in the field. But these notions were often vaguely defined, and important groups were likely to have inconsistent or opposing positions. What was happening at Willowbrook was very important, but that situation was regarded as unique. In Kingdon's terms, closure was still in the primal soup of policy.

The 1987–88 Budget as the Catalyst and Framework for a Closure Policy

The budget process is the quintessential policy stream. It created the impetus and set the timing and framework for the closure policy decision. The fiscal year in New York begins on April 1. Agencies usually start budget preparations in the previous spring and submit the budget proposals to the Division of Budget (DOB) around Labor Day. The *Executive Budget* is presented to the legislature in late January. Spending plan adjustments, negotiations, and discussions about the budget within and between agencies and DOB are continuous.

By 1986, the large scale and pace of deinstitutionalization was creating a situation where OMRDD was, in budget office terms, "competing with itself" for new resources. That is, the full annual costs of the residential and day programs that typically opened late in the fiscal year created substantial out-year obligations. Moreover, as described earlier in the discussion of the "third header" problem, deinstitutionalization resulted in disproportionately high costs for "institution" staff vis-à-vis the number of residents in the centers as well as imbalances in DOB-approved direct care and clinical staff-to-resident ratios.

OMRDD had been consistently successful in getting its "fairer share" of appropriations. However, the percentage increases needed to sustain its pace of development loomed large even in the context of overall surpluses in the state budget. The Division of the Budget was anticipating recommending layoffs of "institution" employees in the 1987–88 fiscal year. These layoffs would include over 400 employees at Bronx, Craig, Manhattan, Newark, and Rome to redress what DOB believed to be large problems in the staff-to-resident ratios at these facilities. However, they were also concerned with the political impact of layoffs at a time when the state's fiscal condition could absorb staffing surpluses and imbalances.

Linking the Policy Streams and Taking the Risk of End-running DOB

The key ingredient for linking the policy streams in this primal soup was a "decision maker looking for work"—a policy entrepreneur. OMRDD Commissioner Webb saw himself in that role. He told his staff, "In any administration, you get one shot at one big decision, and closure is it for OMRDD in the second Cuomo administration." He and the senior staff of OMRDD moved to link the problem and the solution to politics.

Another key ingredient of entrepreneurship is risk, and Webb decided to take a big risk with the1987–88 budget request. OMRDD submitted its budget proposal to DOB in September 1986 without any indication of a closure policy. At the same time, it opened discussions with staff in the governor's office to craft and get approval for a broad-based closure policy. These discussions remained secret not only because of the risk of incurring the wrath of the Division of Budget but also because the parties did not want the potentially problematic issue of closures to be raised in the 1986 gubernatorial campaign, even though Governor Cuomo was expected to win re-election.

In a state with a very strong executive control over the budget process—in its formulation, passage, and implementation—the Division of the Budget (DOB) exercises extraordinary power (DOB 1981). The governor's office program staff maintains oversight over the agencies within each staff member's portfolio. By tightly controlling expenditures from appropriations in a process akin to perpetual "sequestering," DOB has long exercised extraordinarily powerful, central control over the finances in New York State government. With its highly recruited and long-serving civil service staff organized in examination units, DOB also plays a dominant role in managing state government operations and policy.

DOB's institutional style is to maintain quiet control, but newly appointed commissioners quickly learn that virtually every important (some would omit "important") fiscal, policy, and political issue must be approved by DOB. DOB has a long institutional memory, and commissioners and agencies who fail to toe the mark, or end-run DOB to the governor's office or legislature run a very big risk of retribution—sooner or later. OMRDD had not only engaged in an end-run of DOB to the governor's office to craft a closure policy, but had used the budget process as a cover. After DOB was brought into the closure policy process, OMRDD and DOB clashed on several issues.

DOB did not want to be locked into an explicit schedule for closing each facility, but OMRDD prevailed with the argument that the DDSO directors needed to have their feet put to the fire by deadlines. DOB was reluctant to close the recently opened Bronx center or Craig where the political scars from an earlier aborted closure attempt lingered, but OMRDD kept those facilities in the plan. DOB thought that it could still go ahead with planned layoffs, but OMRDD worked with the Governor's Office of Employee Relations to create the widespread impression that closure included a "no layoff" policy. DOB's understanding that an 80-20 state-to-private agency development allocation was agreed upon became a more costly 90-10 split. DOB objected to a "technical" closure bill passed by the legislature because it did not want its hands tied in future consolidations, but OMRDD convinced the governor to sign the bill (Patrick 1987). DOB was extremely upset that OMRDD's "overdevelopment" of community beds in Rome prior to closure resulted in a deficiency budget proposal that DOB was forced to accept. And when DOB felt that it was "sandbagged" by the leak to key legislators of additional community development projects in the pipeline that DOB wanted curtailed, relations reached a new low.

Once the governor announced the closure policy, DOB proceeded with its elements of the implementation process. However, the OMRDD-DOB experience in crafting the 1987 closure policy added long-lasting antagonism to the natural tensions between the program and budget agency. It would reemerge in the 1991 decision to close all developmental centers by 2000 and the reversal of that decision in 1995.

Need for Prison Space

OMRDD's closure policy was crafted with a keen awareness that prisons, not developmental centers, were the primary concern of the governor's staff in 1986. The so-called "Rockefeller Drug Laws," with their mandatory sentencing provisions, were creating serious overcrowding in the state prisons. OMRDD's plans to close several developmental centers meshed nicely with the administration's need for additional prison space.

The need for additional prison space would solve two alternate use issues for OMRDD and provide economical additional capacity for the Department of Correctional Services (DOCS). DOCS could occupy the remainder of the Craig campus (where depopulation had reached a point where a planning committee in that district had proposed creation of a statewide nursing facility to justify its continuation) and Rome (where OMRDD's capital reconfiguration plan showed large diseconomies of scale).

Closing Problem Centers

Another factor in the closure decision was the increasing difficulty in maintaining Medicaid ICF/MR certification in a many developmental centers. There were severe physical plant limitations at Manhattan Developmental Center, and since most of its residents were Willowbrook class members, the problems there received particular scrutiny. Continuing problems in maintaining certification at the Bronx Developmental Center also made that facility a candidate for closure because the projected costs for refurbishing that relatively new facility were enormous. OMRDD was also under pressure from New York City to place children languishing in municipal Health and Hospital Corporation facilities into OMRDD residential programs. Vacant space in OMRDD's centers in New York City was an unwanted invitation to expand services to a variety of dependent populations.

In upstate New York, Newark Developmental Center was one of the oldest facilities, and the newly appointed district director had already indicated his own version of a closure policy by announcing his intention to bring the census at the center to "zero." Staff imbalances at Bronx, Craig, Manhattan, Newark, and Rome made them targets for layoffs in DOB's plans for the 1987–88 fiscal year. OMRDD effectively finessed the issue by proposing to the governor's office that these "problem" facilities could be closed *and* a large part of the prison space problem could be solved at the same time.

Locking in a Multiyear Commitment

Despite the surplus in the budget during the 1986–87 fiscal year, Webb and a executive staff known for its fiscal expertise, wanted to lock in a broad-based, multiyear commitment that would carry beyond the fiscal downturns that were inevitable and, in fact, began two years after the decision. A long-term strategy was also likely to forestall any significant litigation, which was important to the governor's office. A broad closure strategy would address structural anomalies in a system that was becoming community-based but still revolved, fiscally and operationally, around institutions. A closure policy encompassing seven of the twenty developmental centers would tip the system irrevocably toward a complete community base.

Minimizing the Fiscal Impact: MCFAA and DCCIP

There were fiscal hazards in a closure policy. The developmental centers still formed a critical part of the revenue foundation of the system, and "protecting the base" was the first principle of budget and fiscal policy. The capital costs of developmental center renovation were part of OMRDD's closure rationale. New legislation expanding the state's bonding capacity (MCFAA) would allow the state to bond state-operated capital development in the community and not have it show up in the operating budget. OMRDD and DOB officials saw this as tilting the closure argument in OMRDD's favor.

The revenue picture was more problematic. A final piece of the puzzle was a Medicaid State Plan amendment modeled on the state Health Department's hospital closure plan. The Developmental Center Closure

Incentive Plan (DCCIP) would provide federal reimbursement in excess of normal allowable standards for state-operated ICF/MR and Day Treatment programs over a three-year period. The reimbursement would be 200 percent over the standard in the first year, 66.7 percent over in the second, and 33.3 percent over in the third. Total DCCIP revenue for three years was projected to be $34.6 million. This minimized fiscal liabilities on the revenue side.

Elements of Closure Policy and Guidelines Shaping the Closure Processes

In his State of the State Address in January 1987, Governor Cuomo stated that OMRDD would close Bronx, Craig, Manhattan, Newark, and Rome Developmental Centers by 1991, in addition to the already announced decisions to close Willowbrook and Westchester. This was significant not only as a statement of overall objectives but also because the governor himself announced it. His personal stamp would be an important factor at some stages of implementation. The governor's announcement placed particular emphasis on the costs of large institutions.

> "As we develop smaller community-based programs for mentally retarded and developmentally disabled individuals, it becomes clear that the continued affordability of this policy requires the closure or conversion of inefficient buildings and, in some cases, entire campuses. If we fail to recognize the necessity of such steps, we will face an unpleasant reality: the high overhead and capital costs of these facilities will consume precious resources which should be invested instead in community programs" (*Message to the Legislature* 1987).

Shortly after the announcement, OMRDD issued its *Developmental Center Closure Plan: 1987–1991* (OMRDD 1987). This document outlined the main features that were ultimately to be contained in the budget, legislation, spending plans, and a variety of other policy documents. In its outline of the major objectives of closure, several new policy principles were articulated, and other important policy principles were restated. The plan stated that closure would be "programmatically appropriate," "fiscally responsible and appropriate," "less costly than maintaining the large institutional base," and would achieve "governmental efficiencies." Other than these broad assurances, other policy principles contained in the plan had very specific meaning to the constituencies to whom they were addressed. They formed a policy framework guiding the direction and shape of closure implementation. The most significant were stipulations about the schedule and assurances to the private agencies, the state work force, other districts, and the affected communities.

Closure Schedule

At the core of the plan was the schedule of closures. The Staten Island Developmental Center (Willowbrook) was to close in 1987. Westchester and Craig would both close in 1988. The Bronx, Manhattan, Newark, and Rome centers would close by 1991. The issue of a specific timetable for closing each center was controversial. In contrast to court-ordered closures, New York's closure plan was self-imposed, and there were no legal requirements for closure by specific dates. The Division of Budget opposed setting a specific closure schedule, recognizing that the schedule carried a strongly implied commitment of resources well beyond the annual fiscal cycles. Of course, OMRDD executive staff pushed for a statement of specific timetables for just this reason. In addition, the agency felt that the deadlines for closure were necessary to keep both the district and central office staffs focused and committed to specific timetables and measurable outcomes.

Definition of Closure

The *Closure Plan* contained three statements on "The Impact on Client Care" that had important implications for the implementation of closure. The plan called for all (1,335) clients currently living in the institutions to be closed to be placed in residences and day programs in the community. Closure would be achieved by the complete evacuation of all buildings, programs and services on the campus. This was a contrast with the experience in other states, Illinois at Dixon for example, that had "closed" institutions by moving the residents to other institutions (Braddock, Heller, and Zashin 1984). The earlier closures of "small" units in New York had shown that this would be a challenging task.

Renewal of Other Commitments: Courts, Private Agencies, and Other Districts

In the "Impact on Other Significant Agency Commitments & Priorities" section of the plan, OMRDD reiterated its long-standing, fundamental agreement with the private agencies and parents of people living at home. OMRDD explicitly committed to allocate 50 percent of new community beds over the next four years to meet the needs of developmentally disabled individuals living at home who were in need of a community placement. The state's commitment to reducing the populations of the other centers, meeting its obligation to place Willowbrook class clients in the community by 1992, continuing to provide crisis residential services in the areas of the centers being closed, and maintaining the quality of care in the remaining centers were also highlighted. This assured the advocates and groups associated with this case and the Consent Decree that closure would not divert attention away from the state's obligations for these individuals.

Commitment to the State Work Force

The "Impact on State Work Force" section of the plan contained a subtle, but extremely important, commitment. The plan stated that by redeployment of institutional staff into new community programs and by reductions in force "through attrition," the impact of the closure plan on state employees was expected to be minimal. This became the basis of a "no layoff policy." As in the case of the commitment to the private agencies, the Morgado Memorandum continued to form an important element in the foundation of the state's policy framework for the staffing of services.

The "through attrition" statement, nonetheless, emerged from sharp controversy within the administration. At the same time OMRDD was secretly negotiating with the governor's office on closure, DOB was planning layoffs at Rome, Newark, and Craig in the 1987–88 fiscal year. While there were other reasons to designate Rome, Newark, and Craig for closure, many believed that preempting layoffs in these centers played a role in their selection.

Other key constituencies, particularly private agencies and groups in nonclosure districts, were becoming very concerned that community development devoted to closure might have a negative impact on them. The administration also came under pressure from public employee unions to increase the commitment to state-operated development from 80 to 90 percent. While neither figure was made explicit at first, OMRDD began operating on the presumption of the 90/10 split. It was later embodied in statutory language requiring quarterly reports on closure progress to the legislature.

The "Impact on Local Economy" section of the plan promised involvement with local governments and local business communities on decisions on alternate employment and alternate use of the state property. A section on "Financial Impact" stated that closures would yield savings in both capital and operating costs and said that these resources would be available for reinvestment in new community programs.

From the outset, closure was cast in a broad political and economic context. Important commitments to private agencies were reiterated, state employees were given what became known as a "no lay-off policy," and local governmental and business communities were given assurances on involvement in decision-making, alternate use of the property, and reinvestment of savings. The *Closure Plan* restated several policy principles that formed a framework that would shape the direction of implementation. One overarching policy principle implicit in the various assurances was that closure would take place in addition to, not in place of, the current initiatives.

Selling the Closure Decision

The development of the closure policy was not typical because it involved a relatively small number of decision makers. Usually, policies of this magnitude and consequence were the product of extensive discussions within the agency, consultations with key constituency groups, task forces, position papers, public hearings, and a variety of other processes. The fact that the governor announced the decision himself lent substantial weight to its importance and indicated that it was not likely to be reversed. OMRDD would have to overcome the natural tendency of many to oppose the policy simply because they had not been involved in the process. The elements of the *Closure Plan* were crafted to anticipate the concerns of each constituency, but selling the decision within and outside OMRDD was an especially challenging task.

Legislature's Impact on Closure Policy

Several events occurred in the 1987 legislative session following the governor's announcement of the closure plan that had important consequences for implementation: public hearings on the plan, the executive budget, the closure legislation, additional appropriation bills, and plans for the Rome Developmental Center.

The Assembly Standing Committee on Mental Health, Mental Retardation, and Developmental Disabilities and the Senate Committee on Mental Hygiene held joint hearings on the closure plan in February. Many groups expressed annoyance that they had no input in the development of the policy, but the overall reaction was support for closure. Parents, state association representatives, private agency executives, union officials, local and state government elected officials, and other state agency officials were among those testifying, submitting statements, or sending letters to OMRDD and legislative leaders. Some advocates emphasized the need to maintain the commitment to people still living at home as closure proceeded (Platt 1987). Other advocates argued that closing developmental centers was important, but the use of Small Residential Units on the periphery of the old centers, construction of twelve-bed residences, and continued use of day treatment and day training programs had more to do with fiscal dynamics and assurances to state employees than the needs of people with developmental disabilities

(Lottman 1987). Parents of residents of the centers to be closed were especially concerned about the need for adequate health and medical services as well as special programs for individuals with challenging behavior (Taylor 1987). Some groups opposed closure. Some state employees, especially safety officers whose positions were not required in community settings, expressed opposition to the closure plan. Very importantly, the New York State Association for Retarded Citizens stated its opposition to the closure plan in its newsletter, *Our Children's Voice* (ARC 1987).

One important result of the hearings was maintaining involvement in the closure plan on the part of key legislators. The Chair of the Mental Health, Mental Retardation and Developmental Disabilities Committee was instrumental in getting specific language in the 1987–1988 appropriations bill that required quarterly reports to the legislature on six issues: (1) projected and actual numbers of residents placed into the community, as well as those placed in special units, (2) projected and actual numbers of residents placed in state-operated and voluntary-operated facilities, (3) the number of full-time equivalents in community and institutional programs and the actual number of employees laid off in each quarter, as well as the efforts to assist employees affected by closure to obtain other employment, (4) development of programs for medically frail individuals, (5) the numbers of residents placed outside the district, and (6) the status of plans for the alternate use of the facilities.

Selling Closure to Public Employee Unions

Winning the support, or at least the acquiescence, of the unionized work force was absolutely essential. Unionized employees had strongly supported Governor Cuomo in his election campaigns, and it was clear that they would not hesitate to take their case to the Executive Chamber if they felt that closure would be harmful. Consequently, OMRDD, at the state and district level, spent an exceptional amount of time and effort selling closure to the unionized employees. The main issue for the unions was an agreement between the state and the employee unions assuring that at least 80 percent of the community residential programs and some substantial portion of the day programs would be state operated. This was a relatively easy commitment for the state to make since the bulk of these programs were already state operated in the upstate districts that were among the early closers—Rome, Craig, and Newark. The other understanding was that there would be "no layoff" policy. These agreements were important because immediately after the decision and in early stages of implementation, the unions adopted a "wait-and-see" attitude rather than active and vigorous opposition.

A problem arose at Rome where the unions had already been closely involved in developing the plan for the "reconfiguration" of the Rome center into a 125-bed facility. This raised almost no initial objections from the unions even though reconfiguration would have a significant impact on many of the support and maintenance workers at the center. However, with the announcement of "closure," the attitudes of the unionized employees changed dramatically. One senior official at Rome recounted a very tense meeting with the maintenance staff in which he outlined virtually the same scenario for their jobs that would occur under the reconfiguration plan. This time, however, there was a very angry reaction even though closure represented only a very small substantive change from reconfiguration. In fact, the state operation of the new community programs as well as the announcement of the building of a prison on the campus would result in at least as many positions in OMRDD and a substantial increase in overall state employment in the area. Consequently, the Rome administration immediately began to characterize the closure plan as the "expansion" plan. This episode indicated the impact of language. In an area that had been losing industrial jobs by the thousands, "closure" seemed to immediately evoke the specter of plant closings and job losses. Even relatively senior staff in several closure districts reported that they had to remind themselves as well as employees that closure would actually be a transition to a community-based system. In many places, use of the term "closure" was discouraged.

Selling Closure to Affected Communities

The announcement of the closure of developmental centers captured the attention of the communities in which they were located. Several of the centers had been in these locales for almost 100 years. While closure most directly affected the residents, staff, and parents, local government officials, business leaders, and other individuals and groups took an immediate interest in the policy. One fact that emerged very quickly was that although these centers had been in those communities for years, many local figures had very limited knowledge of what a developmental center was, who lived there, and what services were provided. Their understanding of community-based programs was limited to the contentious site selection processes involved in establishing group homes. So, one important element of selling the closure of the center was to first describe the overall system of developmental services and the importance of a community rather than institutional structure. This involved getting as many community people on a large number of task forces and committees with district staff to plan closure implementation.

Employment was the primary concern. Although the creation of community residences and day programs would likely result in no loss in overall employment in the area, the dispersal of this employment was a concern for local government officials and business people. In Westchester, the booming economy at the time of closure made the employment issue virtually invisible to the local community. At Rome, the simultaneous announcement of the conversion of the center campus to a correctional facility ensured a concentration of state employment at this site. While the OMRDD employees remained concerned about their eventual job location, community leaders could look at an overall increase in state employment in the area.

Another concern of the community at-large was the use of the facility subsequent to closure. OMRDD was sensitized to the importance of this issue in the Willowbrook closure. Consequently, OMRDD made alternate use plans a primary concern. Each district was instructed to ensure that community lenders were well-represented on alternate use advisory committees.

The closure at Rome provided an example of efforts to secure the cooperation of the community. The "Accessing Resources Committee" of the overall closure task force focused on preparing for the influx of more people with disabilities into the community. As concerns about the co-location of a prison at Rome grew, the administration introduced supplemental budget legislation for $2 million for special projects in the community associated with the Rome closure. The intent was to use these funds to establish resources not only for people with developmental disabilities coming out of the center but also for people with other disabilities who lived in the community. The money was used to renovate the YMCA pool to accommodate people with disabilities, to make the city library physically accessible, and to renovate two city parks to make them accessible.

Selling Closure to Private Agencies and Legislators in Non-Closure Districts

The most important questions raised in nonclosure districts concerned the impact of closure on the amount and pace of community program development in these areas. In early 1987, the state's economy was healthy, and OMRDD and private agencies had developed over 1,500 new residential beds in each of the previous three years. Nonetheless, representatives of private agencies were skeptical, arguing that closure could absorb the resources needed for people waiting for residential and day services in other parts of the state. The state assured provider agencies and advocates and parents in nonclosure districts that the scale and pace of development across the state would be maintained.

Selling Closure to Parents and Advocacy Organizations

Parents and relatives of the people living in the developmental centers were especially interested in the implications for medical services. The bulk of specialized medical, dental, and other health services were at the centers and used by provider agencies and private individuals. Consequently, assurances that health and medical services would be at least maintained, and in some respects enhanced, were necessary to enlist the support of parents for closure. In Rome, the commitment by the state to purchase a small hospital to operate as an intensive medical ICF was instrumental in gaining the support of parents.

Parents often felt that particular staff members at the institution had established a long-standing or special relationship with their family member. The DDSOs spent a great deal of effort working with parents to convince them that the staff arrangements in their family members' community program would be appropriate, even if the same staff did not follow the individual.

Rome Co-Location Case: A Hard Sell

The Rome Co-location case, very early in closure implementation, was a prime example of how the state took a hard line in selling the decision. The state's need for additional prison space had been a background issue in the overall closure decision, and, in 1985, the Department of Correctional Services (DOCS) did take over a large portion of the Craig campus and "co-located" the Groveland Correctional Facility there. The possible use of the Rome campus for a medium security prison was an issue that percolated just beneath the surface of the closure decision. Rome was to close by 1991 in the original closure plan. However, with the prison system already over capacity, extraordinary pressure was brought on OMRDD to move up the Rome closure date so DOCS could convert the campus to a prison. An amended budget bill added $8.9 million for state-operated community services to accelerate the closure at Rome. The budget for DOCS also provided funds for the conversion of the Rome campus to a medium security prison for about 2,000 inmates. To reinforce a positive reaction by local government officials, $2 million was appropriated for improvements for handicapped accessibility in such local facilities as the city swimming pool and library.

As OMRDD district office managers were assuring local governments, businesses, and employees that closure actually meant reconfiguration of current employees, DOCS officials and elected state officials were promoting the prisons as a major additional source of near-term construction and long-term corrections jobs. The public employee unions at Rome, still concerned about the implications of closure for them, were delighted by the announcement of new sources of jobs.

These developments were not greeted with enthusiasm by the provider organizations in other districts or the local parents. Private agencies in other districts saw these requests, especially for additional money for state-operated programs at Rome, as a shift in funds that would result in the abandonment of over forty private agency projects. They immediately lobbied for and were able to get renewed assurances from the legislature and administration that prior levels of private development would continue.

The local parents and statewide advocacy organizations were not as easily mollified. Many advocates were already opposing the construction of the Small Residential Units on the periphery of the centers as not really community settings (ARC 1987; Lottman 1987). The reservations about the prison became acute as the decision to accelerate the closing of Rome from 1991 to 1989 was made in the early summer. And virtually as soon as the accelerated schedule was announced along with the expanded size of the prison, DOCS began to bring pressure on OMRDD to vacate the northern part of the campus. As the parents' opposition grew, OMRDD, DOCS, and the governor's office enhanced their appeals to the broad community. DOCS announced that the prison at Rome would house 800 more prisoners than initially planned, adding up to 600 more jobs than originally estimated. DOCS began aggressive site preparation as soon as possible, and the ARC brought suit to prohibit the occupation of any portion of the campus for a prison as long as any residents remained. DOCS moved swiftly to occupy its portion of the campus. OMRDD moved the Rome residents to buildings in another section of the campus, and the pleasant setting of brick buildings and wide lawns was quickly turned into a noisy, large-scale construction project. Heavy equipment, temporary rerouting of roads, unfamiliar buildings, and high, double fencing topped with ribbon wire did little to soothe their feelings, and once construction got underway, there were few who argued that closure should be stopped. Most wanted it hurried.

Implementation of Closure

Good policy helps but does not guarantee successful implementation. The closure of seven large developmental centers between 1987 and 1991 was a remarkable example of implementation success and was crucial to the decision to close all developmental centers by 2000 (Castellani 1992, 1996).

Overcoming the Barriers to Implementation Success

There were several problems in closure implementation. The first set of problems revolved around how the policy to close developmental centers changed as it was being implemented. Closure policy was actually a set of not entirely consistent policies with often conflicting or ambiguous objectives—a problem of "goal multiplicity" (O'Toole 1989). Closing the developmental centers was operationally defined as moving all residents off the campuses to community settings as well as setting up day programs and establishing medical, dental, and other specialized services in communities. However, it became quickly apparent that these were complex and problematic objectives. Was scouring a multicounty rural area for a replacement for a recently constructed rehabilitation facility on the edge of the Newark campus a better choice than using the existing building? How would OMRDD deal with varying needs for highly sensitive medical services provided on developmental center campuses?

OMRDD established its own mini-hospital at Rome by purchasing a defunct hospital in a community to accomplish this policy goal. At Craig, OMRDD was committed to reorganizing the way medical services were provided by relying much more heavily on HMOs, private practitioners, and contracts with medical groups. During implementation, OMRDD had to contend with parent and constituent groups in seven closure locales who questioned, made favorable and unfavorable comparisons, and generally advocated for the "policy" being implemented in another locale. Parents and advocacy groups (and managers) in other, nonclosure, districts demanded the adoption of model programs being developed in closure districts.

To gain consensus on the closure policy, the state gave strong commitments to employee unions that the state work force would be maintained. The Employee Services Office (ESO) which worked so well in helping employees at Willowbrook move to community positions was adopted at the next closure site at Westchester. There, a booming service economy in the area, the close proximity of two other state institutions, and experience in the relocation task all encouraged a large number of employees, especially many in hard to recruit clinical positions, to leave the institution staff for similar or better jobs. The state then had to pay bonuses to try to temporarily retain these individuals so that minimum levels of staffing could be maintained.

As closure implementation progressed, support for the policy eroded. Early in the process, OMRDD was able to invoke the authority of the governor's office to resolve resource and timing problems at Rome. However, the ability to bring that authority to bear evaporated as closure implementation became more routine or involved less politically sensitive locales and circumstances, and the attention of executive office policy makers naturally shifted to other issues and problems. The policy priorities of OMRDD were not always matched or sustained by the other organizations on which success depended.

Closure implementation placed OMRDD in a web of relationships with many other state agencies, public authorities, local governments, private contractors, private agencies, banks, federal agencies, landlords and others whose approval, cooperation, and involvement was necessary to completion of the projects. A changing mix of policy makers in these organizations had a substantial impact on implementation success (Bardach 1977; O'Toole and Montjoy 1984). Virtually all of the major problems in implementation took place at "the seams of government," reinforcing the importance of its essential intergovernmental and interorganizational nature (Elmore 1986). These relationships changed from locale and circumstance and as new actors became involved. The sheer number of potential sources of problems in the critical path was daunting, and it seemed that every variation occurred at some time.

As implementation progressed the state's fiscal situation worsened. The state's ability and willingness to devote additional resources to resolve an implementation problem, for example by paying contractors bonuses for early completion, diminished. Less evident but also very problematic was the general caution, hedged commitments, and longer time frames that became pervasive as actual or anticipated freezes and cutbacks affected virtually all of the agencies and organizations. The implementation of closure also varied significantly across locales. What worked in upstate New York often did not work as well in New York City. Financial instability in some private agencies slowed development, and the problems surrounding transfer of property from the city to the state government proved almost insurmountable.

Time was a factor in implementation success as managers found that meeting the timetables and specific policy objectives of closure were very difficult. While deadlines could be extended, closure was ultimately an either/ or situation, and this tended to shift the focus of implementers' efforts to the last and most difficult problems. Closure did not proceed in an orderly, measured pace. There were often surges of demand for time, effort, and other resources, particularly towards the final stages. In each instance, the problem was to enlist other agencies and individuals to share the urgency for processing contracts, allocating funds, certifying new facilities, and completing the many other tasks that were out of the hands of OMRDD.

Implications of Implementation Success

The deadlines for the closure of Willowbrook, Westchester, Rome, Newark, and Craig were met, and Bronx and Manhattan closed within months of the original schedule. This was, by far, the largest, most rapid, and successful closure of state-operated institutions in the United States. It was successful in several important respects. In contrast to other states where closure almost always focused on a single facility under court order, New York's closure policy was self-initiated and covered several institutions. In contrast to closure by means of transferring institution residents to other state or private facilities, the residents of the developmental centers closed in New York went, almost without exception, directly to community residential and day programs. Closure in many other states entailed drawn-out and bitter conflict among institution employees, private agencies, and advocates for closure. In New York, the extensive use of state-operated community programs, "no layoff" guarantees, and the continuation of development in private agencies in and outside closure districts were among the factors that made New York's closure experience relatively free of political and interorganizational conflict. The implementation of closure in New York not only overcame the normal turbulence of implementation, but it was achieved in the face of several important changes and variations in the political, economic, and organizational context of implementation. The most important demonstration of the success of the closures announced in 1987 was that as this round of closures was coming to its end, a policy to close all of New York's institutions was emerging. It appeared that closure was not only "the right thing to do" but also the smart thing to do.

Chapter 10

Rebranding the Cash Cows:
Not Closing Institutions

Institutions as we knew them have closed.

—Anonymous

In January 1991, Governor Mario Cuomo directed OMRDD to develop a plan to close all its developmental centers by 2000. In January 1995, newly elected Governor George Pataki suspended the closure of additional developmental centers pending a review of the policy. New York then adopted a "case-by-case" approach during a controversy surrounding the nonclosure of an institution already designated for closure and later announced plans to expand some existing developmental centers and build a new institution. This was a remarkable reversal of what had seemed to be an inevitable process of institution closure. It was the beginning of a new phase of developmental services in New York, one in which the role of public institutions was reaffirmed as integral to the financing and organization of services.

Foundation of a Decision to Close All Institutions:
The Success of the 1987 Policy

The 1991 plan to close all of OMRDD's remaining developmental centers by 2000 was different in many respects from the decision to close Willowbrook, Westchester, and five other institutions. It was made at a time of multibillion dollar deficits in the state budget, and the state and nation were in a prolonged recession. There was a new Commissioner of OMRDD. In contrast to the secretive crafting of the 1987 decision in its early phases, the decision to close all institutions was reached as the culmination of a long process of public discussion in which the legislature played a prominent role in the

241

framing of the policy. The 1991 decision also rested on the successful implementation of the 1987 decision, an implementation that had a number of positive outcomes.

Closing Developmental Centers on Schedule

The closing of Willowbrook in September 1987, followed quickly by the closure of Westchester Developmental Center, was an occasion of celebration and provided an early boost to the overall closure process. Prompted by the need for prison space, Rome was closed two years early with all of its program goals met. The closures of Craig and Newark were proceeding with no more than the normal turbulence of implementation, and many of the problems experienced later in the New York City facilities were not widely known or ever became critical to overall implementation. Although the national economy and the state's fiscal situation began to worsen, the state was still able to maintain its continuity of employment commitments to the unions, its level of community development in other areas of the state, and the agreed upon growth in private agencies (Castellani 1992).

Positive Impact on Residents and Staff

The outcomes of closure for the residents were a primary concern for policy makers and advocates. Thousands of developmental center residents had already moved to community programs over the several years of deinstitutionalization, and a number of studies showed very positive outcomes for former residents as well as satisfied families (Conroy and Bradley 1985; Gollay et al. 1978; Heller et al. 1988; Lord and Pedlar 1991). The positive impact of deinstitutionalization in New York was confirmed in the testimony from parents, consumers, private providers, and state managers in five-year plan forums and the Senate Committee on Mental Hygiene hearings on closure.

There had been no layoffs of staff, and not one employee went to a lower paying position. In fact, hundreds of employees in the closure districts moved to higher paying positions in OMRDD and other state agencies (Gold 1990). Training programs prepared staff for civil service exams for community positions and jobs outside OMRDD and assisted workers without high school diplomas to earn their General Education Diplomas. When closure was completed, the more highly skilled workforce had a long-term positive economic impact for these individuals and their communities.

Impact on Capital and Operating Costs, Revenue, and Local Economies

As the 1987 closure initiative proceeded and the issue of additional closures was being considered, OMRDD contracted with Grant-Thornton, an accounting and management consulting firm, to conduct an analysis of the fiscal and economic impact of the first phase of closure. The Grant-Thornton report and other analyses of the impact of the 1987 initiative on capital and operating costs, revenues, and local economies were crucial to the decision to close all institutions.

The OMRDD 1986-1991 *Capital Plan* was a catalyst in the development of a 1987 closure policy (OMRDD 1985). With a variety of physical plant problems in the developmental centers, the costs of rehabilitating these facilities, especially with most fixed costs such as security, power plant, and groundskeeping remaining the same for diminishing numbers of residents, was a major factor in the closure decision. Maintaining federal financial participation through continued certification was a paramount issue for OMRDD, and in certification surveys and look-behind audits, auditors increasingly found that large institutions were physically and operationally incompatible with ICF/MR standards. In the first three centers closed (Rome, Craig, and Westchester), the Grant-Thornton analysis estimated that $60,528,000 in maintenance and rehabilitation would have been required in the relatively near term to maintain standards for federal certification (Grant-Thornton 1990). Grant-Thornton also looked at the capital cost implications of using the closed developmental centers for other purposes. The Westchester center was on the grounds of the Harlem Valley Psychiatric Center, and the vacated buildings could be used by that facility. More important were the capital cost savings of converting the Rome and Craig centers to medium security prisons. Using Department of Corrections cost experience for construction of medium security facilities compared with the lower cost of rehabilitating the developmental centers, Grant-Thornton estimated a savings of $107,000,000 for Craig and Rome alone. The Grant-Thornton analyses showed a total net capital cost savings at these three centers of $112,107,000 (Grant-Thornton 1990).

A major savings in operating expenditures was realized by moving developmental center residents into private agency community programs where lower salaries and fringe benefits made them less costly than institution or state-operated community programs. Other operating cost savings were realized in nonpersonal service areas where contracts for maintenance and repair of community facilities were switched to private vendors. Grant-Thornton analyzed these various savings in operating costs and found, in the first six 1987 closures, an overall 9.2 percent decrease in *net* operating costs (Grant-Thornton 1990).

In selling the 1987 closure decision, the local economic impact was an important issue. Community leaders were concerned about the dispersal of employment. Overall, a balance was struck between relocating residents throughout the broader locale and maintaining a level of employment in the vicinity of the original institution. In the six closure districts in the 1987 initiative, the level of employment in OMRDD declined slightly, from 3,043 to 2,942, largely as a result of attrition and transfer to other agencies. However, the increase in other state positions in closure districts was 1,487. This does not include additional positions in such nonstate organizations as community colleges, local special education services, and school district programs that resulted from their use of the developmental center campuses. Increases in local employment had a positive impact on local personal income as construction labor used to build new community programs for OMRDD in the Rome and Craig areas alone was estimated to be $6.9 and $1.5 million annually over a three-year period (Grant-Thornton 1990). The overall permanent increase in personal income as a result of alternate use of the campuses was estimated to be $47.4 million in Rome and $9.5 million a year in the Craig area (Grant-Thornton 1990).

The operation of one or two community residences or day programs could have an important economic impact in small villages and towns, and local governments and business people lobbied OMRDD to locate those programs in their towns (NYSACRA 1998). Many centrally managed contracts with statewide vendors for supplies were switched to purchases from local vendors. Overall, the additional local expenditures due to both the shift in spending by OMRDD and new local spending by other state agencies was almost $3 million a year in the Rome area and $600,000 a year in Craig—a 44 percent increase at Rome and a 17 percent increase at Craig (Grant-Thornton 1990).

Federal revenue generated by the state institutions and state and private community ICFs and Day Treatment programs was a critical issue that lurked in the background of the Grant-Thornton report. The report focused largely on the potential loss of revenues from decertification of outmoded and dysfunctional institutions and said almost nothing about the relative impact on revenues from institutions vis-à-vis community programs. The Grant-Thornton report was issued late in the implementation of the 1987 closures and used to confirm OMRDD's initial claim that closure would be fiscally prudent— "cost neutral." As the first round of closure was nearing completion, the report added momentum to a growing call to close all the state's remaining developmental centers. The question of the impact of closing all developmental centers on federal revenue was still unanswered to the satisfaction of decision makers in the Division of the Budget.

Crafting a Decision to Close
All Developmental Centers by 2000

Governor Cuomo's 1991 directive to plan for the closure of all developmental centers by 2000 involved a very different policymaking process than that which led to the 1987 decision to close several developmental centers. The broad and open participatory policymaking process under new OMRDD leadership included the active involvement of the legislature.

A Change in Leadership

Commissioner Arthur Webb, who had engineered the 1987 policy, was named to head the state's substance abuse program in 1989. Elin Howe, OMRDD's Executive Deputy Commissioner, succeeded Webb. Howe, widely regarded as an expert in operations and fiscal management, had been responsible for day-to-day running of the agency and implementation of the 1987 policy. Howe had spent almost her entire career in OMRDD with several assignments in the field, including director of Willowbrook at a crucial stage in that center's history, director of the New York City Regional Office, and director of the region that included the district of the chair of the Senate Committee on Mental Hygiene. Howe's experience and low-key management style differed from Webb's and resulted in a different strategy in crafting the 1991 closure policy.

OMRDD's Five-Year Plan

Every Commissioner of OMRDD used the 5.07 Plan process to get input from its constituencies and as a vehicle to test new policy concepts. Policy papers on various topics were circulated, and forums were held around the state using the papers as focal points of discussion. The agency then published a five-year plan that featured the revised policy papers as centerpieces for a theme or policy direction.

In early 1990, OMRDD began the formal plan process with one of the policy papers devoted to closing developmental centers. The public testimony from a wide range of constituencies around the state supported the closures initiated in 1987. In the five-year plan, *The Community Challenge*, OMRDD made "Continue Developmental Center Closures and Deinstitutionalization" one of its six main objectives for the coming five years, and the plan stated, "Deinstitutionalization will continue, and during the 1990-1995 period, a decision on additional closures will be made" (OMRDD 1990a, 205). This was a clear signal of OMRDD's intentions and reading of the sense of its constituencies.

Encouraging the Legislature to Take a Lead Role

The legislature did not play a direct role formulating the 1987 decision. Following the governor's January 1987 announcement, the legislature became involved with alternate use plans (especially at Rome), some revisions of the original plans, and in staking out an oversight role, especially by chairpersons of the committees with jurisdiction over OMRDD and legislators from closure districts.

By late 1988, the state's fiscal situation was turning from surpluses to multibillion dollar deficits. Private agencies feared that scarcer resources would be devoted to programs for residents of the centers being closed rather than for developing services for people living at home. The New York State ARC took a strong position opposing any lessening of commitment to private agency development (ARC 1989). The Chair of the Senate Committee on Mental Hygiene proposed legislation to stop the closures announced in 1987 unless the state maintained its commitment to those individuals living at home and the private agencies serving them. In the midst of large cuts in virtually every public program, OMRDD was successful in getting much of the original cuts restored in the budget negotiations with the legislature. The closure initiative, as well as development for people living at home, continued at about the same pace.

The topic of closing developmental centers was again a major issue raised in the budget hearings in the early months of 1990. Several legislators pressed the commissioner to indicate a new phase of closures. The Senate Committee on Mental Hygiene also held hearings on the future of existing developmental centers. Commissioner Howe opened the hearing by endorsing the concept of closing all developmental centers. Testimony from parents, advocates, local government representatives, labor unions, and local and statewide provider agency groups strongly supported the closure of the remaining centers. Formerly reluctant legislators were now taking a lead role. Chairperson Spano stated:

> "It is the recommendation of the Committee that all developmental centers in the State of New York be permanently closed by the year 2000." (New York State Senate Committee on Mental Hygiene 1990)

Local Planning for Closure and a Statewide Conference: The Canary in the Mineshaft

OMRDD directed every one of its district offices to convene a closure study group comprised of consumers, family members, providers, and OMRDD staff to "discuss the implications and impact of closure of their developmental center and to formulate recommendations on how services would then be delivered in the B/DDSO" (OMRDD 1990b). The recommendations of these local closure study groups were to be the basis of a statewide meeting in November 1990 to "discuss future closures, develop a closure policy, and begin formulation of a comprehensive closure plan" (OMRDD 1990b). Almost every district meeting held during the late spring and summer of 1990 ended with an endorsement of closing the developmental center, although four of the twenty districts indicated some continuing use of the center for "special populations" beyond 2000.

As the local conferences were underway, a planning group for the statewide "Charting the Course" conference was established. The reports from the local conferences were synopsized as the basic material for panel discussion at the conference. The panel topics placed heavy emphasis on the successes of the 1987 policy and were strongly oriented to implementation of a new closure policy. Panel chairs (selected from district offices undertaking closure) and members, as well as other invitees, were selected from those who had expressed support for closure in the five-year plan forums, the legislative hearings, and the district study groups.

The Charting the Course conference was canceled virtually on the eve of its opening. Like the death of the canary in the mineshaft, this small, almost invisible event, had large implications. OMRDD's executives assumed the responsibility for canceling the conference, pointing out that deficits in the state budget projected for the coming fiscal year would make it imprudent. There was speculation that the Division of the Budget had a strong hand in the cancellation, signaling their concern about the revenue impact of closing all developmental centers rather than the relatively small cost of an in-house conference.

Closure Planning Continues

OMRDD tried to maintain the momentum toward a new closure policy by conducting a survey of the one hundred invitees to the canceled conference and reported virtually unanimous agreement that all developmental centers should be closed as soon as possible (OMRDD 1990d). Meeting the needs of "special populations" with complex medical and behavioral problems, addressing the difficulties of development in New York City, the need for training, and endorsement for continued "partnership" with private agencies and state-operated community programs were other issues about which the respondents expressed opinions which were consistent with the directions of the 1987 closure policies and implementation.

At the same time, important constituency groups were also joining the groundswell of support for closure. The ARC adopted a resolution in support of closure at its November 1990 meeting, and the editorial in its December 1990 statewide newspaper was titled, "Goodbye to Institutions" (ARC 1990). At a conference for direct care staff, the president of the largest public employee union, the Civil Service Employees Association, announced his support for the closure of developmental centers.

OMRDD moved to consolidate the support for closure, and in December 1990, it published, *A Mandate for the 1990s: Closing Developmental Centers in New York State* (OMRDD 1990c). This document featured the endorsements of closures by consumers, parents, advocacy groups, private providers, union leaders, local government officials, and state legislative leaders around a recap of the positive experience of the 1987 policy and the various forums that focused on additional closures. It concluded, "Now is the time to make it the public policy of the State of New York by mandating the closure of all remaining developmental centers by the year 2000!" (OMRDD 1990c, 13). The publication on the eve of the governor's State of the State Address signaled OMRDD's victory in the internal tussle over a "close-all-developmental centers" policy, and that was confirmed in the Governor Cuomo's 1991 Message to the Legislature in which he recommended that additional closures begin in the 1991–1992 fiscal years and stated,

> "I am directing the Office [of Mental Retardation and Developmental Disabilities] to proceed with these closures and to develop a long term plan to close the remaining developmental centers and restructure community-based services. The result will be a service system that is less costly while still allowing for expansion of services to all persons with developmental disabilities, especially those living at home with their families."

Decision to *Not* Close All Institutions

Governor Cuomo's 1991 directive, like the decisions to close Willowbrook, Westchester, and five other developmental centers, was marked by announcements by the governor, extensive plans, legislative hearings, and public statements and endorsements by legislators and representatives of major constituency groups. The decision to *not* close all developmental centers was the culmination of almost invisible events, ambiguous messages, and the pursuit of alternate agendas that ultimately undermined the 1991 directive.

Hidden Messages

Governor Cuomo's directive seemed to be an unambiguous endorsement of a continuation of the 1987 policy. However, it contained almost imperceptible warnings for those who carefully parse these statements for hidden or veiled messages. The governor stated that the "restructured service system" was to be less costly—the first time this ephemeral standard had been explicitly stated as an outcome of closure. The resulting service system would also have to allow for the expansion of services, especially for those living at home with their families. The careful parsers saw in this the expression of the concerns of the private agencies about the competition between *their* waiting lists and remaining institution residents for new beds. The governor directed OMRDD to develop a plan to close all remaining developmental centers even though OMRDD already had a plan. And there were those who still worried about DOB's role and message in the cancellation of the conference on closing all developmental centers. Nonetheless, almost everyone proceeded on the assumption that the policy problem of closing all developmental centers had been solved, and, in light of the rapid closure of several institutions, that implementation of that policy was virtually guaranteed.

Slow Going: 1991 to 1995

By 1991, OMRDD had closed seven large developmental centers and moved several thousand residents to community settings. Deinstitutionalization continued to reduce the census in the other developmental centers, and when Governor Cuomo directed OMRDD to develop a plan to close all developmental centers by 2000, there were 6,350 individuals living in the remaining developmental centers (OMRDD 1991).

Some of these remaining developmental centers were moving toward closure virtually as an inevitable result of their substantial downsizing. Nevertheless, no additional institutions were closed until 1993 when J. N. Adam Developmental Center in western New York and the Long Island Developmental Center closed. The closure of Long Island, however, demonstrated that the chronic problems of finding adequate community settings for the more challenging residents remained, especially in the New York metropolitan area. Its closure was achieved by moving more than 150 of its residents to clusters of Small Residential Units on the institution perimeter.

Alternate Use and Bonding

The long-term bonding for the construction of new and refurbishing of existing developmental centers began to create problems in the early 1990s that also raised concerns about closing all developmental centers. Ensuring appropriate alternate use of the vacated developmental centers was a key criterion in the initial closures. The occupation of the Willowbrook campus by the CUNY College of Staten Island as well as by some community organizations was regarded as a major achievement. Despite some problems around co-location, the use of the Craig and Rome campuses for the exponentially expanding prison system quickly and easily resolved those problems of alternate use. The Newark Campus was turned over for use by a variety of local government activities including a community college. The Manhattan building, which was never originally intended for patient care, was converted to OMRDD's New York City Regional Office. However, easy conversions of developmental center campuses to alternate use dwindled.

Even what had been expected to be easy conversions ran into problems. Plans to sell the vacated campus of Long Island Developmental Center to Canon Corporation for offices were torpedoed by community opposition despite the enthusiastic endorsement of state and local government officials. Similar problems were encountered in other closure sites. Alternate use, a secondary and readily solved issue in the first wave of closures, now began to loom much larger as closing all centers were being planned.

At the core of the problem were the tax-exempt bonds used to construct and refurbish the institutions. If the buildings were leased or sold to private operators or no longer used for a governmental purpose, the tax-exempt status of the bonds would be nullified. Moreover, 1986 amendments to the federal tax code required the government to sell tax-exempt bonded buildings at fair market value. Beginning in the late 1980s, New York's growing fiscal problems led it into extensive bonding and rebonding of its facilities. At one point, the state "sold" some of its highways to a public benefit corporation that paid the state from the proceeds of tax-exempt bonds it issued. This desperation financing extended to OMRDD facilities where virtually anything that didn't move was bonded. The bonded indebtedness of the facilities far exceeded their fair market value.

The bonding problems with alternate use began at Bronx. Schemes for using what had always been a dysfunctional institution as a high-tech park foundered as the state's Urban Development Corporation and other coordinating bodies were unable to put together plans for private or public alternate use because of lack of agreement on who would be responsible for what portion of the bonded indebtedness. Some of these problems were eventually worked out, but this issue contributed to a growing lack of enthusiasm for closing all developmental centers. Despite the fact that OMRDD had plans on top of plans for closure of all developmental centers and had public support for the policy from the full range of leaders and constituencies, the pace of closures slowed dramatically.

Other Paradigms to Shatter: Supported Living

Even though the pace of closures slowed, most key constituencies thought that this was simply an implementation not a policy problem. With the belief that the institutional paradigm was shattered, advocates and analysts turned their attention to reforming community services (Bradley et al.1994).

Throughout deinstitutionalization and closure, critics pointed out that the overwhelming majority of people who moved out of the developmental centers or family homes into community residential and day programs lived highly structured lives shuttling between Medicaid-funded ICFs/DD, Day Treatment programs, clinics, and other disaggregated institutional settings in agency-owned (and Medicaid-financed) vans. While virtually everyone conceded that group homes were superior to large institutions, many pointed out that essential elements of life in them and the large day programs were institutional: determined by regulation, shift staffing, and professional and administrative oversight (Smull 1989).

Reform was a prominent theme in the early to mid-1990s, and there was a plethora of approaches and frameworks from which to choose as reinventing government and managed care joined total quality management, Medicaid reform and long-term care reform on the menu. Some approaches, such as managed care, were tried and quickly abandoned (Smith and Ashbaugh 1995; Ashbaugh and Smith 1996). Aspects of these various approaches lingered in one way or another, but the agenda for the reform of institution-like community services eventually coalesced into what became known as supported living.

The supported living movement was characterized by three major elements: new kinds of activities, new types of provider organizations, and new ways of funding services. Supported living was to be individualized and person-centered rather than congregate (Bradley et al.1994; Mount 1994). Primary emphasis was to be placed on empowering individuals to choose packages of services and supports that fit their own needs. Independent case managers, job coaches, life coaches, personal care attendants, and others were put primarily at the direction of the person with a disability to assist the person to achieve life objectives, and those objectives would be broader than the clinical outcomes typical of medical models. Housing, transportation, personal care attendants, and job coaches were seen as more important than clinical services.

Supported living also involved recommendations about the organization of services. Advocates argued for organizational arrangements that would be more informal, flexible, participatory, and consumer-centered than traditional program models (Ferguson et al. 1990; Gardner 1992; O'Brien and O'Brien 1994; Racino 1991; Taylor, et al. 1991). Consistent with the aims of supported employment, advocates called for the elimination of sheltered workshops. Twelve-bed ICFs/DD and other congregate care living arrangements were to be replaced by much smaller, individual living situations in the supported living approach. Advocates for this approach also argued that provider agencies should be much smaller then those typical in New York (Taylor et. al. 1991). These new agencies were expected to be bureaucratically thin, have low caps on administrative costs, and generally eschew therapeutic and professional norms and objectives (Ferguson et al. 1990). Since there was limited expectation that traditional providers of developmental services could change, heavy reliance was placed on recruiting new and smaller organizations to meet these criteria. People with disabilities were expected to get supports and services from a broader array of sources in communities rather than from specialized developmental services agencies.

The third major element of supported living was a new approach to funding services. Cash subsidies, vouchers, rent subsidies, and other direct supports to the individual were also to be made more widely available. These included informal supports, including resources to pay neighbors and others for certain services, greater reliance on so-called generic services, and access to market sources of support.

Meeting the Challenge of Reform

The closing of several developmental centers resulted in a substantially reorganized service system, but one in which fewer and smaller institutions still played important roles. Deinstitutionalization and closure of several developmental centers also resulted in a much larger and fiscally stable private provider industry as well as a strong state-operated community services system staffed by public employees with strong political and economic clout. A directive to plan for the closure of all developmental centers by 2000 could not be easily ignored. Calls for the reform of institution-like community services were less compelling, but policy makers and providers also saw that the appeal of reengineered organizations, reinvented government, consumer satisfaction, vouchers, cash subsidies, and market solutions would have to be addressed.

Reform was not opposed; it was used to strengthen and refinance the prevailing system of community services. Support for studies of best practices, conferences, and pilot projects were linked to a major refinancing of community services with a Medicaid waiver. Demonstration projects and the rhetoric of individualized services were linked to a waiting list initiative for financing thousands of new "beds" in existing provider agencies. Closing all developmental centers would not be opposed; closing all developmental centers "as we knew them" would be accomplished by rebranding existing and building new institutions for "special populations" that would be even more important to financing all developmental services.

Embracing the Rhetoric of Reform: Supported Living and Medicaid Waivers

OMRDD appeared to embrace the supported living movement with a burst of conferences and meetings. It funded explorations of "best practices," joined a national supported living pilot program, conducted studies of supported living pilots in other states, hired some leading proponents as consultants, and organized "practicums" to instruct its district managers and private agencies on achieving the objectives of supported living. OMRDD and the ARC jointly called for the closing of sheltered workshops. By the mid-1990s, the agency's plans and other documents were thoroughly suffused with the rhetoric of consumers and individualized approaches to services. However, very little changed in the lives of the great majority of individuals in state or private agency programs. What did change was the way community programs were financed.

Medicaid reform began almost as soon as Medicaid was implemented. Medicaid waivers allowing states to set aside ("waive") certain Medicaid requirements (e.g., statewideness, specific state plan services, eligibility) to curb costs and/or deliver more services for the same money had been available to states virtually since the inception of Medicaid. With a few limited exceptions such as the "Katie Beckett waivers" for severely disabled infants, OMRDD had eschewed Medicaid waivers since its Medicaid maximization strategies had been successful in shifting large portions of overall costs to the federal government. However, in the context of the reform environment in the early 1990s, OMRDD embarked on a new strategy and submitted its application for a 1915(a) Home and Community-Based Services (HCBS) waiver.

New York's HCBS waiver was approved by the federal Health Care Financing Administration for implementation in 1991 and was originally targeted to four of OMRDD's districts. The waiver was quickly made statewide, and within a few years, New York's waiver program grew from the initial 160 enrollees to 35,650 in Fiscal Year 1998–1999—the largest HCBS program in the country, "fully funding 85% of New York's dramatic expansion in supports and services" (HCFA 2000). As the HCFA Final Report on New York's waiver pointed out, OMRDD's stated intention was "to reorganize the state's delivery system to establish an individualized services environment, or ISE, for waiver participants" (HCFA 2000, 8). OMRDD's Individualized Service Environment (ISE), the report explained, "allows the design of uniquely tailored packages of supports and services that help each person pursue his or her goals in life" (HCFA, 2000, 9). HCFA praised OMRDD for "embracing consumer empowerment and inclusion," "increasing emphasis on person-centered approaches," and "focusing the future of the service system on personal choices and needs" (HCFA 2000, 9).

HCFA and OMRDD shared the same rhetoric of reform, but the reality was that very little changed as the same individuals lived in the same large group homes, operated by the same agencies, and attended the same day programs—all now properly documented and reviewed by HCFA as having been the outcome of these consumers' choices. The reality was that private agencies and OMRDD district offices "converted" existing programs to Individual Residential Alternatives (IRAs), "residential habilitation," "day habilitation," "case coordination," and the other categories of individual service environments. Existing Medicaid-funded programs such as ICFs/DD converted, and OMRDD launched work groups to convert non-Medicaid programs such as the remaining Community Residences to IRAs (OMRDD 1998). A number of issues had to be addressed: whether the residents were Medicaid eligible; how to make conversion "cost neutral" as the waiver required; and what regulatory changes were needed. There was no expectation of or plan for substantial reorganization in where people lived or what they did each day. Some restrictive features of the ICF/DD were modified. However, in the overwhelming majority of cases, the same residents remained in the same group homes doing what they had done before. The waiver allowed the provider agency to do this with less staff while getting reimbursed for at least the same, or often more, under a variety of waiver "pricing" mechanisms.

The rhetoric of reform conjured notions of individuals getting services and supports from a variety of sources in communities aided in this by "case coordinators"—individuals who might be "independent case managers" directly employed by the consumers working through independent "fiscal intermediaries" rather than the agencies for whom services were being coordinated. The reality was that unbundling services provided yet another opportunity for revenue maximization.

Case management was already unbundled into Comprehensive Medicaid Case Management (CMCM), now a separately reimbursed service instead of its previous inclusion in the overall ICF/DD rate. As the report of the New York State Commission of Quality of Care (CQC), *Shifting the Costs to Medicaid: The Case of Financing the OMRDD Comprehensive Case Management Program* pointed out, "As with all Medicaid-funded services, there is a potential for duplicate payments which can arise when the same or similar services are furnished by other programs or as an integral aspect of another covered Medicaid service" (CQC 1995, iv). And indeed, CQC did find: that fees for CMCM were set at a rate 45 percent higher than justified by actual costs; that CMCM payments duplicated payments already being received for other services; that 21 percent of claims lacked adequate documentation; that requirements of consumer choice of a case manager were not complied with; that duplication of costs was motivated largely by a desire to supplement the funding of community residences; and that these findings were part of OMRDD's "long history of unorthodox methods of financing and supplementing programs and services" (CQC 1995, iv–vi). OMRDD's response to the criticisms of CMCM was to launch a "New Service Coordination Paradigm," which "embraces consumer choice" and would focus specialized service coordination "only when needed" (OMRDD 1996). The core of the new paradigm would "allow flexibility" for financing. The approach OMRDD and the private provider industry took with various iterations of case management was also used in other services such as clinics and transportation where the unbundling and renaming of services under the overall rationale of individualizing them allowed agencies to maximize reimbursement.

Doing more with less may have been the rhetoric of waivers, but the reality was consistent with the thirty years of the unintended consequences that marked Medicaid. New York did less (or the same) with more. In federal fiscal year 1998–1999, New York's 35,650 HCBS waiver enrollees were generating $1.7 billion in income, almost 6 percent of New York's total Medicaid costs (HCFA 2000).

Pataki Defeats Cuomo

In November 1994, George Pataki, a little-known state senator, defeated Governor Mario Cuomo in his bid for reelection for a fourth term as governor. An electorate weary of twelve years of a Cuomo governorship and a Republican surge across the country that produced majorities in the House of Representatives and the Senate were among the explanations for Pataki's victory. No significant statewide or local issues surrounding developmental services or closure arose in the campaign. Three actions by newly elected Governor Pataki, however, did have significant implications for closing developmental centers in New York: keeping the OMRDD executive team intact; suspending the decision to close all developmental centers; and dealing with the nonclosure of O.D. Heck. However, before Governor Pataki acted, indeed before he was inaugurated, the increasingly fragile consensus around closing all developmental centers ripped apart.

Shortly after the 1994 election, the executive director of the ARC, Marc Brandt, sent a letter to Governor-elect Pataki (with copies to the newspapers) with a proposal to address the budget deficit the new governor would face after his January inaugural. The ARC's primary proposal was "a fully privatized single tier system of mental retardation providers" (ARC 1994). By dismantling the state-operated portion of the service system, Brandt estimated that the state could save "nearly 100 million dollars a year" (ARC 1994).

This ripped the already-stretched fabric of consensus around closing all developmental centers. James Sheedy, the President of the New York State Public Employee Federation, the union representing the bulk of professional, scientific, and technical staff, responded with a letter to Pataki. Sheedy called Brandt's position "dead wrong," and "designed to advantage himself and others in his line of business" (Sheedy 1995). Sheedy charged that "Mr. Brandt and his colleagues rely heavily on state taxpayers to feather their management nests," and pointed to the fact that while the bulk of funding for these "quasi-public" operations came from public funds, 112 of these organizations paid their top executives more than the commissioner [$100,000]. Sheedy went on to accuse Brandt and the private agencies of lobbying law makers to create private empires while PEF worked cooperatively with OMRDD on institution closures. And then it got nasty.

The private provider agencies had matured organizationally and financially by 1994. Brandt's letter to Pataki was the private sector's coming out politically. With an incoming Republican governor, the major private provider organization was placing its bets on privatization and downsizing regardless of its impact on the broad consensus on closing all developmental centers that had heretofore been regarded as essential to the policy's success. Sheedy's note that PEF had "worked cooperatively" in the past on closures was a clear declaration that state-operated community programs were inextricably linked to closing institutions. The ARC's proposal to privatize the entire community sector kicked out one of the key supports of that long-standing policy. However, the fabric of a consensus around closing all developmental centers by 2000 had already stretched thin.

Keeping the OMRDD Administration

In 1993, Commissioner Elin Howe resigned, and Governor Cuomo named Thomas A. Maul as her successor as Commissioner. Maul had played a key role in the revenue and budget functions of the agency for more than twenty-five years, and he had been credited with inventing and aggressively implementing a number of OMRDD's rate-setting and reimbursement strategies.

Pataki's defeat of Cuomo in 1994 was stunning, and it put a Republican in the governor's office for the first time since 1974. Commissioners and their top executives started packing their bags as Republicans who had been shut out of appointments in the executive branch for twenty years prepared to take over. While virtually every other state agency's top executives were being replaced, Governor Pataki renamed Maul as Commissioner of OMRDD, and not one appointee in the top OMRRD executive staff was replaced. The incoming Pataki administration knew that it would inherit yet another huge budget deficit. They decided that the OMRDD managers who had raised and nurtured the cash cows were the best people to ensure the herd continued to produce. Maximizing revenue had become one of the (if not the) critical tasks of the agency.

Retaining the existing OMRDD leadership also was the best prospect of keeping the family feud between the private sector and public employee unions from turning into internecine warfare. Governor Cuomo had done a great deal to alienate public employee unions, and exit polls showed that Pataki had garnered surprising support from these unions' rank-and-file. In a state with a Democrat party enrollment advantage and a long tradition of liberal Republican office-holders, it was unlikely that Pataki was going to appoint an aggressive privatizing administration at OMRDD. In fact, while there were some layoffs of public employees, most job losses were due to attrition and early retirement incentives, and Pataki's administration was not marked by radical privatization initiatives.

Suspension of the Decision to Close All Developmental Centers: System Review

The status of the Cuomo administration's decision to close all developmental centers by 2000 was one of the first questions administrators within OMRDD and private provider agencies asked following Pataki's election. The very slow pace of closures had already raised the anxiety of those hoping for an implementation as rapid as that following the 1987 policy. Few were surprised when the Pataki administration announced that there would be a "suspension" (some heard "moratorium") of additional closures pending a "system review." The careful parsers of bureaucratic language worried over the long-term implications of "suspension" or "moratorium," but the system review carried out within OMRDD by the same program analysts, planners, and budget experts for the same executive team that had been in place before the election produced no surprises (OMRDD 1995). What was clear was that the governor (and his Division of the Budget) and the "new" OMRDD administration was not going to be locked into the Cuomo administration's policy of closing all developmental centers by 2000.

Not Closing O.D. Heck: Case-by-Case

The first Pataki *Executive Budget*, 1995–1996, was essentially the last Cuomo budget, largely constructed in the summer and fall before Pataki's inaugural. The *Executive Budget* for 1996–1997 was wholly Pataki's, and included provisions for the closures of Wilton and Letchworth Village Developmental Centers, where reductions in the census had already brought them to the brink, but not O.D. Heck Developmental Center that had been formally targeted for closure. The nonclosure of O.D. Heck was a clear indication of a new approach. If there were any doubts about what this meant, what followed at O.D. Heck erased them. As it became apparent that O.D. Heck was not included in developmental center closures, the administration at that institution began a local campaign to be reinstated in the closure plan. It was a campaign that put the OMRDD administration between the governor's office and one of its district directors.

O.D. Heck went public by participating in (some suggested instigating) a several-day feature on the institution in the area's major newspaper, the Albany *Times Union*, in January 1996—at the same time the governor's *Executive Budget* appeared without the announcement of the closure of O.D. Heck. In one article, "Life for residents to remain the same" (Grondhal 1996), Elllie Pattison, the past president and longtime member of the Board of Visitors and a player in the fight to not open the facility originally, used the "escape" metaphor that had been prominent in arguments for institution closure. Pattison was quoted as stating, "The others got out, but now we're saying there's no more money to bring in more lifeboats" (Grondhal 1996, C-3). The article stated, "The administrators and staff who run O.D. Heck say life in the community is more humane, and they pushed to have their own institution closed by last year" (Grondhal 1996, C-3). The article stated that there were 138 people "committed to a large institution in the Capital Region," and, "The director wants them to be free to live in community homes. So do staff members, who say there is compelling evidence that they are happier and do better outside the walls of the institution. But the O.D. Heck residents are trapped. By their own profound disabilities. By a fearful public. By government inaction and budget constraints."

The articles also focused on the cost issues. They pointed out that the 500,000 square foot facility was originally designed to house over 700 people, had about 360 residents at its peak, and now housed 138 individuals. "The heating and lighting bill alone is incredible," Director Michael Dillon was quoted as saying. OMRDD officials said they didn't have precise figures on the yearly operating costs at O.D. Heck, but an overall average cost of $124,000 per individual per year was cited in contrast to the $58,000 to $94,000 per year cost in a community setting. Director Dillon went on to say in the article,

> "It's frustrating after all these years. This is no longer an experiment. We know these people are better served in small community settings. We are certain that closure of O.D. Heck is the right thing to do. We were supposed to be closed by now. We haven't been able to deliver on that promise."

The article included a juxtaposition of statements, first by OMRDD, "OMRDD spokeswoman Rausch says individuals may be moved out of O.D. Heck gradually this year, on a case-by-case basis. There is no plan for closure at this time," Rausch says. "O.D. Heck was not mentioned specifically in the governor's budget. That means business as usual." This article ended with the following statement,

> "For most [of] the 138 people stuck in the institution, 1996 will be just another year like the 25 years before it—full of promises and bureaucratic wrangling, but no lifeboats waiting for them to make their escape." (C.3)

Dillon was reassigned to a staff job in the New York City Regional Office and later fired.

Dogs That Didn't Bark—Again: Employees, Advocates, and Providers

The lack of reaction to the announcement that Westchester Developmental Center would close was the key signal to OMRDD and the governor's office that allowed the 1987 policy formulation to proceed. The absence of protest by the major constituency groups or legislators (from either party) who had endorsed the 1990 closure plan and the governor's 1991 directive was a mute, but powerful, signal that support for the plan to close all institutions was a mile wide and an inch deep. Explaining why these dogs didn't bark is difficult, but an examination of some evidence as well as an analysis of the costs and benefits of closure (and no closure) to these key constituents and groups sheds some light on this nonevent. Who stood to gain by closing all institutions? Who stood to lose?

New York's remaining institutions were not relics of an earlier era. Their importance and persistence were grounded in the new roles they played. By the end of the Cuomo administration in December 1994, there were only 3,611 individuals still living in the remaining eleven facilities. However, almost all of them were frail elderly, behaviorally problematic, or criminally involved (OMRDD 1994). The institutions had changed once again. Now they served "special populations."

The frail elderly had no parents and few surviving relatives advocating for repatriation and a community residence close to home. Moreover, OMRDD was rethinking a policy of "aging in place" which would require extensive and costly renovations of community residences to accommodate aging and increasingly infirm individuals. A controversy arose in California around a series of studies that showed higher death rates for some individuals living in community settings vis-à-vis institutions (Borthwick-Duffy et al. 1998; Strauss and Kastner 1996). While researchers argued about statistics, policy makers were paying closer attention to public hearings, editorials, and parent protests. It was easier to effectively turn portions of the remaining developmental centers into skilled nursing facilities than testify at legislative hearings on the death of individuals moved to community residences, especially if staffing for their special needs produced additional reimbursement.

The notions that everyone deserved to live right at home right in your neighborhood began to give way to heightened concerns for community safety. The early 1990s were marked by a series of statutes and court decisions intended to protect the community from various types of dangerous individuals, especially sexual predators. Megan's Law in New Jersey and Kendra's Law in New York resulted in registries and civil commitment of sex offenders. Several years before the United States Supreme Court in *Hendricks v. Kansas* upheld Kansas' Sexually Violent Predator Act, which allowed predatory sex offenders to be paroled from jail to mental hospitals or kept in mental hospitals, New York and other states were already refocusing attention on individuals in their service systems who fit these profiles. Administrators began paying more attention to risk assessments in discharge plans, and the number and census in "special units" of developmental centers—Multiply Disabled Units (MDUs), Regional Intensive Behavior Units (RIBUs), and

Centers for Intensive Treatment (CITs)—grew to insulate these individuals from the community.

It became apparent that few of these individuals were ever going to be placed in the community. Institution employees' jobs were likely to continue or not be disrupted by transfers to community programs. Moreover, caring for special populations in MDUs, RIBUs, and CITs meant higher staffing ratios and substantially upgraded positions—for example, from Developmental Center Aide (G-9) to Secure Care Developmental Aide (G-13).

The controversy around the nonclosure of O.D. Heck (and the removal of the director) effectively eliminated vigorous advocacy for closing all institutions within OMRDD. The main advocacy community in New York was, for the most part, the provider community or closely tied to the provider community. Other advocates had moved on to supported living and other community challenges. New York was no longer the prime target for national advocacy groups promoting institutional closure, and analysts in this area largely reported on the inevitable demise of institutions, occasionally spotlighting another small state that had closed an institution (Braddock 1995; Lakin et al. 1999).

The provider industry had never been an enthusiastic supporter of closure. The ARC had been a reluctant plaintiff in the Willowbrook suit. The historic agreement around the ICF Plan of Compliance between New York and the ARC and other private providers which was implemented with generous start-up support through Purchase of Services contracts and highly favorable rate mechanisms eventually allowed the private provider sector to emerge as a partner rather than a vassal of OMRDD. In the 1987 closure decision, the private sector was understandably concerned that closure would absorb the bulk of resources for community development and was able to get guarantees from the legislature that levels of development in private agencies in and outside of closure districts would not be diminished. In 1990, the private sector endorsed the call for closing all developmental centers by 2000. However, as the state's budget deficits grew in the early 1990s, their enthusiasm for complete closure waned as the prospect of competing for scarcer resources loomed. It is virtually impossible to document waning enthusiasm, but the absence of any protest, opposition, or concern about the new "case by case" closure policy on the part of major private providers or their statewide organizations was an important signal to the Pataki administration. The industry was not simply going to be unopposed to the suspension of closures, it would have an alternative, positive, and more politically popular agenda. There was no directive that explicitly said that developmental centers would not close by 2000. Nonetheless, the O.D. Heck example, the lack of opposition to the decision, and the fig leaf of a "case-by-case" policy, made it clear that policy and practice in New York were now operating in a post-closure world.

Post-Closure World of Institutions and Developmental Services

The post-closure period, from 1995 to at least the early years of this century, was not a time during which policy and practice drifted. In fact, the vacuum of no-closure was quickly filled by important issues that were politically, fiscally, and operationally popular.

Waiting List

At the end of World War II, the Department of Mental Hygiene pressed the U.S. Army to return Willowbrook, pointing out that 800 to 900 infants were on a waiting list for admission to the state's institutions (Lerner 1972). In 1985, OMRDD did a study of the status of residential waiting lists in the state and found that 12,400 individuals were on waiting lists for out-of-home placement (OMRDD 1985). In 1987, the National Association for Retarded Citizens conducted a survey of waiting lists in each state, and New York reported that 9,674 people were waiting for an out-of-home placement (NArc 1987). OMRDD revised its data collection instrument (the DDP-4) several times to eliminate duplication and individuals who were not likely to need out-of-home placements for several years and found that 5,659 individuals were in "immediate need of residential service" (OMRDD 1990d, 15). OMRDD continued to update its instruments and data collection, but there were a number of problems in identifying needs for residential services: they were largely self-reported, they tended to overstate the urgency of need, and there were no independent assessments of need or even eligibility for residential services. Nonetheless, OMRDD routinely used the waiting lists in its budget justifications to argue that it could identify specific individuals whose families said they needed an out-of-home placement.

In the mid-1990s, the private provider agencies began to make the waiting lists their issue. The private agencies claimed that the numbers of individuals waiting for residential services were much larger than those counted by OMRDD—over 9,000 in New York City and pointed to OMRDD's 1985 survey showing 12,400 people statewide waiting (AHRC 1997). They also demanded that New York State fund "residential development" which clearly meant beds. Finally, they pointed out that thirty years after the peak of institutional census overall residential capacity in the state remained essentially the same.

When Governor Pataki took office in January 1995, there were 32,400 individuals living in twenty-four hour care residential settings operated by the state and private providers (OMRDD 1996). In 1967, the year the census in the state's institutions peaked at 27,554, there were 30,594 individuals in those facilities, family care, and other settings (DMH 1968). Not only had capacity remained flat, but OMRDD had assumed responsibility for individuals with developmental disabilities other than mental retardation. The thirty years of deinstitutionalization, closure, and creation of community residential services had substantially reorganized developmental services in New York, but the amount of those services had only increased modestly. With a new administration, the private provider community escalated the waiting list to the top of their political agenda.

The private provider agencies had come a long way from the days of taking over abandoned rectories and convents to now owning and leasing large amounts of property, especially through subsidiary property corporations, for residential and day programs. By the end of the century, the private agencies owned more than two thousand properties and leased (often from related corporations) another fifteen hundred properties. "Conservative estimates" of the value of the 4,654 state and privately owned community properties was $582 million (OMRDD 1999). Moreover, similar to the rebonding of the institutions, the state engaged in extensive rebonding of these public and private community program properties. OMRDD and the private provider industry adopted the rhetoric of supported living, but the reality was that they owned beds that needed to be filled and refilled in order to generate the reimbursement needed to pay off the bonds and mortgages. There were no easy alternate uses for twelve-bed ICFs/DD.

The national ARC launched another waiting list campaign with another state survey. Governors in other states announced commitments to address the waiting list problem, and OMRDD initiated another revision of its needs identification instrument aimed at getting a more accurate count of those waiting as well as more reliable information on the urgency of their need. OMRDD used the waiting lists effectively to generate overall support for its budget requests but became defensive in the face of private agency charges that it was not addressing a crisis. New York was also turning its attention to another aspect of the waiting list problem—the reemergence of the federal courts as players in policy making. This had the potential of becoming a major crisis, *or* an issue on which the state and the private provider industry could resolve the waiting list rift and recement cracks in the political and fiscal foundations.

Return of Federal Courts: Doe and Olmstead

In early 1998, a three-judge panel of the 11th U.S. Circuit Court of Appeals upheld a lower court order directing Florida to make ICF/MR services available to all qualified Medicaid recipients within ninety days of determining that they needed such services. In their original suit (*John/Jane Does v. Chiles, et al.*), plaintiffs, all on waiting lists for admission to *private* agency ICFs/MR, challenged the decision of the Florida legislature to place a moratorium on the certification of additional ICF/MR beds. The plaintiffs claimed that Florida was violating their rights, contending that the state was failing to meet its obligations under federal statutes to furnish services covered under its Medicaid plan "with reasonable promptness to all eligible individuals" (42 USC 1396(a)(8).

Florida conceded the existence of lengthy waiting lists. In 1996, the Florida Department of Children and Families had a waiting list of over 8,000 individuals awaiting developmental services statewide, of whom 1,700 were in need of ICF/MR placements. The state argued (as had New York and all other states) that it was not obligated to make Medicaid services available on the basis of open-ended funding, citing the bed capacity limit and the subsequent moratorium imposed by the legislature.

The *Doe v. Chiles* case exposed a fundamental inconsistency in the states' use of Medicaid funding for long-term care services. The original federal statute focused primarily on the delivery of acute medical services to low-income recipients. Consequently, states had to agree to provide those services promptly to all qualified individuals without respect to state funding limitations. However, as states used Medicaid funding for long-term care services where they traditionally regulated access on the basis of available appropriations and regulated supply and maintained waiting lists, the potential for conflict between federal and state statutes and practices grew. Despite a Medicaid entitlement, over the years, states limited optional services in their Medicaid plans and imposed amount, duration, and scope restrictions on existing services. Congress and HCFA acquiesced to these state strategies by repealing or watering down Certificate of Need requirements and encouraging expansion of Medicaid waivers to provide services to people with developmental disabilities, the frail elderly, persons with physical disabilities, and persons with severe and persistent mental illnesses outside general and psychiatric hospitals, nursing homes, and ICF/MR beds.

The *Doe v. Chiles* suit had been active since 1992, but Florida's enactment of a so-called "Cut Law" (H.R. 1621) eliminated coverage of private ICF/MR services from the state's Title XIX plan and required transfer of the 2,176 individuals then residing in private ICFs/MR to the state's home and community-based waiver programs. A consortium of private providers brought a new class action suit, *Cramer v. Chiles,* which challenged the legality of the statute. The federal district court ruled in *Cramer* that the plaintiffs had an enforceable civil rights action, that the state's Title XIX plan must provide that *all* individuals wishing to make application for medical assistance under the plan shall have the opportunity to do so, and such assistance shall be furnished *with reasonable promptness* to *all eligible individuals.* The time standards for determining eligibility could not exceed ninety days for applicants who applied on the basis of disability and forty-five days for all other applicants.

For Florida, the consequences seemed obvious: an entitlement to ICF/MR services rather than capped appropriations and waiting lists, substantial expansion of ICF/MR and Medicaid funded services, and implementation of procedures for eligibility determination and access within much shorter time frames than currently in place. Florida officials estimated that the state would have to spend at least an additional $1 *billion* annually on specialized developmental disabilities services to ensure that all qualified Medicaid recipients were served within the time frame specified in the court order.

The *Doe v. Chiles* ruling was reaffirmed and refined by the 1999 United States Supreme Court decision in a Massachusetts case, *Olmstead v. L.C.* (119 S. Ct. 2176). However, well before the *Olmstead* ruling, several major private provider agencies in New York let it be known that they were contemplating a similar suit. OMRDD, the governor's office, and the Division of the Budget began intensive analyses and discussions on how to address the threat.

New York State Cares

On August 19, 1998, Governor Pataki announced his New York State Cares initiative, a "comprehensive five-year plan to virtually eliminate the waiting list for residential services" (NYS 1998). This initiative (for what OMRDD and DOB decided were the 6,700 individuals on a waiting list) would create "4,900 new *beds.*" New York had forestalled additional closure lawsuits in the 1980s by its initiative to close several of its developmental centers. Many would see the New York State Cares initiative as a similarly bold move that forestalled intervention of federal courts with potentially enormous fiscal consequences, addressed the demands of the private provider industry for a continued input of clients into their existing facilities, and as an opportunity to expand overall capacity.

The initial New York State Cares proposal called for all of new development to be in the private provider agencies. The public employee unions mounted strenuous protests against further privatization and argued that state employees should be able to continue to provide services for "special need kids" (PEF 1998). The Governor relented and included state-operated residential development as part of the multiyear plan. This solidified union political support for the governor, but OMRDD had already estimated that the private agencies in New York City and the metropolitan area would likely not meet their development targets. Twenty-five years after the Willowbrook Consent Decree and the ICF Plan of Compliance, the prospects of residential development in New York City commensurate with its population remained dim. A rapid expansion of new beds would necessarily be concentrated upstate with its strong state-operated community sector. The private provider sector was guaranteed a renewed influx of funding for bed development in their existing facilities as well as whatever new programs they could establish. Public employees were assured that they would participate in additional community residential development.

The fault lines around supported living and the waiting list were not as deep as those that led to Willowbrook, but they were leading to a split in the fundamental public-private and institution-community integration of services that grew out of the post-Willowbrook consensus. But like the Willowbrook Consent Decree, the ICF/MR Plan of Compliance, and the Morgado Memorandum, the resolution of these problems with Medicaid waivers and New York State Cares, for public as well as private community development, demonstrated the resilience of the political coalition.

Rebranding the Cash Cows—The Patient Income Account

The Pataki administration effectively ended the "close all developmental centers by 2000" policy, and no significant player or group attempted to rekindle enthusiasm for it, especially as they realized the growing importance of developmental centers in the state's fiscal situation. The remaining twelve developmental centers housed only 3,600 residents, and, along with the state-operated ICFs/DD and Day Treatment programs, had become even more important in the state's overall fiscal picture. They were generating far more revenue in federal reimbursements, for private as well as public agencies, than their costs.

Table 8.3 in Chapter 8 showed the large increases in Institutional Reimbursement Rates from 1975 to 1987 when the *per diem* rate reached $218.85 (OMRDD, 00). From the end of fiscal year 1987 to the suspension of closure at the end of fiscal year 1995, the increases in the *per diem* rate skyrocketed.

In the 1960s, the New York State ARC and other advocates opposed Governor Rockefeller's scheme to bond the construction of new institutions because they argued the residents would be held hostage for the parental fees and other income required to repay the bondholders. The waiving of parental liability in New York's Medicaid law and the Medicaid eligibility for the residents of those institutions may have exempted residents and parents from individual fiscal responsibility, but their bondage was largely transferred. Repaying construction bonds was no longer the major fiscal issue. The revenue institution residents and those enrolled in small ICFs/DD, Day Treatment, and other Medicaid-reimbursed programs produced and paid into the Patient Income Account (PIA) had assumed a major role in offsetting the tax-based income accounts of the state budget.

Table 10.1
Developmental Center Per Diem Reimbursement Rates:
1987–88 to 2000–01

Fiscal Year	Per Diem Rate
1987–1988	252.34
1988–1989	291.53
1990–1990	347.81
1990–1991	388.53
1991–1992	442.25
1992–1993	551.55
1993–1994	653.74
1994–1995	935.59 (Closures Suspended)
1995–1996	1,093.34
1996–1997	1,309.77
1997–1998	1,522.33
1998–1999	1,724.97
1999–2000	1,929.97
2000–2001	2,148.81

OMRDD, 2000

By 1995, federal reimbursement from the state operations (developmental centers and other Medicaid reimbursable programs) far outpaced the amounts being paid by state taxes into the General Fund. In fact, as shown in Table 10.2, the large increases in Medicaid reimbursement, channeled into the state budget through the Patient Income Account, allowed the state to *decrease* the proportion of total funds appropriated from state tax support. Federal reimbursement had gone from important to *most* important.

Table 10.2
Medicaid [PIA] Contribution to the General Fund
(Amounts in Millions)

	Total State Purposes	Medicaid (PIA)	Total General Fund (GF)	PIA % of GF
Fiscal Year				
1990–1991	852	701	1,553	45.1
1991–1992	719	798	1,516	52.6
1992–1993	757	839	1,595	52.6
1993–1994	744	880	1,624	54.2
1994–1995	791	994	1,785	55.7
1995–1996	778	998	1,776	56.2
1996–1997	670	1,207	1,877	64.3
1997–1998	720	1,206	1,926	62.6
1998–1999	721	1,214	1,935	62.7
1999–2000	740	1,250	1,990	62.8

OMRDD, 1999

At the time the state was planning to close all developmental centers (1991–1992) Medicaid began contributing more revenue to the state's General Fund (GF) than the tax-based appropriations (State Purposes). By the time all developmental centers would have been closed (1999–2000), Medicaid was contributing close to two-thirds (62.8 percent) of the General Fund operations of the state.

These figures, however, do not show the entire picture. A large additional impact of developmental centers on the fiscal picture results from unofficial estimates by long-time budget and fiscal experts that the *per diem costs* for each developmental center resident were substantially lower than the *per diem reimbursement rate*. Some of the difference was accounted for by institutional costs expended outside the institution, in OMRDD central office for example, which were included in the rate. Nonetheless, as the *per diem* developmental center rate topped $2,000 by the end of the century, unofficial estimates of OMRDD's actual costs per day for each developmental center resident were around $200. Similarly large gaps exist between the *rates* and *costs* in small ICFs/DD, Day Treatment, and other Medicaid programs. By 2000, it was unofficially estimated that Medicaid was generating at least a $300 million a year surplus of *costs* versus *rates*—with a great deal of this "surplus" spilling over from the State Purposes to the Local Assistance portion of the state budget and effectively underwriting local Medicaid costs not covered under 620/621 and "overburden" exemptions.

Institutions were the most productive cash cows, but state-operated community ICFs/DD, Day Treatment, and other Medicaid-funded programs contributed their share to the surplus. Outside the state budget, the surpluses private agencies generated in their ICF/DD, Day Treatment, and other Medicaid-funded programs became their miniversions of cash cows.

It was the growing and crucial fiscal importance of institutions and other state and private agency programs producing surpluses from Medicaid reimbursement that was most important in dampening any lingering enthusiasm for closing them.

A New Institution

On September 29, 1998, one month after Governor Pataki announced the launch of the New York State Cares initiative to virtually eliminate the waiting list, the governor announced the plan to build a new institution—the first new institution the state had built in more than twenty years. A Center for Intensive Treatment (CIT) would be built to provide "specialized secure services" for individuals who had "serious criminal involvement (Governor's Office 1998). The governor's announcement said that the new facility would "enable the State to better provide for the safety and welfare of all its citizens." The governor pointed out that the new facility would create more than

200 permanent jobs as well as 500 jobs for the construction of the facility in the district of the Chair of the Senate Mental Hygiene Committee. The senator "applauded" the governor's efforts to provide local residents employment opportunities, and various other "beaming" state and local officials added their enthusiastic support for a project that would provide jobs and spin off other benefits for the local economy.

Public Safety, Jobs, and Medicaid Revenue

"Institutions as we knew them had closed" was a phrase that became increasingly popular. The remaining developmental centers and new facilities served "special populations"—the frail elderly, behaviorally challenging, and criminally involved—special populations with no constituency expecting or wanting them to be served in typical community settings. The new institutions provided guaranteed, higher paying jobs for the 25,000 public employees employed by OMRDD (OMRDD 1996b). The new institutions continued to be a source of economic well-being for the communities within which they were located. The "special populations" in the new institutions that required upgraded facilities and increased staffing generated more Medicaid reimbursement. They became cash cows on hormones.

Community developmental services were refinanced. A handful of supported living pilot projects seemed sufficient to occupy advocates for reform, especially those with consultant contracts from OMRDD. A Medicaid waiver refinanced the community system of services. ICFs/DD and Community Residences became "Individualized Residential Alternatives," "Residential Habilitation," and "Day Habilitation," even though the same individuals were living in the same group homes and going to the same day programs provided by the same agencies with their more than 50,000 full-time equivalent employees as prior to the waiver (OMRDD 1996b). New York State Cares was a multiyear guarantee of funds for new development of "beds" to private provider agencies, and public employees were assured of their participation in new bed development as well as "backups" for problems in the private sector.

Public officials applauded. Unions endorsed. Private agency executives supported. Community business leaders beamed. Institutions as we knew them had closed.

Conclusion

From Snake Pits to Cash Cows

Doing Well While Doing Good.

—Rosabeth Moss Kanter and David J. Summers

What explains the perseverance and vitality of public institutions?

Public institutions for people with developmental disabilities persevered and remained vital in New York because they generated federal revenues that exceeded their direct costs to state taxpayers and underwrote a substantial proportion of the costs of private and public community services. Billions of dollars of Medicaid-reimbursed expenditures funded the growth and financial well-being of a tightly organized industry that had a significant impact in many local economies. Public institutions for special populations produced extraordinarily large amounts of revenue, guaranteed the jobs of public employees, and acted as backups for private and public agency community programs. These factors supporting the perseverance of public institutions were not coincidental but central to a long-term strategy that was forged in the mid-1970s and carefully managed since then; a strategy that turned political adversaries into allies, parents into providers, and competitors into partners.

Their Fiscal Importance

From 1935 to 1965, New York State policy makers were preoccupied with the capital construction costs of new and expanded facilities and the other tax-supported expenditures to care for the growing numbers of younger and more severely disabled individuals. From 1965 to the end of the century, the fiscal dynamics were almost completely reversed. Construction and maintenance of public institutions were largely removed from the state budget and financed through moral obligation bonds sold and managed by public authorities and repaid by patient fees. The passage of Medicaid in 1965, and the federal

269

government's agreement to allow states to certify their public institutions as ICFs/MR, created a set of fiscal incentives that New York used to shift a large and increasing share of the costs of public institutions to the federal government. The federal government's acquiescence in states' use of the ICF/MR model for community programs also allowed New York to shift the costs of its privately and publicly operated community services to the federal government.

Medicaid ICF/MR reimbursement rates, which topped $2,000 per day for developmental center residents in 2000, were calculated using complex formulas for fixed and variable costs—aggressively captured in base year cost-finding surveys. Base year rates were trended forward in ways that produced substantial surpluses over the actual direct expenditures. While the greatest relative return was in the large (institution) ICFs/MR, surpluses were also generated in private and public small (community) ICFs/MR, day treatment programs, clinics, and a variety of support and ancillary services which were brought under Medicaid financing. The revenue surpluses in the Patient Income Account of the state budget were also used to offset the state and local government shares of Medicaid and other costs not covered by Medicaid. Rather than being fiscal burdens for the state, public institutions were part of an integrated, mutually reinforcing, public and private sector, state and local government fiscal strategy which resulted in the federal government paying the majority of the costs of all developmental services in New York State.

Their Economic Importance

Despite the emblematic role Willowbrook in New York City assumed, public institutions in New York were largely located in upstate, rural areas where they became more economically important as smoke stack industries left and as these institutions employed larger numbers of staff. The treatment requirements of the ICF/MR and other Medicaid-funded programs also made that staff increasingly professional and in New York, unionized. Public institutions and other developmental services, with more than 75,000 (largely federally funded) public and private agency full-time equivalent jobs—along with psychiatric hospitals, prisons, and colleges—became *the* major source of good jobs and economic well being in much of upstate New York. The economic impact was enhanced by the concentration of the bulk of routine services in large horizontally and vertically integrated super-agencies that held either monopolies or carefully managed major shares of services in those locales where they were often the largest employers.

Their Political Importance

Beyond the natural political importance of a multibillion dollar industry, other features of New York's experience contributed to strong and deep support for public institutions and related services. The historic accommodations of the 1970s transformed the antagonism between the state and the mental retardation constituency into a partnership that avoided partisan cleavages along public-private sector lines. The geographic distribution of public and private services in the state also cemented exceptionally strong bipartisan support for developmental services. In upstate areas, Republican legislators (who controlled the State Senate for all but a few years between 1935 and 2000) and local business interests allied with unionized public employees to support public expenditures for jobs in institutions as well as in community services. In New York City and the metropolitan area, private agencies maintained close ties with Democrat legislators (who controlled the Assembly from 1965 to 2000) to ensure that sufficient funds were appropriated for their program maintenance and expansion. Parent and advocacy interests were almost completely subsumed within provider agencies and contract arrangements. In New York, the public and private sectors were fiscal, organizational, and political partners rather than adversaries, and public institutions were one important element of the overall accommodation among the interests.

Their Operational Importance

The resilience of public institutions was also a result of their integration into the overall system of public and private services. The early adoption of the "small" ICF/MR as the primary community model, the conversion of privately operated Community Residences to ICFs/MR, and the later assumption of the bulk of developmental services and supports under the Home and Community Based Services waiver effectively eliminated the regulatory and fiscal distinctions between institutions, group homes, and individualized services in community settings. They were all larger or smaller, aggregated or disaggregated variations of the same Medicaid-funded programs. There were virtually no functional or regulatory barriers to the movement of people with developmental disabilities—and, very importantly, employees—within, among, or back and forth between "institution" and "community" settings operated by either public or private agencies. Public institutions became simply one component in a functionally and fiscally integrated system.

Their Adaptation and Specialization in New Roles

Public institutions adapted to serve special populations and took on new roles in the overall service system. At the beginning of the twenty-first century, the bulk of individuals remaining in New York's developmental centers were the frail elderly, the behaviorally problematic, and the forensically involved. Serving "special populations," with richer state employee staffing and higher Medicaid reimbursement rates, became the primary operational rationale for the perseverance of existing and construction of new public institutions. The regulatory, fiscal, and programmatic integration of large and small ICFs/MR added the crucial "backup" role as individuals who were difficult to serve or presented risks in community settings were moved to public institutions.

Quality of Services in Public Institutions

Investigations by oversight bodies showed that the problems of abuse and neglect had not disappeared in public institutions *or* in public and private community programs. Nonetheless, newly constructed and refurbished, smaller, and better staffed facilities *appeared* to be providing more humane and better care, and even the harshest critics and advocates would likely concede that abuse and neglect were no longer endemic in public institutions. By 2000, the professional literature and popular media rarely dealt with the problems that were recurring topics from at least the Moreland Act Commission of the mid-1940s through the exposés that led to the parents' suit at Willowbrook. In fact, most critiques of services faulted the unnecessary clinical features of these Medicaid-funded programs rather than neglect. Occasional organized efforts by parent groups were invariably in support of continuing public institutions.

The assumption of developmental services under Medicaid financing also brought additional federal oversight—a concern for quality of care honed by substantial fiscal penalties for noncompliance. The perseverance of public institutions was supported, in part, by the absence of any important or sustained argument that poor conditions or care existed in them. The fact that public institutions were no longer poorhouses was another factor contributing to their perseverance. No apparent social stigma was associated with gaining access to Medicaid-funded entitlements on the part of middle-class parents, and these parents were better equipped and more likely to maintain oversight over the care of their family members.

Lessons and Implications for Understanding
The Problem of Institutions

Since the mid-twentieth century, advocates, analysts, and historians assumed that declines in the numbers and census of public institutions and increases in services delivered by private agencies in community settings were reliable indicators of progress toward solving the problem of public institutions like Willowbrook—indeed the key to resolving most of the other problems in this arena. A myopic focus on these apparently inexorable trends was bolstered by a political ideology in which closing institutions was the "right thing to do" and analyses of the cost and size of institutions that claimed that closing them was the smart thing to do. The rapid declines in public institutions appeared to deflect attention away from explaining either increases in the numbers and censuses in other types of institutions or, as described by some advocates and analysts, the institutional features of most day and residential services delivered in private and public community agencies.

The problem of institutions was not who lived in them. In 1935, the Albion and Naponach State Institutions for Defective Delinquents housed 1,223 of that era's "special populations." Sixty-five years later, New York, having gone from the prewar schools, farms, and colonies housing relatively less-disabled adults, the overcrowded infant infirmaries of the postwar era, and the modernized ICF/MR active treatment model, was building new institutions for the same types and numbers of individuals who had been in Albion and Naponach. Changes in the types of residents were closely linked to changes in the fiscal, economic, and operational roles institutions played turning from poorhouses and burdens on the state treasury to vital sources of revenue, opportunities for well-paying jobs, and engines of local economic development.

The problem of institutions was not one of size, auspice, or unique patterns of daily life. At the beginning of the twenty-first century, the overwhelming majority of individuals living in so-called community services were in congregate residential and day programs that replicated the highly routinized patterns of daily life typical of the downsized state institutions. Individuals living inside and outside formally designated institutions still received elaborately prescribed and monitored clinical-therapeutic services rather than supports for daily living most needed and would likely prefer. Moreover, in New York, very large fiscally and operationally integrated public and private community agencies controlled the overwhelming bulk of residential and day services and had been successful in rebranding many congregate and routinized programs under various "individualized" labels.

The problem of institutions was not simply their location. Many "community" programs housed hundreds of former institution residents in clusters of group homes on the periphery of closed facilities. Large numbers of group homes were located in isolated rural areas, and others were concentrated in "human services zones" in marginal urban areas that were not the idealized communities in which many reformers hoped these individuals would live.

Institutions "as we knew them" may have closed, but other types of institutions persevered, adapted, and achieved widespread professional and political support as their residents, their roles, and their relationship to other organizations continued to change. New York's experience showed that the problems of institutions, as they have been traditionally posed—state auspice, size, location, condition, routinized patterns of life, and social isolation—were not solved. New York's experience since 1935 is not simply a demonstration that public institutions persevere and that private and public community services have institutional characteristics. Explaining who gets what kinds of services, where they get them, how they get access to them, what are the conditions within which they are delivered, and who pays how much must not be limited or skewed by a focus on public institutions. The answers to these questions must instead be pursued within the framework of all developmental services.

Organization of Services: A Framework for Examining Key Issues

Aside from Sparer's (1996) examination of the effects of where Medicaid rate-setting authority was located in a state, relatively little attention has been devoted to how features of the organization of services have significant implications for who gets what services, how they are delivered, and how much they cost. New York's experience showed why its allocation of responsibility for delivering and paying for services among the public and private sectors and federal, state, and local governments laid a new foundation for developmental services in the state. It showed how local management authorities were structured and how program certification, rate setting, and quality assurance functions were located had enormous consequences. It explained the significant impact of decisions to give private agencies substantial control over eligibility determination, access to services, needs assessment, and measuring the characteristics of recipients. New York's experience showed that strategic choices to make parent-advocacy agencies, along with state-operated programs, the bases of community services; to expand existing rather than develop new agencies; to encourage horizontal and vertical integration of the full range of services within those agencies; and to manage the market shares within locales had long-term implications.

Other states have widely varying, and often multiple approaches, to organizing and financing developmental services (Castellani 1997, 2000, 2001). Yet most comparisons among states usually do not go beyond statewide measures of service volume and overall expenditures to consider how major features, and important "technical" aspects, of the organization of services have important consequences for who gets them and who pays. Comparisons using these broad measures do little to explain why apparently similar states take different approaches to the use of institutions and other types of services. Examining important features of the organization of services that are not usually considered helped explain what happened in New York and provides guidelines to studying the experience of other states and for comparisons among states.

Definitions, Demographics, and Capacity

New York's sixty-five-year experience shows that understanding the perseverance of institutions and other important elements of state's service systems needs to take into account the differences and changes in the numbers and characteristics of those served. Analysts looking at rapidly rising costs in Medicaid expenditures have focused on the growth in the numbers of disabled individuals eligible for services and the extraordinarily high and lifelong costs of these services (Vladeck 2003). New York's experience showed how disability definitions, the demographics of disability, eligibility for Medicaid, and the availability of different types of services were linked and had substantial, and often unexpected consequences. Differences between categorical and functional definitions of developmental disabilities were debated within professional circles at the beginning of the twenty-first century. In practice, the trend was to include more types of low-incidence and uncertain conditions within the developmental disabilities framework where high levels of well-regarded, publicly funded services were provided. These individuals (with sometimes difficult-to-define disabilities) accounted for more than 20 percent of those in residential services in New York State (Castellani 2000).

The lack of agreement on definitions of disability was compounded by uncertainty about the numbers of individuals with developmental disabilities. The errors in the plans of the 1960s were a result, in large measure, of analysts forced to fit their calculations of incidence, prevalence, and utilization into predetermined 1,000-bed institutional models. However, the wide and unexplained variations in New York and other states about the numbers on waiting lists showed that estimates of incidence, prevalence, utilization, and need were still widely off the mark.

As far back as the explosion of overcrowding after World War II, the relationship between need and institutional capacity could be characterized as: if you build them, they will come. The decisions to admit infants, to build institutions upstate and not in New York City, to deinstitutionalize large numbers of former New York City residents in upstate communities, and to eliminate the waiting list in five years were policy choices that had much more impact on the availability of services in New York than any scientific assessments linking needs to where and what type of service capacity to build. In New York, changes in the overall capacity of residential services over sixty-five years were unrelated to changes in the state population.

The implementation of the *Olmstead v. L.C* decision has been highlighted as a critical problem for states (Vladeck 2003), but as the waiting list issue moved to the top of the policy agenda, the wide and unexplained variations in definitions, demographics, and capacity that lurked below the surface began to emerge. Two surveys of waiting lists done by the national Arc (formerly Association for Retarded Citizens) were crucial to highlighting the issue in states and formed the background for decisions in the federal courts. However, there were radical and anomalous changes within and among states in the numbers waiting for residential services between the two surveys done by the Arc, and these were unrelated to the wide and unexplained variations among states in overall residential capacity consistently reported in less policy-charged descriptions (Braddock 1995; Prouty and Lakin 1997).

As New York and many other states launched "waiting list" initiatives (often to stave off *Olmstead* challenges), they were beset by the inability to accurately count the numbers of people waiting for services, determine their eligibility, distinguish the differences between Medicaid eligibility and "eligibility" for other services, assess the level and urgency of needs, and manage access over the limited time frames set for eliminating the waiting list. Despite a great deal of effort on these issues in New York, definitional and demographic problems had not been solved. New York's experience points to the unforeseen and unintended consequences of substantial differences among states in their capacity to resolve these definitional and demographic problems that affect policy choices about funding additional services.

Lessons and Implications for Explaining Policy Making and Administration

Importance of History and Context

New York's experience demonstrates the importance of examining a significant public policy issue over a long period of time. Decisions made in the mid-1960s to mid-1970s were shaped by policies and actions taken decades before; for example, where to build what kind of public institutions, whether to admit infants, or whether to grudgingly tolerate or integrate parent-based community organizations. The decisions to close public institutions and early implementation successes led most analysts to declare the resolution of that policy problem, move on to other issues, and ignore the important changes in policy and practice that ensured their perseverance. A short-term focus on the conflicts surrounding Willowbrook missed such significant, indeed radical, changes as the transformation of the parent groups into major providers of community services and organizational and political partners with the state administration. Predictions about the inevitable closing of all public institutions rested on assumptions about the course of policy decisions and actions that a long-term view showed had important unintended outcomes.

A great deal of the policy discussions about public institutions and developmental services and much of the literature in this area continues to be characterized by a mid-1960s world view when Willowbrook typified public institutions, community services were underfunded, parent groups were advocates suing the state, and the state was preoccupied with the costs of construction and operation of overcrowded facilities. It fails to account for the fact that public institutions have undergone radical change, parent-advocacy groups now operate multi-million dollar super agencies, the state is more concerned with revenues than costs, and people with developmental disabilities are sources of income rather than burdens.

Using a historical context also captured the importance of a number of long-term situational factors; for example, the difficulties of building large public institutions in New York City, and later, the lack of either adequate congregate care or individually accessible housing for people with disabilities in the city. This had a profound impact on the pace and geographic distribution of people across the state, their characteristics, the services they received, and whether they received them from private or public agencies.

The history of public institutions in New York reconfirmed the importance of examining public policy making and administration in their social, economic, and political contexts. The changes in public institutions that contributed to their vitality were heavily influenced by post-World War II changes in attitudes in middle-class families and professional opinions about placing disabled children in public institutions. Late twentieth century concerns for public safety were important supports for building new and reconfiguring existing institutions for individuals at risk of criminal behavior. The economic importance of public institutions also changed as their costs were converted to the basis for their fiscal benefits to the state. Their conversion into ICFs/MR made them important sources of large numbers of professional jobs, and their location in communities suffering the loss of industry made them crucial to the economic well-being of their locales. The partisan clashes around public institutions that flared in the 1960s (that included presidential ambitions and battles for state party control) gave way to an historic set of political compromises that largely removed public institutions from the arena of partisan politics.

Importance of Strategy in Policy Making and Administration

The perseverance of public institutions in New York was not accidental, but rather the outcome of a series of pragmatic and bold decisions, made within a relatively short period in the mid-1970s, that were forged into a long-term and consistent strategy. One of the first principles of New York's strategy for developmental services was to maximize Medicaid. Virtually from the inception of Medicaid (and at the same time it was cutting back on eligibility for the aged and medically infirm), New York used the program to fund its public institutions for people with mental disabilities. From 1965 to 2000, every expansion, extension, and reorganization of services in New York was first and foremost considered in relation to its impact on Medicaid reimbursement. Dealing with the federal courts was another element in the strategy. By entering into the 1975 Willowbrook Consent Decree, New York effectively pushed federal courts to the margins of policy making. While Willowbrook would continue to "drive the agency" in many important management and programmatic ways, the federal court became a goad to action and arbiter of disputes between the parties rather being centrally involved in decision making as the court was in other states.

The ICF Plan of Compliance was another strategic decision as New York promised to radically revamp and permanently close thousands of ICF beds in public institutions. By adopting a massive ICF Plan of Compliance, the state resolved, for a number of years (with deadline extensions), the problem of the federal government's concern about how New York was using the large ICF/MR program in its public institutions. Its implementation required the creation of thousands of residential and community services in a short period of time and led to the historic agreement with the parent organizations to rapidly expand their embryonic community programs into a full-fledged and integrated residential and day services community system while retaining control over key elements of access to those services. After a start-up period involving extensive operational, technical, and fiscal assistance (Purchase of Service contracts), the state made yet another strategic decision and instigated the massive conversion of small private agency Community Residences to the "small" ICF/MR program.

The final important element of the New York strategy of the 1970s was its agreement (memorialized in the Morgado Memorandum) with its public employee unions that the state, as well as private agencies, would operate residential and day services in communities using public employees and would develop those programs at the same level as private agency development.

A distinguishing feature of New York's experience with public institutions and all other developmental services from 1965 to 2000 was that it was formed by a set of intentional, cohesive and consistent public policy decisions, approaches, and agreements. They were strategic because policy makers and key interests in the field reconstructed and built anew the political, economic, fiscal, organizational, and operational foundation for developmental services in New York State. Key elements of that strategy were solidified in the mid to late 1970s, linking decisions made earlier after the adoption of Medicaid and the ICF/MR program. The strategy was consistently pursued, expanded and solidified in the following decades: shift the state's costs to the federal government, make parents partners, and make adversaries allies. This was the framework for public and private sector, state and federal, and state and local government and established a consistent approach toward financing, organizing and staffing public and private as well as institutional and community developmental services.

Importance of Nondecisions and Nonactions

The fact that many aspects of New York's strategic approach were often obscure and seemingly inconsequential is a lesson on the importance of understanding nondecisions and nonactions in public policy making. The federal government failed to take early and preemptive action against New York and other states who were aggressively using the ICF/MR program to shift the costs of public institutions and public and private community services to the federal government. The federal government was reduced to rearguard audits and reviews of an already-entrenched and comprehensive system of services. The failure of oversight bodies to challenge vulnerable aspects such as Medicaid eligibility in the wholesale conversion of Community Residences to ICFs/MR allowed OMRDD to undertake this massive refinancing of its private community services. The effective withdrawal of the ARC from the Willowbrook suit left relatively marginal civil rights organizations and Willowbrook parents as the only challengers to OMRDD. The almost complete silence by the advocates, parent provider organizations, and policy makers in the face of the state's suspension of the decision to close all developmental centers by 2000 was as important as many explicit actions and decisions.

Related to nondecisions were preemptive actions by New York policy makers, such as the Willowbrook Consent Decree in 1975, the 1987 decision to close several institutions, and the 1998 Waiting List initiative that were designed in large part to keep important decision making out of the federal courts. Other policy decisions and actions (e.g., Chapters 620 and 621, District 98, and the Padavan Site Selection statute) were intended to effectively put local governments at the periphery of policymaking. At a number of critical junctures, nondecisions, nonactions, and virtually invisible actions were features of policy and practice.

Importance of Policy Management and Management Capacity

Underneath the strategic lay a set of critical policy management decisions and actions. In contrast to most other states, New York concentrated the key regulatory functions of program certification, rate setting, and quality assurance within the operating agency (first the Department of Mental Hygiene and later OMRDD). OMRDD's establishment of twenty Developmental Disabilities Services Offices (DDSOs) had major policy management implications. The well-staffed DDSOs had direct line control over the public institution *and* state-operated community services in the locale, and exercised substantial control over program certification, local quality assurance, and contract approval for the private agencies in the district. At the statewide level, policy issues with the private providers were carefully managed through residential and day provider councils, a large number of advisory committees, and astute use of the 5.07 five-year, DDPC, and Local Government plans. OMRDD and the governor's office used appointments and contracts to manage and coordinate policies with the Developmental Disabilities Planning Council, the Commission on Quality of Care for the Mentally Disabled, and the Office of the Advocate for the Disabled. The governor's office and legislators played important roles at certain times on certain issues, but overall after 1975, they relied on OMRDD to use these various statewide and local administrative structures, arrangements, and mechanisms to manage policy: to coordinate and control, to generate more federal revenue, to keep disputes out of the public and political arena, and to accommodate potentially troubling advocates and interests. In return, OMRDD and its public and private partners enjoyed their "fairer share" of resources.

New York's experience also demonstrated the importance of management capacity to the successful implementation and continued performance of its strategy. New York made an early decision to enhance its management capacity in developmental services when it increased staffing in revenue and reimbursement offices even as it was cutting back staff in other areas during the continuing fiscal crises of the 1960s and 1970s. The adoption of the ICF/MR program had the effect of increasing management capacity as its clinical requirements called for larger numbers of supervisory and management positions (which produced many of OMRDD's senior managers in the district and central offices). In light of the decades-long antagonism between advocates and the psychiatry-dominated Department of Mental Hygiene, OMRDD quickly adopted a nonmedical management approach that created greater opportunities for professional managers. The well-staffed DDSOs with comprehensive local authority allowed the agency to deal with problems as they arose, to provide the technical and other assistance to the private agencies in their early stages of development, and to effectively manage deinstitutionalization.

OMRDD also hired federal staff who had drafted the ICF/MR regulations to assist in writing its regulations, retained a prestigious Washington law firm to represent the agency in dealings with HCFA, and contracted with major accounting and management consulting firms on continuing and *ad hoc* issues of rate-setting, reimbursement, and administrative reorganization.

Implementation, Privatization, and Interorganizational Management

The management capacity New York State built within and closely linked to OMRDD was essential to the success of its Medicaid maximization strategy. But it was its capacity for interorganizational management that was crucial in the rapid creation of private community services in the 1970s, the implementation of the closure of several public institutions in the 1980s, and the ongoing management of a large and complex public and private array of institutional and community services. Much of the literature on privatization conveys the image of one-time, one-way transfers of public functions to private agencies, a delayering of middle managers, and oversight by contract managers. While this may be the case for such routine functions as cleaning, food service, and security, New York's experience shows that the management of large and complex arrays of health and human services required substantial, indeed enhanced, interorganizational management capacity.

New York's experience showed that the successful management of the public-private array of services required the state's continuing provision of direct technical, operational, and administrative assistance to private agencies. The state's provision of ancillary services for the operation of those private agencies, and the state's maintenance of a variety of central fiscal, legal-regulatory, and administrative functions in OMRDD was also essential to the functioning of a system of private and public agencies. Especially important were the experienced middle managers with both administrative and clinical backgrounds working at the seams of public and private organizations. New York's experience demonstrates the importance of understanding the linkages among policy making, policy management, and management capacity. It also shows that successful privatization and ongoing management success requires *more* — not less — middle-interorganizational management capacity.

By creating a comprehensive system of services based on the ICF/MR program — both large and small, public *and* private — New York built a highly integrated system that greatly enhanced movement of service recipients from public to private, from institution to community services as well as the ability to move individuals from private to public institutions for special populations and "back up" services.

Public institutions in New York State persevere because they are vital components in this integrated public and private system. Fewer and smaller public institutions are much different from those of the Willowbrook era in their clientele and the roles they play and the fiscal and economic benefits they generate. Public employees who fought deinstitutionalization have better-paying jobs caring for "special populations." Many of the parent-based agencies that struggled for survival have become supermarkets of services and are doing well while doing good. Public institutions have gone from being snake pits to cash cows.

Bibliography

Anderson, L. L., K. C. Lakin, T. W. Mangan, and R. W. Prouty. "State Institutions: Thirty Years of Depopulation and Closure." *Mental Retardation* 36 (1998): 431–443.

Anderson, L. L., R. W. Prouty, and K. C. Lakin. "Closure of Large State Facilities and Reductions of Resident Populations: Trends and Milestones." *Mental Retardation* 38 (1999): 509–510.

Ashbaugh, J. and G. Smith. "Beware the Managed Health-Care Companies." *Mental Retardation* 34 (1996): 189–193.

Association for Retarded Citizens of the United States (NARC). *A National Status Report on Waiting Lists of People with Mental Retardation for Community Services.* (Arlington, Texas: Association for Retarded Citizens of the United States, 1987).

———. *A Status Report to the Nation on People with Mental Retardation Waiting for Community Services.* (Arlington, Texas: Association for Retarded Citizens of the United States, 1997).

Association for the Help of Retarded Children. (AHRC). "The Residential Waiting List: Who Matters? The Crisis of Those Who Sit at Home and Wait." *Chronicle* (New York: Association for the Help of Retarded Children, 1997).

Axelrod, D. *Shadow Government: The Hidden World of Public Authorities—and How They Control Over $1 Trillion of Your Money* (New York: John Wiley and Sons, 1992).

Bank-Mikkelson, N. E. "A Metropolitan Area in Denmark: Copenhagen." In R. Kugel and W. Wolfensberger, eds. *Changing Patterns in Residential Services for the Mentally Retarded* (Washington, DC: The President's Committee on Mental Retardation, 1969).

Bardach, E. *The Implementation Game: What Happens After a Bill Becomes a Law* (Cambridge, MA: MIT Press, 1977).

Benjamin, G. and T. N. Hurd. *Rockefeller in Retrospect: The Governor's New York Legacy* (Albany, NY: The Nelson A. Rockefeller Institute of Government, 1984).

Berkowitz, E. D. "The Politics of Mental Retardation During the Kennedy Administration." *Social Science Quarterly* 61 (1980): 128–143.

Berkowitz, E. D. *Disabled Policy: America's Programs for the Handicapped* (New York: Cambridge University Press, 1987).

Beyer, B. K. *Thomas E. Dewey 1937–1947: A Study in Political Leadership* (New York: Garland Publishing Co., 1979).

Bird, W. A., P. J. Castellani, and C. Nemeth. "Access to Early Intervention Services in New York State." *Journal of Disability Policy Studies* 1 (1990): 66–84.

Blanck, P. D. "Employment Integration, Economic Opportunity, And The Americans With Disabilities Act: Empirical Study from 1990–1993." *Iowa Law Review* 79 (1994): 854–923.

Blatt, B. and F. Kaplan. *Christmas in Purgatory* (Boston: Allyn and Bacon, 1966).

Blatt, B. *Exodus from Pandemonium: Human Abuse and Reformation of Public Policy* (Boston: Allyn and Bacon, 1970).

Boggs, E. M. "Behavioral Fisics." In J. J. Bevilacqua, ed. *Changing Government Policies for the Mentally Disabled* (Cambridge, MA: Ballinger Publishing Co., 1981).

Boggs, E. K., K. C. Lakin, and S. Clauser. "Medicaid Coverage of Residential Services." In K. C. Lakin, B. Hill, and R. Bruininks, eds. *An Analysis of Medicaid's Intermediate Care Facility for the Mentally Retarded Program* (Minneapolis: Center for Residential and Community Services, 1985).

Borthwick-Duffy, S., K. F. Widaman, and H. J. Grossman. "Mortality Research, Placement, and Risk of Death: Basic Research, the Media, and Public Policy." *Mental Retardation* 36 (1998): 416–422.

Braddock, D., ed., *Disability at the Dawn of the 21st Century and the State of the States* (Washington, DC: American Association on Mental Retardation, 2002).

Braddock, D., T. Heller, and E. Zashin. *The Closure of the Dixon Developmental Center: Public Policy Monograph No. 1* (Chicago. IL: Institute for the Study of Developmental Disabilities, 1984).

Braddock, D., R. Hemp and R. Howes. *Public Expenditures for Mental Retardation and Developmental Disabilities in the United States* (Chicago, IL: Institute for the Study of Developmental Disabilities, 1984).

Braddock, D. and T. Heller. "The Closure of Mental Retardation Institutions II: Implications." *Mental Retardation* 23 (1985): 222–229.

Braddock, D., R. Hemp, G. Fujiura, L. Bachelder, and D. Mitchell, D. *The State of the States in Developmental Disabilities* (Baltimore, MD: Paul H. Brookes, 1990).

Braddock, D., R. Hemp, L. Bachelder, and G. Fujiura, G. *The State of the States in Developmental Disabilities,* 4th ed. (Washington, DC: American Association on Mental Retardation, 1995).

Braddock, D., R. Hemp, S. Parish, and J. Westrich. *The State of the States in Developmental Disabilities,* 5th ed. (Washington, DC: American Association on Mental Retardation, 1998).

Bradley, V. J. "Implementation of Court and Consent Decrees: Some Current Lessons." In R. H. Bruininks and K. C. Lakin, eds., *Living and Learning in the Least Restrictive Environment* (Baltimore, MD: Paul H. Brookes, 1985).

Bradley, V. J., J. W. Ashbaugh, and B. C. Blaney, B. C. eds., *Creating Individual Supports for People with Developmental Disabilities: A Mandate for Change at Many Levels* (Baltimore, MD: Paul H. Brookes, 1994).

Butterfield, E. C. "Basic Facts About Public Residential Facilities for the Mentally Retarded." In R. B. Krugel and W. Wolfensberger, eds. *Changing Patterns in Residential Services for the Mentally Retarded* (Washington, DC: President's Committee on Mental Retardation, 1969).

Caro, R. H. *The Power Broker* (New York: Alfred A. Knopf, 1974).

Castellani, P. J. "The Impact of Judicial Policy Outputs on Mental Hygiene in New York State" (Ph.D. diss., Syracuse University, 1975).

Castellani, P. J., W. E. Epple, and L. Sirmans, L. *Homer Folks Transitional Center: A Report on an Intensive Short-Term ICF Program for Individuals with Maladaptive Behaviors* (Albany, NY: New York State Office of Mental Retardation and Developmental Disabilities, 1985).

Castellani, P. J., N. A. Downey, M. B. Tausig, and W. A. Bird. "Availability and Accessibility of Family Support Services." *Mental Retardation* 24 (1986): 71–79.

Castellani, P. J. *The Political Economy of Developmental Disabilities* (Baltimore, MD: Paul Brookes, 1987).

Castellani, P. J. "Closing Institutions in New York State: Implementation and Management Lessons." *Journal of Policy Analysis and Management* 11 (1992): 593–611.

Castellani, P. J., S. E. Segore, M.C. Brown, and W. A. Bird. *An Overview of Service Agencies in New York State* (Albany, NY: New York State Office of Mental Retardation and Developmental Disabilities, 1995).

Castellani, P. J. "Closing Institutions in New York State: Policymaking and Implementation Issues." In J. Mansell and K. Ericsson, eds. *Deinstitutionalisation in Scandinavia, the United States and Britain: Changing Patterns of Intellectual Disability Services* (London: Chapman and Hall, 1996).

Castellani, P. J. "Managing Alternative Approaches to the Provision and Production of Public Goods: Public, Private, and Nonprofit." In J. J. Gargan, ed. *Handbook of Local Government Administration* (New York: Marcel Dekker, 1997).

Castellani, P. J. "The Administration of Developmental Disabilities Services in State Government." In J. J. Gargan, ed. *Handbook of State Government Administration* (New York: Marcel Dekker, 2000).

Castellani, P. J. "Managing Learning Disabilities Services in the United States." *Tizard Learning Disabilities Review* 6 (2001): 33–40.

Clauser, S. B., L Rotegard, and C. White. "State Reimbursement Policies." In K. C. Lakin, B. Hill, and R. Bruininks, eds. *An Analysis of Medicaid's Intermediate*

Care Facility for the Mentally Retarded Program (Minneapolis: Center for Residential and Community Services, 1985).

Cohen, H. J. "Obstacles to Developing Community Services for Mentally Retarded." In M. J. Begab and S. A. Richardson, eds. *The Mentally Retarded and Society: A Social Science Perspective* (Baltimore, MD: University Park Press, 1975).

Conley, R. W. *The Economics of Mental Retardation* (Baltimore, MD: Johns Hopkins University Press, 1985).

Conroy, J. W. and V. J. Bradley. *The Pennhurst Longitudinal Study: A Report on Five Years of Research and Analysis* (Philadelphia: Temple University Developmental Disabilities Center, 1985).

Crissey, M. S. and M. Rosen, eds., *Institutions for the Mentally Retarded: A Changing Role in Changing Times* (Austin, TX: Pro-Ed, 1986).

Deutsch, A. *The Shame of the States* (New York: Harcourt, Brace, 1948).

Disability Experience in America. "Fighting to Keep 'Em In: California Foes of Community Living Fight De-Institutionalization." *Ragged Edge* (Rochester, NY: Disability Experience in America, 1998).

Elmore, R. F. "Graduate Education in Public Management: Working the Seams of Government." *Journal of Policy Analysis and Management* 6 (1986): 69–83.

Ferguson, P. M. *Abandoned to Their Fate* (Philadelphia, PA: Temple University Press, 1994).

Ferguson, P. M., M. Hibbard, J. Leinen, and S. Schaff. "Supported Community Life: Disability Policy and the Renewal of Mediating Structures." *Journal of Disability Policy Studies* 1 (1990): 9–35.

Gardner, J. F. "Quality, Organization Design, and Standards." *Mental Retardation* 30 (1992): 173–177.

Gargan, J. J. "Consideration of Local Government Capacity." *Public Administration Review* 6 (1981): 649–658.

Goggin, M. L. *Policy Design and the Politics of Implementation: The Case of Health Care in the American States* (Knoxville, TN: University of Tennessee Press, 1987).

Gold, G. G. "How Deinstitutionalization Created New Roles for Managers and Supervisors at the Rome Developmental Disabilities Service Office." In J. M. Rostow and R. Zager, eds. *New Roles for Managers* (Scarsdale, NY: Work in America Institute, 1990).

Gollay, E., R. Freedman, M. Wyngarrden, and N. R. Kurtz, N. R. *Coming Back: The Community Experience of Deinstitutionalized Mentally Retarded People* (Cambridge, MA: Abt Books, 1978).

Grant-Thornton. *The Fiscal and Economic Impact of Developmental Center Closure, 1987–1990* (Albany, NY: The New York State Office of Mental Retardation and Developmental Disabilities, 1990).

Grob, G. N. *From Asylum to Community: Mental Health Policy in Modern America* (Princeton, NJ: Princeton University Press, 1991).

Grob, G. N. *The Mad Among Us: A History of Care of America's Mentally Ill* (New York: The Free Press, 1994).

Grondahl, P. "For Residents, Life to Remain the Same at O.D. Heck Center." *Albany Times-Union.* 15 January 1996, C-1.

Grondahl, P. "Integration Only Partly Achieved." *Albany Times Union.* 16 January 1996, C-5.

Heller, T., M. A. Bond, and D. Braddock. "Family Reactions to Institutional Closure." *American Journal on Mental Retardation* 92 (1988): 336–343.

Hendrickson, P. "Lawsuit Against Prison Co-location Sends Shockwave Through RDC." *Rome Sentinel.* 27 October 1987.

Hemp, R., D. Braddock, and J. Westrich, J. "Medicaid, Managed Care, and Developmental Disabilities." In D. Braddock, R. Hemp, S. Parish, and J. Westrich eds. *The State of the States in Developmental Disabilities,* 5th ed. (Washington, DC: American Association on Mental Retardation, 1998).

Hevesi, A. G. *Legislative Politics in New York State: A Comparative Analysis* (New York: Praeger, 1975).

Hughes, R. *The Shock of the New* (New York: Alfred A. Knopf, 1991).

Janicki, M., ed., *Group Homes: Here to Stay* (Baltimore, MD: Paul H. Brookes, 1985).

Kantor, Rosabeth Moss and David V. Summers. "Doing Well While Doing Good: Dilemmas of Performance Measurement in Nonprofit Organizations and the Need for a Multi-Constituency Approach." In Walter W. Powell, ed. *The Nonprofit Sector: A Research Handbook.* New Haven, CT: Yale University Press, 1987).

Kingdon, J. W. *Agendas, Alternatives, and Public Policy,* 1st ed. (New York: Harper Collins, 1984).

Kugel, R. B. and W. Wolfensberger, eds., *Changing Patterns in Residential Services for the Mentally Retarded* (Washington, DC: President's Committee on Mental Retardation, 1969).

Krugel, R. B. "Why Innovative Action." In R. B. Krugel and W. Wolfensberger eds. *Changing Patterns in Residential Services for the Mentally Retarded* (Washington, DC: President's Committee on Mental Retardation, 1969).

Lakin, K. C. and R. H. Bruininks. "Contemporary Services for Handicapped Children and Youth." In R. H. Bruininks and K.C. Lakin, eds. *Living and Learning in the Least Restrictive Environment* (Baltimore, MD: Paul H. Brookes, 1985).

Lakin, K. C., C. C. White, B. K Hill, R. H. Bruininks, and E. A. Wright. "Longitudinal Change and Interstate Variability in Residential Services for Persons with Mental Retardation." *Mental Retardation* 28 (1990): 343–351.

Lakin, K. C., L. Anderson, R. Prouty, R., and B. Polister. "State Institution Populations Less Than One Third of 1977, Residents Older with More Impairments:
Trends and Milestones." *Mental Retardation* 37 (1999): 85–86.

Lakin, K. C., B. Prouty, D. Braddock, and L. Anderson. "State Institution Populations
Smaller, Older, More Impaired: Trends and Milestones." *Mental Retardation* 35
(1997): 231–232.

Lakin, K. C., D. Braddock, and G. Smith. "Closure of Large State Facilities and
Reductions of Resident Populations: Trends and Milestones." *Mental Retardation*
37 (1999): 509–510.

Lakin, K. C., D. Braddock, and G. Smith. "Leveraging Federal Funding in the States
to Address Olmstead and Growing Waiting Lists: Trends and Milestones." *Mental
Retardation* 39 (2001): 241–243.

Laski, F. J. "The Right to Habilitation and the Right to Education: The Legal Foundation." In R. H. Bruininks and K. C. Lakin, eds. *Living and Learning in the
Least Restrictive Environment* (Baltimore, MD: Paul H. Brookes, 1985).

Lerner, H. J. *The State Association for Retarded Children and New York State Government, 1948–1968* (New York: New York State Association for Retarded Children, 1972).

Lord, J. and A. Pedlar. "Life in the Community: Four Years After the Closure of an
Institution." *Mental Retardation* 29 (1991): 213–221.

Lottman, M. S. Testimony Regarding the Office of Mental Retardation and Developmental Prepared for the Assembly Committee on Mental Health, Mental
Retardation's Plan to Close Six State Developmental Centers. (Albany, NY: Assembly Standing Committee on Mental Health, Mental Retardation, and Developmental Disabilities and the Senate Committee on Mental Hygiene, 1987).

Mansell, J. and K. Ericsson, eds., *Deinstitutionalisation in Scandinavia, the United
States and Britain: Changing Patterns of Intellectual Disability Services* (London: Chapman and Hall, 1996).

Marmor, T. *The Politics of Medicare* (Chicago: Aldine, 1970).

Martiniano, R. *The Willowbrook Consent Decree: A Case Study of the Judicial Impact
on Budgeting* (Albany, NY: The Rockefeller Institute of Government, 1984).

McClelland, P. D. and A. L. Magdovitz. *Crisis in the Making: The Political Economy
of New York State Since 1945* (New York: Cambridge University Press, 1981).

Missal, J. E. *The Moreland Act: Executive Inquiry in the State of New York* (New York:
Crown Press, 1946).

Morgado, R. J. *Implementation of Major Mental Hygiene Initiatives. Memorandum To
Howard F. Miller, James Prevost, and Thomas A. Coughlin* (Albany, NY: New
York State Executive Chamber, June 15, 1978).

Mount. B. "Benefits and Limitations of Personal Futures Planning." In V. J. Bradley, J. W. Ashbaugh, and B. C. Blaney, eds. *Creating Individual Supports for People with Developmental Disabilities: A Mandate for Change at Many Levels* (Baltimore, MD: Paul Brookes, 1994).

Nakamura, R. T. and F. Smallwood. *The Politics of Implementation* (New York: St. Martin's Press, 1980).

New York State Association of Community and Residential Agencies (NYSACRA). *Serving Persons with Mental Retardation and Developmental Disabilities: The Impact of Residential and Community Facilities on the Local Economy* (Albany, NY. New York State Association of Community and Residential Agencies, 1998).

New York State Association for Retarded Children. (ARC). *Our Childrens' Voice* (Delmar, NY: New York State Association for Retarded Children, 1987).

———. Co-Location at Rome D.C. Rumored—State to Close Facility Earlier Than Planned. *Our Childrens' Voice* (Delmar, NY: New York State Association for Retarded Children, 1987).

———. *Our Childrens' Voice* (Delmar, NY: New York State Association for Retarded Children, 1990).

———. *Our Childrens' Voice* (Delmar, NY: New York State Association for Retarded Children, 1994).

New York State Association for Retarded Children (ARC). *40 Years: A Chronicle of Adversity, Resolve, Change* (Delmar, NY: New York State Association for Retarded Children, 1989).

New York State Association for Retarded Children (ARC). *Directory of Chapters' Programs and Services* (Delmar, NY: New York State Association for Retarded Children, 1994).

New York State. *A Comprehensive New Master Plan for Mental Disability* (Albany, NY: 1965).

New York State Planning Committee on Mental Disorders. *A Plan for a Comprehensive Mental Health and Mental Retardation Program for New York State* (Albany, NY: 1965).

———. *Reports of the Sections on Mental Health and Mental Retardation, Volume I.*

———. *Reports of the New York City, Long Island, Hudson River, Catskill and Binghamton Regional Planning Committees, Volume II.*

———. *Reports of the Buffalo, Rochester, St. Lawrence, Syracuse and Albany Regional Mental Health Planning Committees, Volume III.*

———. *Reports of the Regional Mental Retardation Committees, Volume IV.*

— — —. *Task Force Reports of the Mental Retardation Section of the State Planning Committee: Coordination, Financing, Education, Training of Professional Personnel, Prevention, Social Welfare, Vocational Rehabilitation and Employment Services, Parent and Volunteer Groups and Community Organizations, Research and Demonstration Projects, Clinics and Hospitals, Mental Retardation and the Law, and Facilities Construction, Volume V.*

— — —. *Source Documents and Data: The Foundations for Planning, Volume, VII.*

New York State Commission on Quality of Care for the Mentally Retarded (CQC). *Converting Community Residences into Intermediate Care Facilities for the Mentally Retarded: Some Cautionary Notes* (Albany, NY: 1980).

New York State Commission on Quality of Care for the Mentally Retarded (CQC). *Willowbrook: From Institution to Community: A Fiscal and Programmatic Review of Selected Community Residences* (Albany, NY: 1982).

New York State Commission on Quality of Care for the Mentally Retarded (CQC). *Missing Accountability: The Case of Community Living Alternative, Inc.* (Albany, NY: 1984).

New York State Commission on Quality of Care for the Mentally Retarded (CQC). *Profit Making in Not-For-Profit Care: A Review of the Operations and Financial Practices of Brooklyn Psychosocial Rehabilitation Institute, Inc.* (Albany, NY: 1986).

New York State Commission on Quality of Care for the Mentally Retarded (CQC). *Safeguarding Public Funds: A Review of Spending Practices in OMRDD Rate Appeals* (Albany, NY: 1995a).

New York State Commission on Quality of Care for the Mentally Retarded (CQC). *Shifting the Costs to Medicaid: The Case of Financing the OMRDD Comprehensive Case Management Program* (Albany, NY: 1995b).

New York State Commission on Quality of Care for the Mentally Retarded (CQC). "HI-LI Administrator Convicted." *Quality of Care Newsletter* (Albany, NY: 1995c).

New York State Council of Economic Advisors. *Annual Report* (Albany, NY: 1972).

New York State Division of the Budget. *The Executive Budget in New York State: A Half-Century Perspective* (Albany, NY: 1981).

New York State Governor's Office. *Governor Pataki Announces Secure Facility Expansion in Norwich.* (Albany, NY: Executive Chamber Press Office. September 29, 1998).

New York State Legislative Commission on Expenditure Review (LCER). *Construction of Mental Hygiene Facilities. Program Audit* (Albany, NY: 1973a).

New York State Legislative Commission on Expenditure Review (LCER). *Community Mental Health Services. Program Audit* (Albany, NY: 1973b).

New York State Legislative Commission on Expenditure Review (LCER). *Persons Released from State Developmental Centers. Program Audit* (Albany, NY: 1975).

New York State Legislative Commission on Expenditure Review (LCER). *Use of State Developmental Centers. Program Audit* (Albany, NY: 1980).

New York State Legislative Commission on Expenditure Review (LCER). *Family Court Orders for Handicapped Children. Program Audit* (Albany, NY: 1984).

New York State Legislative Commission on Expenditure Review (LCER). *Capital Funds for Developmental and Psychiatric Centers. Program Audit* (Albany, NY: 1986).

New York State Moreland Act Commission (Moreland). *The Care of the Mentally Ill in the State of New York. A Report by a Commission Appointed by Honorable Thomas E. Dewey, Pursuant of Section 8 of the Executive Law to Investigate the Management and Affairs of the Department of Mental Hygiene of the State of New York and the Institutions Operated By It.* (Albany, NY: 1944).

New York State Office of Planning Coordination (OPC). *New York State: Economic Outlook for the Seventies* (Albany, NY: 1969).

New York State. *Executive Budget, Fiscal Years 1935–2001.* Albany, NY.

New York State. *Message to the Legislature 1935–2001.* Albany, NY.

New York State Department of Mental Hygiene and Mental Hygiene Facilities Improvement Fund. *Master Plan* (Albany. NY: 1962).

New York State Department of Mental Hygiene (DMH). *Annual Reports, 1935–1975.* Albany, NY.

New York State Department of Mental Hygiene (DMH). *Mental Hygiene News* 30, Nov. 1959, 1.

New York State Department of Mental Hygiene (DMH). *Report to the Governor: Major Goals, Construction Program* (Albany, NY: 1967).

New York State Office of Mental Retardation and Developmental Disabilities (OMRDD). *Five-Year Comprehensive for Services to Mentally Retarded and Developmentally Disabled Persons in New York State: 1979–84. (5.07 Plan)* (Albany, NY: 1978).

New York State Office of Mental Retardation and Developmental Disabilities (OMRDD). *Deinstitutionalization in New York State: An Update from the New York State Office of Mental Retardation and Developmental Disabilities* (Albany, NY: 1979).

New York State Office of Mental Retardation and Developmental Disabilities (OMRDD). *Comprehensive Plan for Services to the Mentally Retarded and Developmentally Disabled* (Albany, NY: 1980).

New York State Office of Mental Retardation and Developmental Disabilities (OMRDD). *Willowbrook Consent Decree: Trainee Manual* (Albany, NY: 1982).

New York State Office of Mental Retardation and Developmental Disabilities (OMRDD). *The 1984–87 Comprehensive Plan for Services to Persons with Mental*

Retardation and Developmental Disabilities in New York State. (5.07 Plan) (Albany, NY: 1984).

New York State Office of Mental Retardation and Developmental Disabilities (OMRDD). *Developmental Centers: Residential Trends, Fiscal Years Ended March 31, 1971 through March 31, 1984* (Albany, NY: 1984).

New York State Office of Mental Retardation and Developmental Disabilities (OMRDD). *Program/Capital Plan: 1986–1991* (Albany, NY: 1985).

New York State Office of Mental Retardation and Developmental Disabilities (OMRDD). *A Report on Residential Waiting Lists* (Albany, NY: 1985).

New York State Office of Mental Retardation and Developmental Disabilities (OMRDD). *Small Residential Units: A Residential Alternative* (Albany, NY: 1985).

New York State Office of Mental Retardation and Developmental Disabilities (OMRDD). *Community Residential Models* (Albany, NY: 1986).

New York State Office of Mental Retardation and Developmental Disabilities (OMRDD). *Voluntary-Operated Community Development, Volumes 1 and 2* (Albany, NY: 1987).

New York State Office of Mental Retardation and Developmental Disabilities (OMRDD). *Developmental Center Closure Plan* (Albany, NY: 1987).

New York State Office of Mental Retardation and Developmental Disabilities (OMRDD). *Strengthening the Continuum: 1987–1990 (5.07 Plan)* (Albany, NY: 1987).

New York State Office of Mental Retardation and Developmental Disabilities (OMRDD). *Report on Community Development* (Albany, NY: 1988).

New York State Office of Mental Retardation and Developmental Disabilities (OMRDD). *Closure Policy and Its Possible Implications: A Survey of Perceived Effects Upon Residents* (Albany, NY: 1989).

New York State Office of Mental Retardation and Developmental Disabilities (OMRDD). *The Community Challenge: A Partnership with Families, Consumers, and Providers. (5.07 Plan)* (Albany, NY: 1990a).

New York State Office of Mental Retardation and Developmental Disabilities (OMRDD). *A Survey of Key Informants on Closure* (Albany, NY: 1990b).

New York State Office of Mental Retardation and Developmental Disabilities (OMRDD). *A Mandate for the 1990s: Closing Developmental Centers in New York State* (Albany, NY: 1990c).

New York State Office of Mental Retardation and Developmental Disabilities (OMRDD). *A Survey: Needs of People at Home with Developmental Disabilities in New York State* (Albany, NY: 1990c).

New York State Office of Mental Retardation and Developmental Disabilities (OMRDD). *InfoFacts: Quarterly Information Reports 1991–2001* (Albany, NY: 1991).

New York State Office of Mental Retardation and Developmental Disabilities (OMRDD). *O.D. Heck Closure Plan* (Albany, NY: 1994).

New York State Office of Mental Retardation and Developmental Disabilities (OMRDD). 1995. *Systems Review* (Albany, NY: 1995).

New York State Office of Mental Retardation and Developmental Disabilities (OMRDD). 1996a. *New Service Coordination Paradigm* (Albany, NY: 1996a).

New York State Office of Mental Retardation and Developmental Disabilities (OMRDD). 1996b. *Workforce Management Plan: 1996–2000* (Albany, NY: 1996b).

New York State Office of Mental Retardation and Developmental Disabilities (OMRDD). 1998. *Conversion of Community Residences to Individualized Residential Alternatives* (Albany, NY: 1998).

New York State Office of Mental Retardation and Developmental Disabilities (OMRDD). 1999. *State and Voluntary Residential Properties* (Albany, NY: 1999).

New York State Office of Mental Retardation and Developmental Disabilities (OMRDD). 1999. *General Fund/PIA Available Appropriations* (Albany, NY: 1999).

New York State Office of Mental Retardation and Developmental Disabilities (OMRDD). 2000. *Institutional Reimbursement Rates* (Albany, NY: 2000).

New York State Office of the State Comptroller (OSC). *Excessive Reimbursement for Voluntary Agency Leases with Related Property Companies. Report 90-S-106.* (Albany, NY: 1990).

New York State Public Employee Federation (PEF). "PEF Fights to Keep Serving 'Special Needs' Kids." *The Communicator* (Albany, NY: 1998).

New York State Senate Committee on Mental Hygiene. *Report on Developmental Closures* (Albany, NY: 1990).

New York State Senate Committee on Mental Hygiene. *Toward Independence: The Future of Developmental Centers in New York State* (Albany, NY: 1990).

New York State Temporary Commission on State Hospital Problems. *Progress Report of the Temporary Commission on State Hospital Problems* (Albany, NY: 1942).

New York State Temporary Commission to Revise the Social Services Law. *The Administration of Medicaid in New York State, Interim Report #6* (Albany, NY: 1975).

New York Times, "Kennedy's Target." 26 December 1965, IV–V, 2.

Nirje, B. "The Principle of Normalization and its Human Management Implications." In R. Krugel and W. Wolfensberger, eds. *Changing Patterns in Residential Services for the Mentally Retarded* (Washington, DC: The President's Committee on Mental Retardation, 1969).

O'Brien, J. and C. L. O'Brien. "More Than Just a New Address: Images of Organization for Supported Living Agencies." In V. J. Bradley, J. W. Ashbaugh, and B. C. Blaney, eds. *Creating Individual Supports for People with Developmental Disabilities: A Mandate for Change at Many Levels* (Baltimore, MD: Paul Brookes, 1994).

O'Neill, J., M. Brown, W. Gordon, C. Hoffman, and R. Schonhorn. *Deinstitutionalizing Individuals Who Are Moderately and Severely Disabled: The Bureaucratization of a Community Program* (New York: United Cerebral Palsy Association of New York State, 1985).

O'Toole, L. J., Jr. and R. S. Montjoy. "Interorganizational Policy Implementation: A Theoretical Perspective." *Public Administration Review* (November/December 1984): 491–503.

O'Toole, L. J., Jr. "Goal Multiplicity in the Implementation Setting: Subtle Impacts and the Case of Wastewater Treatment Privatization." *Policy Studies Journal* 18 (1989): 91–102.

Padavan, F. *Site Selection of Community Residences for the Mentally Disabled: Historical Perspective and Legislation. A Report by the Chairman of the New York State Mental Hygiene and Addiction Control Committee* (Albany, NY: 1979).

Parish, S. L. "Forces Shaping Developmental Services in the States: A Comparative Study." In Braddock, D., ed. *Disability at the Dawn of the 21st Century and the State of the States* (Washington, DC: American Association on Mental Retardation, 2002).

Patrick, H. Memorandum from Hal Patrick (OMRDD Deputy Counsel) to Ilene Margolin (Governor's Director of Human Services) re: S.3705/A.6786 SIDC Closure. (Albany, NY: 1987).

Pense, A. W. "Trends in the Institutional Care of the Mentally Defectives." *American Journal of Mental Deficiency* 50 (1945–46): 455.

Platt, I. Testimony Regarding the Office of Mental Retardation and Developmental Prepared for the Assembly Committee on Mental Health, Mental Retardation's Plan to Close Six State Developmental Centers. (Albany, NY: Assembly Standing Committee on Mental Health, Mental Retardation, and Developmental Disabilities and the Senate Committee on Mental Hygiene, 1987).

President's Commission on Mental Retardation. *The National Reform Agenda and People with Mental Retardation: Putting People First* (Washington, D.C.: 1994).

President's Panel on Mental Retardation. *A Proposed Program for National Action to Combat Mental Retardation* (Washington, D.C.: 1962).

Prouty, R. and K. C. Lakin. *Residential Services for Persons with Mental Retardation and Related Conditions: Status and Trends Through 1996* (Minneapolis, MN: Research and Training Center on Community Living, 1997).

Rothman, D. *The Discovery of the Asylum: Social Order and Disorder in the New Republic.* Boston: Little, Brown and Co., 1971.

Rothman, D. *Conscience and Convenience: The Asylum and its Alternatives in Progressive* America (Boston: Little, Brown and Co., 1980)

Rothman, D. and S. M. Rothman. *The Willowbrook Wars* (New York: Harper and Row, 1984).

Scheerenberger, R. C. *A History of Mental Retardation* (Baltimore, MD: Paul H. Brookes, 1987).

Sheedy, J. J. Letter to The Honorable George E. Pataki, January 3, 1995.

Smith, G. and J. Ashbaugh. *Managed Care and People with Developmental Disabilities: A Guidebook* (Alexandria VA: National Association of State Directors of Developmental Disabilities Services and Human Services Research Institute, 1995).

Smull, M. W. *Crisis in the Community* (Alexandria, VA: National Association of State Mental Retardation Program Directors, 1989).

Sparer, M. S. *Medicaid and the Limits of State Health Reform* (Philadelphia, PA: Temple University Press, 1996).

Starr, Paul. "Medicine and the Waning of Professional Sovereignty." *Daedalus.* 1978.

Sterner, Jerry. *Other People's Money: A Play in Two Acts.* (New York: S. French, 1989).

Strauss, D. and T. Kastner. "Comparative Mortality of People with Mental Retardation in Institutions and the Community." *American Journal on Mental Retardation* 101 (1996): 26–40.

Storrs, H. C. "An Administrative Structure for an Institution for the Mentally Deficient." *American Journal of Mental Deficiency* 50 (1945–46): 473.

Taylor, J. Testimony Regarding the Office of Mental Retardation and Developmental Disabilities Prepared for the Assembly Committee on Mental Health, Mental Retardation's Plan to Close Six State Developmental Centers. (Albany, NY: Assembly Standing Committee on Mental Health, Mental Retardation, and Developmental Disabilities and the Senate Committee on Mental Hygiene, 1987).

Taylor, S. J., R. Bogdan, and J. A. Racino, eds. *Life in the Community: Case Studies of Organizations Supporting People with Disabilities* (Baltimore, MD: Paul H. Brookes, 1991).

Trent, J. W. *Inventing the Feeble Mind: A History of Mental Retardation in the United States.* Berkeley, CA: University of California Press, 1994.

Tyor, P. L. and L. V. Bell. *Caring for the Retarded in America: A History* (Westport, CT: Greenwood Press, 1984).

United States Department of Health and Human Services. Health Care Financing Administration. (HCFA). *Final Report: Review of New York's Home and Commu-*

nity-Based Services Waiver (New York: Health Care Financing Administration, Region 2, 2000).

Vladeck, Bruce C. "Where the Action Really Is: Medicaid and the Disabled." *Health Affairs* 22 (2003): 90–100.

Ward, M. J. *The Snake Pit* (New York: Random House, 1946).

Webb, A. Y. *Closing Institutions: One State's Experience* (Albany, NY: New York State Office of Mental Retardation and Developmental Disabilities, 1988).

Wolfensberger, W. *The Principle of Normalization in Human Services* (Toronto: National Institute on Mental Retardation, 1972).

Yarbrough, T. E. "The Judge as Manager: The Case of Judge Frank Johnson." *Journal of Policy Analysis and Management* 1 (1982): 386–400.

Index